T0413912

North Korean
Nuclear Weapon and Reunification of the Korean Peninsula

Other Related Titles from World Scientific

Politics, Culture and Identities in East Asia: Integration and Division
edited by Peng Er Lam and Tai Wei Lim
ISBN: 978-981-3226-22-7

Political Parties, Party Systems and Democratization in East Asia
edited by Liang Fook Lye and Wilhelm Hofmeister
ISBN: 978-981-4327-94-7

East Asia: Developments and Challenges
edited by Yongnian Zheng and Liang Fook Lye
ISBN: 978-981-4407-82-3

Regionalism in East Asia: Why Has It Flourished Since 2000 and How Far Will It Go?
by Richard Pomfret
ISBN: 978-981-4304-32-0

North Korean Nuclear Weapon and Reunification of the Korean Peninsula

Sung-wook Nam
Korea University, South Korea

W JERSEY • LONDON • SINGAPORE • BEIJING • SHANGHAI • HONG KONG • TAIPEI • CHENNAI • TOKYO

Published by

World Scientific Publishing Co. Pte. Ltd.

5 Toh Tuck Link, Singapore 596224

USA office: 27 Warren Street, Suite 401-402, Hackensack, NJ 07601

UK office: 57 Shelton Street, Covent Garden, London WC2H 9HE

Library of Congress Cataloging-in-Publication Data

Names: Nam, Sung-wook, 1959– author.
Title: North Korean nuclear weapon and reunification of the Korean Peninsula / Sung-wook Nam.
Description: Hackensack, NJ : World Scientific, [2019] |
Includes bibliographical references and index.
Identifiers: LCCN 2019025704 | ISBN 9789813239968 (hardcover)
Subjects: LCSH: Nuclear weapons--Government policy--Korea (North) | Nuclear weapons--Korea (North)--History. | Nuclear disarmament--Korea (North) | Nuclear arms control--Korea (North) | Korean reunification question (1945–) | Korea (North)--Foreign relations--United States. | United States--Foreign relations--Korea (North)
Classification: LCC U264.5.K7 N37 2019 | DDC 327.1/747095193--dc23
LC record available at https://lccn.loc.gov/2019025704

British Library Cataloguing-in-Publication Data

A catalogue record for this book is available from the British Library.

For any available supplementary material, please visit
https://www.worldscientific.com/worldscibooks/10.1142/10982#t=suppl

Desk Editor: Jiang Yulin

Typeset by Stallion Press
Email: enquiries@stallionpress.com

Contents

About the Author

Dr. Sung-wook Nam is an East Asia expert with the theoretical and practical experience in academia, government and intelligence services on North Korea and China. He has worked as an analyst for Korean National Intelligence Service and an advisor to Ministry of National Defense, Ministry of National Unification and Ministry of Foreign Affairs.

Nam is Dean of Graduate School of Public Policy, Korea University since 2016 and director of Center for North Koreanology at the Asiatic Research Institute, Korea University since 2013. He received his PhD in Applied Economics from the University of Missouri-Columbia, USA. He also works as a commentator on international affairs at the Korea Broadcasting Service since 2008. His academic career includes four years as Professor of North Korean Studies at Ewha Women's University and five years as the head of the School of National Intelligence Academy.

His positions in the government since entering academia in 1999 include the President of Institute for National Security Strategy in 2008–2011. Also, he was the general director of National Unification Council Advisory (vice-minister level) in 2012–2013. In addition to numerous papers and books, he is the author of *North Korean Food Shortage and Reform of Collective Farm* (Munchen Germany: Hertze Verlag, 2006). He is co-author of *South Korea's 70-Year Endeavor for Foreign Policy, National Defense, and Unification* (Singapore: Palgrave Macmillan, 2018).

Email: namsung@korea.ac.kr

Preface

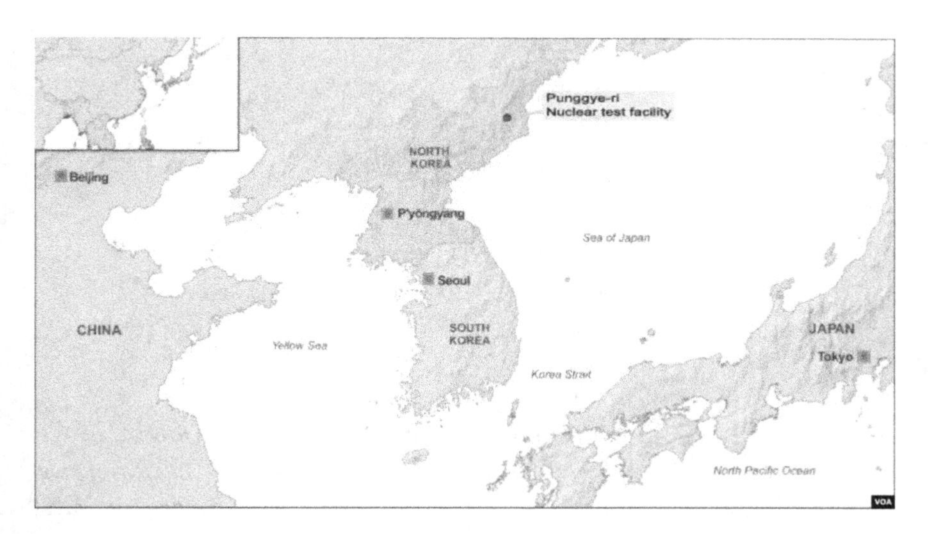

Figure 0.1 East Asia and Korean Peninsula

Source: Voice of America (https://www.voanews.com/).

Figure 0.2 North Korean main cities

Source: Central Intelligence Agency (www.cia.gov).

North Korea has been preparing for nuclear development much longer than most people think. The time when North Korea was supposed to have decided to develop nuclear weapons for the first time dates back to the time of the Korean War (1950–1953). On November 30, 1950, US President Harry S. Truman announced, "We are actively reviewing the use of all weapons, including nuclear weapons, to prevent the invasion of Communists on the Korean Peninsula." It was the very day after Douglas MacArthur, commander in chief of United Nations troops in South Korea, proposed bombing Manchuria. General MacArthur asked the Joint Chiefs of Staff George Marshall Jr. of the US Department of Defense to use 34 atomic bombs on the eve of Christmas. The target area included 21 cities and the Maritime Province of North Korea including

Manchuria. However, President Truman rejected MacArthur's request to use the atomic bombs. On April 5, 1951, the Joint Chiefs of Staff of the Ministry of National Defense ordered General MacArthur to retaliate with the use of atomic bombs only when the Chinese forces entered the North Korean border on a large scale or when the Soviet bomber attack began. Six days later, President Truman dismissed General MacArthur, who did not follow his orders obediently. President Truman had determined that it was not appropriate to give General MacArthur, a stubborn and uncompromising figure, the right to use dangerous nuclear weapons. General Matthew Ridgway, who was appointed as successor to General MacArthur, requested 38 atomic bombs from the US Joint Chiefs of Staff in May, but as with General MacArthur, he did not get approval from Washington.

Even though North Korea defined the threat of US nuclear use as blackmail, the nuclear threat of US embarrassed the regime. The talk of possible use of nuclear weapons by President Truman and the counter-pressures of communist regimes resulted in hundreds of thousands of refugees moving from the north of the peninsula to the south. President Kim Il-sung had watched Japan, which had the loyal military forces of the Emperor in August 1945, surrender unconditionally after the dual use of nuke or atomic bomb weapons by the United States. On November 30, 1950, President Kim Il-sung was frustrated by President Truman's statement that the use of nuclear weapons and the atomic bombing could become a reality in North Korea. The fear of nuclear weapons felt by the leadership of North Korea, including President Kim Il-sung, would have been the first motive to recognize the necessity of nuclear weapons for self-defense. From that time, Kim Il-sung decided to hasten the development of nuclear weapons in order to achieve a nuclear balance with the US.

North Korea began to develop nuclear weapons in September 1950, when General MacArthur landed at the Incheon port and deployed the military forces of South Korea and the United States on a 38th parallel. In October 1952, before the armistice, North Korea established the Korea Institute of Science and Technology

(KOSE) to systematically study science and technology and established the Atomic Energy Research Institute under the Chosun Academy of Sciences. Around the same time, in 1954, the People's Armed Forces Department set up a nuclear-armed defense force to take measures against the US military attack. Accordingly, the United States focused on identifying North Korea's intentions to develop nuclear weapons. Finally, the United States began to prepare for the threat of North Korea's nuclear weapons development through the deployment of nuclear weapons by the Chairman of the Joint Chiefs of Staff of Radford, and by Dwight D. Eisenhower's tactical remarks in January 1955. The United States announced the deployment of long-range missiles on the Korean Peninsula in May 1955 and began to deploy tactical nuclear weapons. Meanwhile, North Korea began to accelerate its nuclear development. North Korea established the Atomic and Nuclear Physics Research Institute in April 1955, and the Soviet Union and North Korea signed an accord on the "nuclear research on the peaceful use of atomic energy." The official objective of North Korea's nuclear development, which was superficially designed to conceal the allegations of nuclear development by the international community, was of course peaceful use.

North Korea also focused on fostering the relevant research personnel needed for nuclear development. The North Korean Academy of Sciences selected young talent in July 1953 immediately after the armistice agreement and sent them to Moscow in order to study nuclear physics systematically. In addition, North Korea had been training staff working in the nuclear sector every year since 1956 at the Dovna Nuclear Research Institute in the Soviet Union. The relevant departments in North Korea steadily pursued various policies including training personnel and establishing facilities to prepare for the development of nuclear weapons. North Korea completed a nuclear power research complex in Yongbyon, North Pyongan Province, officially known as a "furniture factory" in November 1962, and invited Choi Hak-geun, a nuclear expert who was working at the Dovna Nuclear Research Institute in the Soviet Union. North Korea introduced the 2MW research reactor IRT-2000 from the

USSR in June 1963 and succeeded in enriching plutonium for the first time in 1965. From 1967, the reactor began to operate in earnest. After China succeeded in their nuclear test in October 1964, Kim Il-sung visited China and asked Mao Zedong to support the development of nuclear technology in North Korea, but there was no real progress. In 1972, President Kim Il-sung decided to pursue nuclear development independently without the active support from China and the Soviet Union and analyzed China's nuclear development strategy. China's nuclear development strategy has three main characteristics: concealment, dispersion and mobilization. Unlike China, North Korea has defined "concealment, dispersion and underground service" as the three main characteristics of its nuclear development. While China maneuvered nuclear weapons because it is located on a wide continent, North Korea chose the underground strategy because it is small in size and contains mostly mountainous terrain. In the end, North Korea pursued its peculiar strategy of developing North Korean nuclear weapons to match its own national strengths, weapons systems and mountainous terrain.

It is only in 1989 that the North Korean nuclear issue was publicized as an international concern, even though North Korea began to show interest in the nuclear issue from the end of the Korean War in the 1950s. Since the 1960s, Kim Il-sung had already made several official references to his desire for nuclear possession. North Korea, which had feared that the United States might use nuclear weapons at the time of the Korean War, rebuilt the People's Army in 1954 and set up a "nuclear weapons defense" division within the People's Army. The reason why North Korea paid much attention to nuclear weapons during the 1950s and 1960s originated from the international situation in which North Korea was involved. First, North Korea was very afraid of the US Air Force and nuclear weapons during the Korean War, and in particular was disappointed by the indifferent behaviors of the Soviet Union during the Korean War and the unwillingness of the Chinese Army to participate in the initial stage of the war. Due to the neutral stance of friendly socialist countries, North Korea was determined to have a military strategy idea of securing its "ability to perform its own war." As the conflict between China and the Soviet Union became very clear in the mid-1960s, North Korea chose the "Juche diplomacy", which maintained a certain distance from China and the Soviet Union. North Korea's nuclear arsenal development had been attempted in the political context of North Korea, while both China and the Soviet Union were seen as unreliable. This book deals with the past, present and future of North Korean nuclear development in three dimensions. It reviews the history and origins of North Korea's nuclear development and analyzes the technical aspects related to the development of nuclear weapons. This book also analyzes North Korea's international politics, which was fiercely operated in East Asia during the period of North Korea's nuclear development, and deduces North Korea's intention and policy implications.

This book includes the asymmetric characteristics of nuclear weapons that overwhelm conventional weapons in terms of destructive power and technological aspects to exactly understand the reality of North Korean military threats. As North Korea conducted six nuclear tests, various sanctions were adopted by the UN Security Council. Despite the enormous sanctions and maximum pressures, however, North Korea claimed to have succeeded in experimenting nuclear weapon and launching the intercontinental ballistic missile (ICBM), a transport vehicle, and also completing its weight reduction, miniaturization and diversification. In recent years, North Korea has threatened that the US mainland has been placed within range of the ICBM strike. Since the unconventional Trump administration was established in 2017, the North Korean nuclear issue has been being deployed at a new level. In 2018, the first summit between the United States and North Korea was held in Singapore. Since then, the two countries have been unable to find any meaningful contact point between North Korea's request for declaration to officially end the Korean War and the lifting of sanctions and the US's claim for reporting, inspection and verification of nuclear weapons and facilities in North Korea. The second summit between the United States and North Korea was held in Hanoi in February 2019. This book carefully anticipates the impact of the unprecedented summit between Washington and Pyongyang on resolving the North Korean nuclear issue and its progress. It also deals with the economic compensation that North Korea strongly desires in pursuit of denuclearization and the scope of denuclearization and the lifting of UN sanctions that had been the roots of "no deal" at the Hanoi Summit in Vietnam. President Donald Trump did not accept the lifting of UN sanctions against North Korea proposed by Kim Jong-un, while the young leader Kim did not also agree the demand of FFVD (Final, Fully Verified Denuclearization) demanded by Trump. The first summit was a result of miscalculation by Trump, while the "no deal" of the second summit was produced by Kim Jong-un's misunderstanding toward the US. This book delves into the case of Vietnam's reform and opening and projects the financial support of the international community when North Korea denuclearizes in the near future like the Ukraine Model pushed strongly by former US Secretary of Defense William Perry in the 1990s. It also describes the situation in which a new Cold War order is constructed and diagnoses new changes in Northeast Asian international politics swiftly developed due to the North Korean nuclear crisis. Before and after the Singapore and Hanoi summits between the US and DPRK, North Korean leader Kim Jong-un visited China four times within a space of 10 months in six years of power and has strengthened friendly Sino–North Korean relations. In fact, Chinese leader Xi Jinping had been in full engagement with Kim Jong-un in advance of the summit with US President Trump as he intended to utilize North Korea as a leverage so that he would be able to resist against the pressure of the United States' demand in the trade war. The complex international order of Northeast Asia is being built on the occasion of the North Korean nuclear crisis. The last chapter looks at the possibility of unification of the Korean Peninsula in various scenarios.

History repeats itself. International politics is also repeated. The Northeast Asian international politics, in which the Cold War frame has not changed much since the middle of the 20th century, is being operated with a fusion of past, present and future, based on tactical strategies of North Korean diplomacy. Kim Jong-un unexpectedly proposed the "four-party talks in 1997" card in his 2019 New Year's address. The young leader said that under close ties with the cease-fire parties, North Korea should actively pursue multilateral negotiations to transform the armistice system of the Korean Peninsula into a peace regime. The parties to the ceasefire are the United States, North Korea and China. South Korea is a party to the problem of the Korean Peninsula. The four-party talks, which took place six times in Geneva, Switzerland during 1997–1999, were attended by delegates from South Korea, North Korea, the United States and China. North Korea announced a card to restore the four-party talks and lead the declaration of the end of the Korean War. In fact, in 1996, South Korean President Kim Young-sam and US President Bill Clinton proposed the four-party talks for the first time at a summit in Jeju Island, South Korea. It was the intention of the United States and South Korea at that time to form a framework for peace settlement on the Korean Peninsula by engaging China, a signatory to the armistice agreement. However, the first four-party talks ended without successful results for the subsequent two years, confirming North Korea and China's own hidden intentions. Pyongyang's Deputy Foreign Minister Kim Kye-gwan, who had been reluctant to the first round of multilateral talks, preferred the direct dialogue between North Korea and the United States. Appearing unenthusiastic throughout the four-party talks, he repeated the existing repertoire such as demanding the withdrawal of the USFK and stopping massive war exercises between South Korea and the United States. China emphasized the declaration of the end of the Korean War, non-interference in the domestic politics and disarmament measures. The four-party talks received much media interest and provided a photo opportunity for the involved parties, but they had not achieved any unique solutions or achievements. It was natural that the results of the four-party talks had not been attained in the international politics of Northeast Asia, which already posed challenges to bilateral talks. But the situations in Seoul, Pyongyang, Washington and Beijing in 2019 are different from 1997. Despite the first summit in Singapore in 2018, denuclearization has not progressed and sanctions against North Korea have been maintained. Kim Jong-un felt the need to have a new frame in international politics in Northeast Asia and establish a new governance to shake up Trump's initiative ahead of the second round of summit. He expressed in the 2019 New Year's address of the North Korean regime of hoping "the United States takes a credible action in response to our proactive and preemptive efforts and responds with appropriate action ..." The new governance was the four-party talks, and it took a concrete action by visiting China in a cold winter season in January 2019. North Korea's Chosun Central News Agency said, "The two leaders of China and North Korea emphasized in-depth and candid communication on the issue of joint research and coordination of the process of negotiations on the Korean Peninsula and denuclearization." The young leader stressed in Beijing that North Korea has a control on the relation between North Korea and the United States. According to the North Korean dictionary, the term "control" means to take initiative and respond with the initiative. It is in line with the New Year's address. Kim Jong-un was led by his own initiative, and North Korea is the Party (A) and the United States is the Party (B). In particular, Kim Jong-un, who has received generous sponsorship from China's elder brother Xi, will have a similar feeling of securing strong supporters. By urging the United States to take preemptive concessions, Kim Jong-un will firmly refuse the US's request for verification of reports and will focus on alleviating sanctions and declaring the end of Korean War.

In the end, North Korea will engage in diplomacy to form a three-to-one relationship with South Korea, North Korea, China on one hand and the United States on the other, and it had already taken a first step in Beijing. Before the second summit in Vietnam, the ball was then on the Washington court. Trump would have to choose whether to hold a meeting poor in substance for propaganda like the first summit, partly accept North Korea's request for the lifting of sanctions and declaration to end the Korean War, or postpone the second round of summit indefinitely. The Trump administration was unhappy with the turbulent domestic politics given that the federal shutdown lasted 35 days due to the disagreement in the passing of the Mexican border barrier budget in December 2018/January 2019 and "difficult issues" in local politics. It is doubtful whether President Trump has properly understood the meaning of the summit between North Korea and China and the three-dimensional strategy of the four-party talks this year.

Paradoxically, Kim Jong-un hopes for the lifting of the US sanctions against North Korea with the four-party talks that the two countries proposed 22 years ago. Trump is still twittered and does not get the concrete product of denuclearization. The confusion and miscommunication between Trump and Kim Jong-un finally resulted in "no deal" in Hanoi in 2019. While writing this book, two summit meetings between the United States and North Korea were held with international attention, but they have not yet found a basic clue to denuclearization. The denuclearization issue in North Korea has been known to the world for 26 years or so, but it is still in progress. Although the United States has tried to solve problems in international politics, the North Korean nuclear issue has to be included in the items that have not been solved for such a long time. For some time, the North Korean nuclear issue will be a serious obstacle to the cooperative Northeast Asian international politics.

This book is informed by my academic and practical adventure in institutions like Korea University, National Security Institute, and Democratic Peaceful Reunification Advisory Committee. I have visited North Korea 14 times for governmental meetings and academic conferences with Kim Il-sung University Professors and business projects with North Korea national economy council, etc. Whenever I had meetings with North Korean counterparts, I felt that even though we speak the Korean language, we were heterogeneous in nature — more so than with the members of the international community. Seventy years have passed since the division of Korean Peninsula. North Korea has been imprisoned by distinctive Juche ideology and self-reliant economy as well as socialist control and observation system since the foundation in 1948. It will take a much longer time to restore the humanism and democratic system in the northern part, even though the nuclear issue will be solved with diplomatic negotiation and the dream of a united Korean Peninsula is to be achieved in the future. The Korean Peninsula has a long way to go before its people realize their dream of a denuclearized and unified Korea.

I hope that this book will help readers to systematically understand the historical aspect and implication of the North Korean nuclear issue and to grasp the rapidly changing situation in Northeast Asia due to the North Korean nuclear crisis. I am deeply grateful to the team at World Scientific. My editor, Jiang Yulin, supported me with patience while many big diplomatic events happened. Without his tremendous encouragement, my book will not be timely completed in the critical period.

Professor Sung-wook Nam
January 2019

Chapter 1

The Beginning and Progress of North Korea's Nuclear Development

North Korea's preparations for nuclear development dating back to the 1950s

Kim Il-sung, the leader of the North Korean regime, worked in the Chinese Communist Party and operated in the Soviet Union during the anti-Japanese struggle period of the 1930s and 1940s. He joined the Communist Party of China in 1931 and started to work in the lower-level organizations in Manchuria. In 1941, following the Japanese invasion, he crossed the Manchurian border with Chinese guerrillas and joined Soviet forces in Siberia, where he spent four years. He might have been hostile to the Japanese military, but he also experienced fear of Japanese imperialism as he suffered tremendous hardships during the anti-Japanese struggle. Kim Il-sung witnessed Japan surrendering unconditionally after the US atomic bombings and felt the importance of power logic in the international community. He confessed that there was no way to survive in the relentless reality of the international community other than to raise military strength.[1]

Immediately after the collapse of Japan, the Soviet army occupied the north region above the 38th parallel on the Korean Peninsula and succeeded in communizing North Korea with Kim Il-sung, who was highly loyal to Joseph Stalin. Kim Il-sung, who was prepared to invade South Korea by military force even after the withdrawal of the Soviet Army in December 1948, maintained strong allegiance to Stalin in order to obtain variety of support from the Soviet Union. Three months after the outbreak of the Korean War in June 1950, when the United States' powerful military power approached the Sino–North Korean border area, China became worried about the collapse of the buffer zone. China sent nearly 1 million People's Liberation Army troops in October 1950 to North Korea to prevent the South Korean and American troops from defeating the North Koreans. When US President Harry S. Truman mentioned the possibility of using nuclear weapons, the North Korean military was very upset. Kim Il-sung focused on managing internal dissent by attacking his opponents and subordinates in a December 21, 1950 meeting in Byulori, a border town in North Pyeongan Province. He was afraid of taking the responsibility of the war loss that resulted from the strategic failure and misjudgment of the US troops operation. He tried to shift responsibility onto his subordinates, and unexpectedly proposed the development of new military capabilities like nuclear weapons. He secured the support from the Soviet Union and China because of the strategic importance of the Korean Peninsula. China participated in the armistice agreement in July 1953, and by 1958, the People's Liberation Army was stationed in North Korea, expanding its influence. The North Korean regime maintained diplomatic relations with the Soviet Union as a satellite state and received military support from China throughout the severe crisis of regime collapse during the Korean War. Until the early 1960s, the two powers could exert strong influence on North Korea.

After Stalin's death in March 1953, the influence of the Soviet Union in North Korea was somewhat reduced. The new Soviet leader, Nikita Khrushchev criticized the worship of Stalin at the 20th Congress of the Soviet Communist Party in February 1956, but North Korea maintained that the practice of worshiping Kim Il-sung was an essential part of its national identity in the socialist revolutionary process. While maintaining the Stalinist dictatorship system, the North Korean regime began to modify the cause and purpose of dictatorship from the liberation of the working class to national liberation. The theory of national liberation led to the promotion of independence by avoiding excessive dependence on China and the Soviet Union in North Korea's foreign policy.

Since the death of Stalin, the Kim Il-sung government supported China's hardline policy against the peaceful coexistence policy of the new Soviet leader, Khrushchev. After the conclusion of the Third Congress of the Communist Party of Romania in June 1960 (Bucharest Convention), the 81st Communist Party conference in Moscow in November 1960 and the 22nd Congress of the Soviet Communist Party in October 1961, the ideological conflict between the lines of China's dogmatism and Soviet's revisionism were deepened. In the 1960s, international politics was rapidly changing. For example, there were South Korea's military coup in May 1961, the Soviet's pro-India position in the Sino–Indian border dispute in 1962, withdrawal of Soviet missiles in the Cuban Missile Crisis in October 1962, and the success of China's nuclear test in 1964. As the Soviet Union ceased military and economic aid to North Korea in 1962, and the communist bloc, including Eastern Europe, which provided 20% of its aid, cooled their relationship with North Korea, North Korea felt a deep sense of isolation. Furthermore, China failed to provide economic rewards to North Korea, and in the ripple of the Cultural Revolution that took place during 1966–1976, there was a lack of diplomatic interest in North Korea. In 1964, as Khrushchev retreated from power and the prospect of economic development in South Korea increased with the conclusion of the South Korea–Japan Agreement in 1965, North Korea sent a delegation to the 23rd Session of the Communist Party of Soviet in March to April 1965 to strengthen its relations with the Soviet Union. Since then, North Korea established a military assistance agreement with the Soviet Union in May 1965, an Economic and Technical Agreement (1966–1970) in February 1966 and an Agreement for Strengthening Military Power in March 1967.

Figure 1.1 North Korean nuclear facilities

Source: RIA (www.ria.ru).

Kim Il-sung recognizes the psychological fear of nuclear attacks and necessity of nuclear development

The Korean War began with the reckless will of Kim Il-sung and Park Hyun-young to unify the two Koreas by military means and was finally decided with the consent of Stalin and Mao Zedong. The ambitious idea of Kim Il-sung to unify the Korean peninsula by force resulted in failure, and he felt the psychological fear of the US atomic bomb.[2] In the absence of the Soviet nuclear umbrella, Kim Il-sung recognized the need to develop his own nuclear weapons. The Chinese People's Support Forces began participating in the Korean War from the end of October 1950. US President Truman said in a press conference on November 30, 1950 that "nuclear is one of our weapons and is actively reviewing the use of nuclear weapons."[3] In December of the same year, the US military authority set up a "SHAKEDOWN" strategy to prepare for the intervention of the Soviet Union in the Korean War, and the US Army assigned to the Far East Command was prepared to launch a retaliatory strike against the Soviet Union. On Christmas Eve in 1950, General Douglas MacArthur, then commander of the Far East division of the US Army, submitted a "blockade target list", which he deemed the necessary use of 26 atomic bombs, and demanded four atom bombs to be used for invading troops, including the enemy air base.[4] President Truman seriously considered using nuclear weapons, but finally decided not to use them because of the enormous damage caused by the war, the fall of international prestige due to the use of nuclear weapons, the possibility of the war expanding to nuclear World War III and the risk of nuclear weapons use by the Soviet Union since 1949.[5] Instead, President Truman sent a B-29 bomber equipped with the atomic bombs of the ninth medium-range bombing squadron to Guam in April 1951. Truman approved the order to increase the number of atomic bombs in the Pacific area and gave the Far East commander limited authority to launch a nuclear retaliatory attack against an air strike from outside the peninsula at the end of April.[6]

The North Korean leadership became nervous after Truman mentioned the possibility of nuclear use on November 30, 1950, and some residents of Pyongyang were pushed south by anxiety and fear of atomic bombs. At that time, the North Korean Workers' Party control of the residents was looser than it had been before. The Labor Party could not prevent the floods of residents from going to Seoul, even though it propagated that "the US could never shoot an atomic bomb, so residents do not go down to South Korea." Amid the strong confirmation over the infeasibility of US atomic attack, Kim-Il-sung firmly recognized the psychological power of humans, not the physical and military power of nuclear weapons.

At the Third Plenary Session of the Labor Party Central Committee (Byulori meeting: Star Duck Conference) held on December 21, 1950,[7] Kim Il-sung talked of weak organizational and discipline causing major military flaws experienced in the Korean War. Kim Il-sung focused primarily on enhancing the organization and control of the Labor Party, but also recognized the need for nuclear development that could fundamentally restrain the opponent's nuclear use. The Nuclear Artillery, a ground-based missile capable of carrying atomic bombs and nuclear weapons, was deployed in South Korea in order to support the "NSC-162/2" policy of the mass retaliation doctrine on January 12, 1954. This was in accordance with the "New Press Defense Policy" of the Eisenhower administration, which increased its reliance on nuclear power in October 1953. Since then, nuclear power management/storage/docking facilities have operated with the command and control facilities in Yongsan, Seongnam, Osan, Uijeongbu, Dongducheon, Daejeon, Gunsan, Dobongsan, Chuncheon and Hooyuk. After 1972, Gunsan was the only base used for storing US nuclear weapons in Asia until the strategic nuclear weapons were exported to a US Air Force Base in Colorado by the declaration of the denuclearization of the Korean Peninsula in 1991. President George H. W. Bush and South Korean President Roh Tae-woo announced in September and December 1991 that there were no longer nuclear weapons in South Korea. The two Koreas agreed to a "Joint Declaration on the Denuclearization of the Korean Peninsula" on December 31, 1991.

The Communist Party of China deployed some 150,000 troops to Xiamen and began shelling at Jinmen Island on September 3, 1954, which was then under the jurisdiction of the Taiwan government. President Dwight D. Eisenhower of the United States announced that he would not hesitate to use nuclear weapons against China. But Soviet leader Khrushchev only blamed the US for mentioning the possibility of nuclear use after the military struggle in the Taiwan Strait, and did not directly mention to any indication of their willingness to use nuclear weapons. China and the Soviet Union signed the Treaty of Friendship Alliance in February 1950, but the Soviet Union did not provide an active nuclear umbrella for China. In 1954, only the US, the Soviet Union, and the United Kingdom had nuclear weapons. North Korea also recognized the peculiar situation in which the Soviet Union's nuclear umbrellas were not provided to China, and strongly felt the need for its own nuclear development.

The Cold War in East Asia in the 1960s and North Korea's response

After the surrender of Japan, North Korean regime was actively supported by the Soviet Union and China in the initial stage of the regime, but it has been diplomatically isolated due to anti-Stalinism and the rigidity of the Chinese Cultural Revolution since the mid-1950s. The Pyongyang regime claimed its own diplomacy under the banner of national liberation in order to maintain a dictatorship system. The United States began experiencing rapid changes both internally and externally in the 1960s. First, there was a proliferation of racial and cultural diversity, and the other was a move to block further nuclear proliferation with nuclear states. These changes led to the tendency of American isolationism and the establishment of the Non-Proliferation Treaty (NPT) system, including the reduction of Asian influence in the 1970s. However, the United States had improved its relations with the Soviet Union in order to minimize the weakening of the hegemony in Asia and Europe, while strengthening cooperation with China and Japan for the multilateral foreign policy that had well controlled the Soviet Union.

The US Nixon administration, which was launched in January 1969, expressed the Nixon Doctrine and set the policy for US priority and isolation. President Richard M. Nixon announced the withdrawal of 25,000 US troops from Vietnam in February 1969. The Nixon–Sato Joint Statement, which increased Japan's role in East Asia, was announced in November 1969. America's status in Asia was lowered, US–Soviet relations had partially improved, and US–Japanese relations had further strengthened. The Soviet Union warned of the unlawful and irresponsible conduct of the North Korean abduction of the US Navy ship Pueblo in January 1968 and US Navy reconnaissance aircraft EC-121 in April 1969 and supported the Nixon Doctrine's relief of tension. China, on the other hand, felt a sense of crisis when the Chinese leader Mao saw the Nixon–Sato Joint Statement as a process of forming anti-communist military alliances between Japan, South Korea and Taiwan. China and North Korea attempted to improve their bilateral relations by sending delegates and senior leaders to their respective countries in October 1969 and April 1970. The US and the Soviet Union had a sharp ideological confrontation between capitalism and communism in the late 1960s. The Soviet Union, which experienced a very dangerous nuclear war crisis surrounding the deployment of missiles in Cuba in October 1962, welcomed the Nixon Doctrine in terms of alleviating tensions with the United States and expanded the influence of Japan in terms of policy conflicts and tensions with China and North Korea. However, China and North Korea were respectively different. It was only 20 years since Japan was defeated, and the pain of the colony had not completely surpassed the first generation. After all, the rise of Japan was a threat to China and North Korea. In response to the Nixon Doctrine,[8] North Korea actively cooperated with China.

However, North Korea and China did not have smooth cooperation in the late 1960s. President Nixon of the United States visited China in February 1972 and announced a joint statement that included efforts to ease tensions on the Korean Peninsula. On the other hand, the North Korean regime had strengthened its independent foreign policy in the new situation of "Cold War Relaxation and

Diversification of the International System". In the new situation, the Soviet Union and China increased their efforts to improve their national interests, mainly by improving their relations with the United States rather than their cooperation with North Korean and socialist camps. Kim Il-sung felt alienated from the new movements of the Soviet Union and China and sought a new way to justify the nation's self-determination. President Nixon's visit to China had increased the international isolation and concern that North Korea seriously felt. Meanwhile, China supported North Korea's interests in diplomatic, economic and military affairs. China also backed North Korea's position on the issue of unification on the Korean Peninsula at the United Nations General Assembly. In addition, China had increased its economic support to North Korea, which was suffering from the accumulation of foreign debt. In 1973–74, after the oil crisis, 1 million tons of crude oil was supplied at favorable prices. In January 1976, an oil pipeline was established to send energy from China to North Korea. Cooperation in the military sector had also been strengthened, and a high-level military mission had visited each other in 1974–75.

As the tensions between the United States, the Soviet Union and China had eased, North Korea became increasingly afraid of international isolation due to the diminishing cohesiveness of its socialist camp. However, on the other hand, the North Korean regime evaluated the situation that the American influence on Asia had been reduced and judged that the international conditions to unify the South Korean region with military force had been matured in accordance with the communization of South Vietnam (April 19, 1975). Kim Il-sung requested a visit to China and the Soviet Union in April 1975 to obtain political and military support for the unification of the Korean peninsula, but the Soviet Union rejected the request. China allowed Kim Il-sung's visit to Beijing, however, it did not actively support the revolutionary line of Kim Il-sung. The Soviet Union extended the validity period of the mutual defense treaty between North Korea and the Soviet Union, which expired in July 1976, by five years, but did not provide large-scale weapons that would encourage military adventure, including the provision of high-performance aircraft (including MIG-23).

China concluded a peace treaty with Japan in 1978. A three-tier cooperation system in the initiative of the United States to counter the Soviet Union was born in East Asia. The United States had recognized mainland China since 1979, as a single government of "one China" and formulated diplomatic relations with mainland China. Chinese Communist Party Chairman Hua Guofeng visited North Korea in May 1978 and Chinese Deputy Minister Deng Xiaoping visited Pyongyang in order to reduce North Korean concerns of security in the new era of détente in September 1978. However, China acknowledged the presence of US forces in South Korea, while North Korea demanded the withdrawal of US forces from the Korean Peninsula. North Korea then recognized that China had a dominant position in the surrounding area. This dominance was the reason that China invaded Vietnam in February 1979. On the other hand, the Soviet Union showed support for North Korea's unification policy and advocated the withdrawal of US forces. The Soviet Union showed the improvement of relations with North Korea in June 1976. The Soviet official media advocated withdrawing the USFK from South Korea and exhibited faithful support for North Korea's unification policy and ethnic self-determination. In response, North Korea also expressed support for the Soviet invasion of Afghanistan.

The Kim Il-sung administration wanted the North Korean region to remain in a vacuum without intervention by the surrounding great powers. A vacuum state means that the surrounding power is balanced by a certain force. The destruction of balance could be acted as a superpower's unilateral pressure on the Kim Il-sung regime. Due to the United States' defense forces in East Asia (USFK) and China's strategic dominance in the Asian continent, the North Korean regime had always tried to find survival strategy in the rapidly changing order of North East. If the USFK and China's suzerain rights are separated or clashed, it is possible for North Korea to maintain the vacuum state. However, if the two elements are combined in the three-tier cooperation and the pressure of the US to the Soviet Union, the vacuum state can be extinguished. The North Korean regime should avoid a situation where the geopolitical interests of the Korean Peninsula are shared between the great powers, arising a difficult scenario for North Korea. Therefore, the North Korean regime needed to strengthen its relationship with the Soviet Union.

In the 1970s, the bilateral foreign policy trend of the United States relaxed the solidarity within the socialist camp and made the North Korean regime feel the alienation and passing. On the other hand, the North Korean regime sensed the vacuum state of the international dynamics of the North Korean region in the context of the relaxation of tensions. In order to overcome the alienation and crisis, the North Korean regime expanded its own lines of political, ideological and military fields while utilizing its strategic position, even though Pyongyang recognized the power vacuum state of the Korean Peninsula as an opportunity that made use of the adventurous period of military expansion. Since the opportunities and crises in the North Korean regime stemmed from the vacuum and intervention of the great powers, it was the worst that the powers' interests in the peninsula were disproportionately shared. Striking the balanced status quo of superpowers in North Korea was a vital diplomatic goal for the North Korean regime.

In the mid- and late-1960s, influenced by strong opposition to the Vietnam War, the United States strengthened its preferential policy and isolationist tendencies to improve relations with foreign countries and relax tensions with the local powers rather than reducing its involvement in Asia. In addition, with the spread of nuclear weapons in the international community, such as France in 1960 and China in October 1964, the United States and the Soviet Union agreed to stop further nuclear proliferation, including atomic weapons from World War II. The Conference of the Eighteen Nation Disarmament Committee (ENDC), in which all related countries participate, was formed. The United States submitted in 1965 a draft of non-proliferation treaty to the disarmament conference. The United States and the Soviet Union agreed on the details of the treaty in August 1967. The UN General Assembly passed a resolution of 95 votes in favor of a Non-Proliferation Treaty (NPT) in June 1968. The NPT was signed in New York on July 1, 1968 by representatives of the United States, the Soviet Union, Great Britain, and 53 non-holders. NPT Article 9, paragraph 3, states that a country that has succeeded in acquiring nuclear weapons before January 1, 1967 is regarded as a legitimate holder and demands nuclear disarmament. The NPT was ratified and became officially in force on March 5, 1970.

From 1950s to 1990s, North Korea had focused on introducing and exploiting nuclear technology from Japan and the Soviet Union

After the discovery of the principle of nuclear fission by European scientists in the 1930s, the United States launched the world's first nuclear development program, the Manhattan Program in September 1942, and succeeded in the atomic bomb test in New Mexico on July 16, 1945. After World War II, the Soviet Union and Great Britain began nuclear development. Japan, which has been stimulated by international nuclear development activities, was beginning to become interested in nuclear development. The mining activities for uranium buried on the Korean Peninsula were conducted by the Institute of Physical Chemistry of Japan and the Geological Imperial College of Science and Engineering, which was newly established in 1941. Satoyasu Iimori, who obtained his Ph.D. in natural science in 1916, joined the Institute of Physics and Chemistry of Japan in 1917. Iimori conducted uranium exploration on the Taedong River and the Cheongcheon River in 1934. In a paper published in the same year, he explained the rare elemental minerals around Sekcheon Hot Springs in the vicinity of the hot spring. Iimori refined the uranium ore from the Korean Peninsula in 1935. In 1940, an engineer of the Geological Survey of Chosun Governor's Office discovered a fergusonite mineral containing 8.4% of uranium in a Gukgun mine located in the Haewol-myeon area of Baewon County, South Hwanghae Province, and developed an emergency mine. Originally, the local mine was a gold mine, but Japanese imperialists stopped the gold mining for the digging of fergusonite in March 1943. The Institute of Chemical and

Biochemical Studies began to employ 1,200 Korean workers in September 1943, and 600 workers escaped by August 1945 due to the hard work of 10 hours per day. Iwase Eiji found red tin in April 1941, in the eastern part of Sangdo-dong, Gilju County, and North Hamgyong Province, which was 2.7 times higher in uranium purity than other surrounding minerals.

Japan's Army Aviation Technology Research Institute commissioned the Institute of Physics and Chemistry to study the development of atomic bombs in June 1941. Following the initials of a researcher Yoshio Nishina, the name of the research project was "Nigo". Nigo research succeeded in producing uranium hexafluoride, a gas for thermal diffusion for uranium separation, but failed to separate uranium (uranium 235 enrichment) and was suspended in April 1945 as the separation facility was destroyed. Radioactive mineral resources were found in hot springs around Kyungsung County, North Hamgyong Province in 1944. The Institute of Physics and Chemistry of Japan instructed the subordinate branch located on the Korean Peninsula to send the fergusonite to Japan in May 1944. The branch collected 3 tons of fergusonite with 4–5% uranium oxide content for 15 months until July 1945 and stored it in Incheon, near Seoul. Under the leadership of the Chosun Governor-General, the "Chosun Major Mineral Emergency Research Team" consisting of researchers and technicians from the Korean Peninsula, Japan and Manchuria was organized. From August to December 1944, a geological survey was conducted. The investigation team reported that the national mine was then the largest uranium source on the Korean Peninsula with fergusonite containing up to 6% uranium oxide.

There was a rumor that the Japanese government succeeded in the initial atomic bomb test at the Yongheung factory in Hungnam District, Hamhung City in South Hamgyong Province.[9] In order to escape the defeat of World War II through the development of atomic bombs, Japan actively carried out nuclear material discovery and nuclear research activities on the Korean Peninsula. The national mine of South Hwanghae, the largest uranium producer on the Korean Peninsula, belonged to the North Korean region after the Korean War and 1,200 Koreans during the Japanese occupation were engaged in uranium mining. There were also Koreans in the Geochemistry Research Institute, Kyungsung Imperial University and the Geological Survey of the Chosun Governor's Office. Considering these points, it was assumed that many Koreans related to uranium extraction partly recognized the development plan of the atomic bomb made in Japan. It was very likely that the Kim Il-sung regime managed those facilities and used them for future nuclear development, because the Japanese nuclear facilities remained in the North Korean region upon the defeat of the Japanese imperialism by US atomic bombs.

The North Korean regime established the Chosun Academy of Sciences in October 1952 and founded the Nuclear Energy Research Institute in December of that year. It signed the "Peaceful Utilization Agreement" with the Soviet Union in March 1953. A physics library was opened in Wonsan, Gangwon Province in September 1953.[10] A nuclear armed forces division was established under the People's Armed Forces in 1954. In June of the same year, Kim Il-sung visited the nuclear power plant that the Soviet Union built for the first time in the world. The Kim Il-sung administration decided to install the Atomic and Nuclear Physics Research Institute at the second general meeting of the Chosun Academy of Sciences in April 1955. The Radiochemical Research Institute was established in March 1956, and in June of the same year, six North Korean scientists attended the Eastern European Science Congress on the peaceful use of nuclear energy.[11] The Kim Il-sung administration concluded an agreement with the Soviet Union to join the establishing of the "Dubna Multilateral Nuclear Research Institute" in Moscow and dispatched 30 nuclear engineers to the institute on March 26, 1956. At that time, the Yongbyon Radiochemical Research Institute was established. Approximately 250 North Korean scientists were estimated to have participated in the study at Dubna, including North Korean scientists dispatched to the Dubna lab in May 1975 and January 1980.

With the success of the Soviet Union's nuclear development in 1949 and the US's nuclear policy statement in November 1950, the

Kim Il-sung regime had the basic infrastructure, including the establishment of nuclear research institutes and organizations. With the establishment of the Soviet Union's Dubna Nuclear Research Institute, North Korea was also able to acquire advanced nuclear technology related to socialist countries such as the Soviet Union in March 1956. Since the criticism of Stalin's personal worship at the 20th Congress of the Communist Party of Soviet Socialism in February 1956, the socialist camp had begun a struggle between revisionism and dogmatism. The founding of the Dubna Nuclear Research Institute almost coincided with the time of ideological struggle. The Soviet Union developed the first atomic bomb among the socialist nations in 1949. Khrushchev had offered incentives to North Korea that the researchers could join the Dubna Nuclear Research Institute in order to elicit support from other socialist countries for his revisionist line. China also dispatched Wang Qingchang, a nuclear scientist, to the Dubna Nuclear Research Institute, and succeeded in developing the atomic bomb in 1964. Unlike Khrushchev's intentions, the line struggle began to intensify in 1960, and in 1964, Khrushchev was defeated. While China and North Korea introduced Soviet nuclear technology from the Dubna Nuclear Research Institute, Mao and Kim Il-sung were able to continue their policy of dogmatism. The Soviet Union took a dual position to separate North Korea and China in 1959. The Soviet Union informed China of the abrogation of the 1957 military new technology agreement and refused to provide a model of atomic bombs. On the other hand, North Korea signed a nuclear agreement with the Soviet Union in September 1959 and therefore could receive the continued support for the Yongbyon Nuclear Research Center from the Soviet Union. At the same time, North Korea signed a nuclear cooperation agreement with China in September 1959. The USFK announced on January 29, 1959 that it had deployed nuclear weapons to South Korea under a massive retaliatory strategy of the United States, which could be regarded as justifying North Korea's nuclear agreement. The Kim Il-sung regime was able to occupy a superior diplomatic position by sending scientists to the Soviet Union's Dubna Nuclear Research Institute and achieving a nuclear agreement with the Soviet Union despite the turmoil of Sino–Soviet diplomatic conflicts.

The Kim Il-sung regime's basic nuclear infrastructures included recruiting and nurturing nuclear researchers. Dr. Lee Seung-gi, who majored in chemical industry at Kyoto Imperial University in Japan in 1939, developed the first synthetic fiber, VINALON, in Asia in 1939. He served as dean of the College of Engineering at Seoul National University in 1945 and became the first director of the Nuclear Research Institute of the Chosun Academy of Sciences, the first nuclear research institute in North Korea. The Kim Il-sung regime succeeded in extracting the plutonium amount in grams for the first time in 1975. Plutonium extraction was a chemical process that Dr. Lee was likely to have been involved in. Dr. Lee was elected to the Supreme People's Assembly and died on February 8, 1996. Professor Do Sang-rok was an author of North Korean physics academics who wrote a book called *Nuclear Structure and Nuclear Theory.* Kim Il-sung publicly praised the book, and appointed Dr. Do as a professor at the Department of Physics at Kim Il-sung University. From late 1950s, Dr. Han In-seok advocated nuclear development for party cadres. Jung Geun, the general manager of North Korea's nuclear development policy enforcement, was a professor at Seoul National University and went to North Korea. Dr. Seo Sang-gook, who received Kim Il-sung's special trust, was presumed to be the head of the first nuclear test of North Korea and had experience in research at Dvina. Choi Hak-gun was also seen as a councilor at the North Korean diplomatic mission in Vienna, Austria, for four years starting in 1974, after passing through the Dubna Institute. It was known that the International Atomic Energy Agency (IAEA) library acquired technical information on nuclear energy. Gae Young-soon had also been known as a specialist in nuclear device and facility construction since the early 1970s, claiming to "build a nuclear power plant with our own strength." Dr. Kyung Won-ha, a father of nuclear technology in North Korea, graduated from Kim Il-sung College of Engineering, but came down to South Korea in 1951 during the Korean War. It was assumed that he studied in Brazil and the US in the 1960s and then went to North Korea in the 1970s to engage in nuclear development programs such as the Yongbyon nuclear reactor (CANDU type heavy water reactor). In April 1969, he published his master's thesis, *Numerical Technique of Spherical Width Axis*, at McGill University in Canada. He published in March 1972 a doctoral thesis at the same university called *Theoretical Study of Spherical Gaseous Detonation Waves*. References to the doctoral dissertation included the *Atomic Bomb Height* published in 1954 by the Los Alamos National Laboratory, the US's first to develop an atomic bomb. After submitting his doctoral dissertation, he resumed his studies in July 1972. North Korea detected a high-performance explosion test from 1983 to 2006 about 70 times, and it was analyzed that it carried out an explosion test (high-tension test) on the finished product high-explosive device just before the nuclear test from 1993 to 1998. North Korea carried out a first nuclear test on October 9, 2006. Dr. Kyung Won-ha was also expected to have participated in the development of North Korea's high-explosive devices since 1972. The tradition of securing nuclear manpower for many years in North Korea explains the reason that the denuclearization of North Korea should include the dismissal of researchers, or knowledge bases, at the same time as the dismantling of nuclear weapons and facilities.

In the 1960s, many nuclear scientists from the Korean Peninsula returned to North Korea by the slanted propaganda of a pro-North Korean organization, the Chosun Federation of Korean Residents in Japan (Chongryon), and worked at the Yongbyon nuclear research center. They had learned about nuclear technology in Japan through the Chosun Science and Technology Association under Chongryon. Since the 1950s, the administration has been able to continuously introduce external nuclear technology through methods such as exchange of scientists with foreign countries. The Soviet Union wanted to monopolize nuclear weapons technology in communist countries by constructing nuclear power plants in communist countries and controlling technology, uranium and nuclear materials and operational personnel. North Korea and the Soviet Union signed a nuclear agreement in September 1959, and the Soviet Union promised

North Korea support for the Yongbyon Nuclear Energy Research Institute. The regime introduced the Soviet heat power 2MW small reactor (IRT-2000) in January 1962 and started installation under the support of the Soviet Union and construction of nuclear research center in Yongbyon and Pakcheon, North Pyongan Province that year. The construction of the Yongbyon Nuclear Energy Research Institute was completed in February 1964, and the North Korean engineers began receiving training on how to operate the Nuclear Energy Research Institute from the Soviet technologists. The administration completed the critical facility and began operating the 2MW reactor in June 1965. Before the commissioning of the nuclear reactor, Kim Il-sung stated in his address to the Higher Education Party that the foreign technology should be actively introduced on February 23, 1965 because it lacked the ability to "process" the fuel in an industrial way.[12] The "treatment of industrial processes" was estimated to refer to the formation of a predecessor fuel cycle and a critical state (fission environment) with reference to the completion of a critical facility and four months prior to reactor operation. The regime built the Yongbyon Nuclear Energy Research Institute under the support of the Soviet Union, but attempted to develop nuclear technology in other ways without depending on the support of the Soviet Union. In 1959, the regime established a nuclear research and development center disguised as a furniture factory signboard on the Kowloon River in Yongbyon City, North Pyongan Province. Kim Il-sung praised the success of China's nuclear test and sent an expert to China in October 1964.[13] However, China expressed its willingness to reject North Korea's request for technical assistance in 1964, China cooperated with uranium mining exploration in areas known to have highly commercialized uranium deposits in 1964, such as Hwanggi-gun in North Hamgyong Province, Hamheung City in South Hamgyong Province, North Gyeongsang Province, Goseong-gun in Gangwon Province, and Pyeongsan in South Hwanghae Province. As a result, about 26 million tons of uranium was reportedly buried in North Korea, the feasible output of total reserves was estimated at 4 million tons. Kim Il-sung emphasized that there was enough nuclear material in North Korea by referring to the Higher Education Council General Meeting held on February 23, 1965. On the Korean Peninsula, unlike South Korea, there is a large amount of uranium in the North. In the context of the strict monitoring of uranium movement in the international community by the NPT, North Korea fully meets the primary conditions for nuclear development.

1960s: Kim Il-sung's policy to strengthen national defense through nuclear weapon

Kim Il-sung actively pursued an aggressive defense policy after the Cuban Missile Crisis in 1962. He actively promoted self-reliant national defense, which maximized defense strength, and put the Juche (self-reliant) idea as a governing ideology. At the Fourth Plenary Meeting of the Korean Workers' Party held in December 1962, North Korea discussed "the issue of strengthening the defense forces in relation to the recent international situation", and adopted "self-armaments principle in defense" that included four military lines like fortification of the whole country, becoming cadres of all soldiers, modernization of the entire military force, and the modernization of the entire army. North Korea secretly pursued nuclear development as a means of self-reliant defense. South Korean President Park Chung-hee secretly tried to develop a nuclear bomb and missile by feeling the sense of danger that security might be threatened by the detente atmosphere of Northeast Asia due to the visit of US President Nixon to China in 1972 and the withdrawal of the US 7th Division from South Korea. The top leaders of the two Koreas ultimately recognized in the late 1960s and early 1970s that fickle conflict and cooperation between the continent and maritime forces needed their own nuclear arsenal rather than relying on their allies to swiftly respond to security threats under rapidly changing international politics. There were some commonalities on both sides at the time.

Kim Il-sung attended a rally organized by the Chairman of the Labor Party and the head of the army in October 1965, and said, "In the near future, North Korea can possess nuclear weapons." Two years later, Kim Il-sung said, "We also produced atomic bombs, and we can use them if the United States uses atomic bombs." Park Sung-chul, who was then North Korea's deputy prime minister in 1970, emphasized, "We will make an effort to manufacture the atomic bomb by 1972" to a delegation of Japanese social scientists who visited Pyongyang. When China refused to support North Korea's development of nuclear weapons, Pyongyang just started operating research reactor IRT-2000 on its own. Since 1965, when North Korea's nuclear technology was not well developed, Kim Il-sung had expressed its willingness to develop nuclear weapons and missiles based on the recognition that North Korea has abundant uranium reserves. He addressed the opening ceremony of the 1965 Hamhung Military Academy, saying, "Once again, the US and Japan also will intervene when the Korean War takes place again," and "We must have missiles to strike the United States and Japan to prevent the intervention of the two countries." He emphasized at the October 1965 Labor Party meeting, "North Korea can possess nuclear weapons at a time not too far away." He also insisted at the military commanders meeting in 1967 that "We also produced atomic bombs." China's leader, Mao Zedong met Kim Il-sung in Beijing on April 18, 1975, saying, "As China developed nuclear weapons, relations with the Soviet Union deteriorated and tens of millions starved to death due to economic difficulties. So if the development of nuclear weapons has been intensely carried out in a country that is small and economically vulnerable like North Korea, the economy will collapse and even socialism itself can't keep up and do not even dream it." However, "The biggest obstacle to North Korea's nuclear development is China, and we can succeed in secreting and steadily securing nuclear development," said Kim Il-sung on a train back to North Korea. The North Korean leader did not listen to Mao's advices and pursued his own nuclear development.

Despite the independent course of nuclear development, Kim Il-sung continued to confirm the strategic importance of a close relationship between North Korea and China, while Sino–Soviet conflict had reduced their influence on North Korea. In addition, he concentrated on getting economic support while lamenting and comforting China even amid criticism of the international community emerging from the nuclear development process. Due to the amendment of Khrushchev in 1956, the Nixon Doctrine in 1969, and the international community's relaxed atmosphere, the regime was not limited to acquiring technology through the Soviet Union. North Korea tried to again acquire nuclear development technology from China that had a negative attitude at the support, and covertly attempted to develop its own aggressive nuclear power based on a large amount of uranium buried as shown in furniture factory signs and nuclear missile development references.

1970s: Continuation of the NPT system and North Korea's nuclear development

In the 1970s, North Korea focused on nurturing relevant personnel to develop nuclear weapons. North Korea's Department of Education established a department of nuclear research related to a number of universities in 1973. North Korea secretly imported Scud missiles, a means of delivering nuclear weapons from Egypt in 1976, and then disassembled them in order to produce counterfeit goods. In the end, North Korea started to introduce and develop missiles, which are vehicles for the use of nuclear weapons, concurrently with the development of nuclear weapons. Kim Il-sung emphasized the importance and necessity of constructing nuclear power plants in various political events in 1974. North Korea succeeded in testing the Scud B missiles made by its own technology in 1984 as a reverse design method. North Korea also succeeded in launching the Scud C missile in a range of 500km in 1986. An exploration for uranium, the raw material for the development of uranium nuclear weapons, was conducted throughout North Korea in 1978. North Korea started the construction of a 5MW reactor in Yongbyon in 1980 and a 50MW reactor in 1985, and the introduction of a 440MW Soviet type VVER light-water reactor. North Korea had to join the NPT in 1985 at the request of the Soviet Union in the process of introducing Soviet nuclear reactors. North Korea intentionally delayed signing the safeguards agreement because of the fear that joining the NPT would hinder the development of nuclear weapons. North Korea was revealed to have been secretly cleared by the US Central Intelligence Agency (CIA) that the NPT was aimed at obtaining nuclear weapons development and military and economic support from the Soviet Union. According to the CIA document, it was estimated that North Korea first extracted plutonium in the late 1980s and early 1990s.

North Korea tried to secretly develop nuclear weapons on the domestic side, but it did internationally smoke-screen tactics. The country joined the International Atomic Energy Agency (IAEA) in July 1974, entered the safety control system of the IAEA, and served as a member of the Council from 1989 to 1991. While South Korea dispatched the director general to the IAEA, North Korea has made every effort to conceal its nuclear arsenal, including resident delegations. Paradoxically, it was South Korea, not North Korea, who was suspected of nuclear weapons from the international community before the 1980s. South Korean President Park Chung-hee continued to receive suspicions about developing nuclear weapons from the US Department of Defense and intelligence agencies before his death in October 1979. In 1977, the story of Dr. Benjamin W. Lee, a genius physicist from South Korea, who died in a car accident at the age of 42 in US state of Michigan, was reported to be related to South Korea's nuclear development. In part, there was a media report that the US CIA interfered with South Korea's nuclear development in response to Dr. Benjamin W. Lee's decision to help develop Park Chung-hee's nuclear weapons program, which simultaneously began with the withdrawal of the USFK from South Korea. At that time, it was not officially confirmed whether

Dr. Benjamin W. Lee's death was directly related to the US's move to stop South Korea from developing nuclear weapons.

North Korea's introduction of nuclear technology through external researchers and exchanges continued into the 1970s. The administration invited eight Chinese nuclear scientists to North Korea and received technical support for nuclear research institutes and reactor construction in April 1971. Dr. Cho Kwang-joo who conducted centrifugation experiments at the Institute of Nuclear Engineering at Tokyo Institute of Technology, went to North Korea in March 1974, and attempted to commercialize monazite buried in North Korea. After studying nuclear fusion at the Nagoya University of Japan after World War II, Dr. Hushimi Kochi visited North Korea in 1987, and he was an advisor to Professor Lee Shi-gu who earned the title of honorary doctorate at the Chosun Academy of Sciences. North Korea sent a delegation to attend the general conference of the Dubna Institute in May 1975. A delegation headed by Kim Kyung-jun was dispatched to Beijing to acquire isotope application technology in 1975 and 1976. Twenty-seven nuclear missile researchers were dispatched to a nuclear test center in China in March 1977.

The top leaders of the two Koreas officially announced the North–South Joint Statement in July 1972, which declared the principle of peaceful coexistence and peaceful reunification for the first time since the Korean War. Since then, President Park Chung-hee enacted the Yushin Constitution on October 17, 1972, which made the legislative functions ineffective in the name of preparation for peaceful reunification. The Kim Il-sung regime promulgated the Socialist Constitution to strengthen the Labor Party's sole control over North Korea in November 1972. It stipulated in the Socialist Constitution adopted in December 1972 that the Labor Party would lead the North Korean regime, strengthening the regime and laying the foundation for succession. South and North Korea's top leaders, after announcing the Inter-Korean Joint Statement, emphasized the importance of strengthening the power of each regime and implementing measures to build a succession system rather than actual measures for inter-Korean relations and reunification. This was presumably intended for local political goals. The Inter-Korean Joint Statement can be interpreted as an expression of anxiety felt by the top leaders of the two Koreas on the unilateral treatment of the Korean Peninsula by the neighboring great powers in an uncertain and changing international situation. The difficult situation of the Vietnam War in the 1970s and the establishment of the NPT system influenced the leaders of the two Koreas who were not nuclear weapons states. In the aftermath of the Vietnam War in January 1968, South Korea President Park Chung-hee felt two anxieties. One was distrust of the alliance. The Nixon Doctrine, announced in July 1969, was intended to step down US influence in Asia. The Seventh Infantry Division of the US Forces Korea was withdrawn from South Korea in March 1971. US troops stationed in Vietnam also began to withdraw from Vietnam in 1969 and was completely withdrawn in March 1973. Eventually, South Vietnam was incorporated by North Vietnam on April 30, 1975. On the other hand, when President Nixon visited China in February 1972 and improved US–China relations, he felt uneasy that the issue of the Korean Peninsula could be determined by one-sided negotiations between the great powers. On September 8, both Koreas issued a joint statement on North–South cooperation to emphasize "independence". South Korea's Nuclear Weapons Initiative was initiated through a document titled "Kinds of Nuclear Weapons and Our Development Direction". In conclusion, South Korea intends to respond quickly to changes in the rapidly changing foreign environment by strengthening the regime through the establishment of the Yushin Constitution in October 1972. Since the commencement of nuclear development, uranium exploration had been carried out on South Korea and it had been confirmed that 240,000 tons of uranium were buried. At that time, the United States recognized that South Korea was most likely to have nuclear weapons inevitably. In 1976, US Secretary of State Henry Kissinger stressed that if South Korea would not give up its nuclear weapons development, it would consider a full withdrawal of US forces from South Korea. Donald Gregg, who was the head of the CIA's Korea branch in 1973–75, noted that Park Chung-hee eventually gave up nuclear development in 1977.

The Kim Il-sung regime held the 5th Congress of the Labor Party in November 1970 and adopted the six-year economic development plan including the use of nuclear energy. The North Korean regime's public declaration of the use of nuclear energy at the Labor Congress included the objection to the NPT regime that took effect in March 1970. North Korean Deputy Prime Minister Park Sung-chul told a Japanese delegation of social science in 1970 that he would "make an effort to manufacture the atomic bomb by 1972." Kim Il-sung instructed in 1972 the Labor Party's nuclear development department to refer to the case of China's nuclear development and to proceed with North Korea's nuclear development under the strategy of "hiding, dispersing, and undergrounding". North Korea joined the IAEA in September 1974 and signed a partial safeguards agreement for 2MW reactors in September 1977 and began receiving regular inspections. However, in 1975, before the inspection, the first g-unit plutonium was extracted from a 2MW reactor. As directed by Kim Il-sung, North Korea had already taken precautionary measures. In November 1978, North Korea conducted uranium exploration throughout North Korea. Uranium exploration proceeded at intervals of about 15 years since 1946. Along with the exploration activities, uranium mining activities were also conducted in mines such as Pyeongsan County in North Hwanghae Province and Suncheon County in South Pyongan Province. North Korea established the Nuclear Physics Department at Kim Il-sung University in 1973 and the Department of Nuclear Engineering at Kimcheg Technical University to strengthen the base of nuclear research personnel. The Atomic Energy Research Institute was changed to the jurisdiction of the General Administration of Atomic Energy in January 1974, and the Atomic Energy Act was enacted in the same year. In order to accelerate nuclear development, institutional and organizational reforms were carried out. Although South Korea abandoned nuclear development plan due to the pressure of the United States, Kim Il-sung strengthened its regime security and kept secretly continuing its nuclear development activities in a vacuum without the influence of powerful nations in Northeast Asia's international politics.

1980s: North Korea completed its production cycle of plutonium and rejects Soviet inspections

In the 1980s, the Kim Il-sung regime attempted to strengthen its own nuclear technology while introducing the Soviet nuclear technology. The Soviet Union demanded North Korea accept the NPT inspections, but the North denied immediate acceptance, delayed it as soon as possible, and used it as a negotiation chip. North Korea concluded a partial safeguards agreement in September 1977 to allow the IAEA to inspect the 2MWt reactor in Yongbyon. North Korea joined the NPT regime on December 12, 1986. Normally, when a particular country joins the NPT regime, it must sign a nuclear safety agreement with the IAEA within 18 months and receive inspections from the IAEA, but North Korea did not sign the nuclear safety agreement until 1991. North Korea signed the IAEA nuclear safety safeguards agreement only after the declaration that both Koreas did not have nuclear weapons on the Korean Peninsula in the second half of 1991 and announced the suspension of the Team Spirit training in 1992. The Kim Il-sung regime had secured a certain level of its own technology and was able to reject the Soviet demands. Even if the conditions for introducing foreign technology deteriorated due to refusal of inspections, North Korea had taken a strategy to gradually secure nuclear technology at home and abroad. It was impossible for a particular country to actually develop a nuclear weapon under an international nonproliferation regime aimed at reducing the use of nuclear weapons and focusing on peaceful uses. The Kim Il-sung regime completed the plutonium production cycle and started its own nuclear development activities to atomize plutonium, making uranium raw materials, reactors and reprocessing facilities and conducting high-level experiments. In November 1982, the uranium refining and conversion facility of Pakcheon County, North Pyongan Province, which was commenced in 1962, started to operate. The construction of uranium refining and conversion facility was started in Pyeongsan County, North Hwanghae Province in 1985.

Before and after the 1980s, North Korea began construction of four nuclear reactors. Although the Yongbyon 2MW reactors were subject to inspection under the Partial Safeguards Agreement in 1977, the North Korean regime began construction of a 5MW reactor in Yongbyon in 1979 with its own technology, reached the critical point on August 14, 1985, and began operation at the end of 1986. During the construction of the 5MW reactor, the administration was supposed to have focused on securing the reprocessing technology based on the plutonium extraction case in 1975, and construction of the reprocessing facility started in Yongbyon in November 1985. In addition, North Korea started construction of a 50MW nuclear reactor in Yongbyon in May 1985, and it built a 200MW reactor in Taecheon, North Pyongan Province in November 1989. According to the request of the Soviet Union, North Korea joined the NPT on December 12, 1985. As a result, North Korea and the Soviet Union concluded an "Economic and Technical Cooperation Agreement for the Construction of North Korean Nuclear Power Plant" on December 25, 1985, and the construction was started in February 1990 by selecting the shore of Sinpo City in South Hamgyong Province.

The regime began construction of a radioactive chemical laboratory and a reprocessing facility in Yongbyon in November 1985. As a result of IAEA inspection in 1992, the annual reprocessing capacity of this facility was estimated to be about 200 tons. Reprocessing is the process of isolating only isotopes suitable for nuclear explosion among the isotopes. The isotope suitable for a nuclear explosion has the same chemical number as the proton number but has different mass numbers for different numbers of neutrons. Both "reprocessing", which separates Pu-239 and Pu-241, and "enrichment", which increases the content ratio of U-235, are the processes of nuclear isotope separation. The precipitation technology is a method that can be reprocessed in the shortest period by the rudimentary remotely operated technique even if the cooling period of the spent fuel is short and the Pu-239 concentration is low. It was estimated that North Korea used the same method in the early stage of reprocessing. There are technical inherent limitations that cannot completely remove (reprocess) Pu-239 from nuclear wastes. Pu can be extracted from nuclear wastes by pyrolysis, precipitation, filtration, solvent extraction and ion exchange. One of the solvent extraction methods, Purex Technology, is a solution of TBP tri-butyl phosphate that is extracted from nitric acid aqueous solution by using four Pu nitrates as an extraction agent, and the process proceeds to complicated processes such as cutting and dissolving spent nuclear fuel, solvent extraction, and storing process solution. Technicians can arbitrarily conceal Pu in this complex process. Since 1983, North Korea has stepped up its high-performance explosion test for nuclear material explosion.

North Korea was detected to have conducted 70 high-performance explosion tests from 1983 to 2006, and it was estimated that the explosion test for the high-performance explosive devices of the final product, the last stage of the nuclear test, was conducted from 1993 to 1998. The first nuclear test in October 2006 officially confirmed that North Korea's high-performance explosive devices operate normally. Nuclear bombs are divided into two types: the gun type (mostly highly enriched uranium) stores nuclear material in two parts and breaks up the gunpowder to fire nuclear material on one side of the gun and nuclear material on the other side so that the two materials are combined to reach a supercritical state, Structure; on the other hand, the traverse width type (mainly plutonium) is a method of rapidly compressing nuclear material into a supercritical state by concentrating the explosive force around a high explosive around a nuclear material having a critical mass and centering the bulbous nuclear bomb. In the 1980s, North Korea proceeded to extract plutonium from nuclear reactors, so the high-performance explosion test would have done by the traverse width devices. North Korea focused on extracting WGPu (Weapons-Grade Plutonium) containing more than 93% of Pu-239, including uranium raw materials, nuclear reactors and reprocessing facilities. Highly enriched uranium (HEU) and weapons-grade plutonium (WGPu) are used as raw materials for nuclear weapons. HEU is superior in quality but difficult to manufacture, while WGPu is widely used because it can be mass-produced in nuclear reactors.

Kim Il-sung emphasized in his 1958 and 1977 New Year's address that nuclear power plants should be built to develop power tools for machine operation in terms of power management and power industry development.[14] North Korea calls the Yongbyon complex the "First Nuclear Power Industrial Base", but there is no electricity generator for converting nuclear energy into electric energy. To utilize nuclear as electrical energy requires additional facilities such as reactors, steam generators, and electricity generators, but this is not the case for the Yongbyon reactor area. The so-called "right to peaceful use of nuclear energy" that North Korea would use nuclear power as an energy source was an external cause for legitimate development of nuclear weapons. Estimates of plutonium produced by North Korea varied from country to country. The United States estimated that North Korea extracted 11–13kg of WGPu through fuel rod withdrawal and reprocessing during 1989–1990. On the other hand, during 1989–1991, South Korea estimated 7–12kg, Japan 16–24kg, and Russia 22kg.[15] Even if the data provided by North Korea were accurate, estimates of plutonium production could differ by up to 30kg for three reasons. First, it was difficult to estimate the actual production of Pu-239 because it was possible to control the degree of combustion and replace the fuel rod when using the graphite moderator like the 5MWe reactor in Yongbyon. The total amount of nuclear fuel in the Yongbyon 5MWe reactor is 50 MTU of 8,010 nuclear fuel rods — these fuel rods are stacked vertically on each of 801 channels. Second, the recovery rate of Pu-239 in the reprocessing process is not constant. Third, a certain amount of loss occurs when metal is processed to make Pu-239 as a bomb.

Because of this technical margin of error, even if a denuclearization agreement is initiated in earnest, there may be disagreement between the Parties and the relevant countries on the way in which the produced nuclear material is calculated. Also, as time passes, the number of cases that must be tracked to calculate the production of nuclear material increases, and the calculation becomes more complicated. A typical negotiation style, in which North Korea rejects the declaration and inspection of nuclear weapons and materials, and takes the negotiation process for a long time, resulted in a vacuum that lacked international surveillance on nuclear development and made it difficult for the NPT and the international community to denuclearize North Korea. This technical error had led to inconsistencies between the data submitted by the North to the IAEA in 1990s and the IAEA inspection results. North Korea rejected special inspections of unscientific and suspicious facilities, and a serious North Korean nuclear crisis took place in 1994. These North Korean suspicious behaviors were being repeated in the conflicts between the Trump administration and the Kim Jong-un regime in 2018.

1990s: Prolonged negotiations for denuclearization and suspicion of nuclear development

On September 15, 1989, North Korea's nuclear issue finally surfaced as the images of secret nuclear facilities, photographed by French commercial satellite SPOT No. 2, became public. The reality of North Korea's nuclear weapons development secretly pursued for the past 30 years had finally been publicly disclosed to the international community by satellite data. 1989 was the year when the communist regimes of the Eastern European countries began to collapse after the declaration of Malta that the US President George H.W. Bush and the Soviet President Mikhail Gorbachev agreed to end the Cold War at the summit. In an international situation where China and the Soviet Union were deviating from socialism and seeking reconciliation with the capitalist camp, North Korea had to worry about the future choice of policies and routes. For North Korea, which had based on the ideology of anti-Americanism, it meant a compromise with the capitalist state and reconciliation with imperialism, which led to a weakening of the rule of regime. The disastrous ending of the dictator Nicolae Ceausescu whom Kim Il-sung imitated, as a result of the 1989 democratic revolution in Romania was a tremendous shock to the North Korean dictator. Kim Il-sung, who, of course, felt extreme fear when he saw the peaceful unification of East and West Germany, acted on the contrary to promote the development of nuclear weapons and to reject the reform and opening. Kim Il-sung, the leader of North Korea judged that the only measure to ensure security in the absence of the guardianship of China and Russia was the development of nuclear weapons. From this time on, North Korea began to publicly threaten to have nuclear weapons in the international community. North Korean foreign minister Kim Young-nam's remarks in March 1990 signaled a public threat to the international community. North Korea's brinkmanship diplomacy through nuclear threat was similar to trying to spread their wings when warts met their enemies. The North Korean diplomats' remarks included a hidden intention to exaggerate their abilities and to expose their enemies to threats to their opponents.

During the Middle East Gulf War (1990–91), the US military recognized that Iraq was developing a nuclear program. The IAEA failed to find a nuclear program in Iraq, despite its inspections of nuclear weapons and facilities. Therefore, the IAEA pursued a strong and detailed inspection of North Korea to avoid repeating the incomplete missile inspections in Iraq. US President Bush announced in 1991 that he would abolish all tactical nuclear weapons on the Korean Peninsula except for the air force and limit plans for the modernization of strategic nuclear weapons. As a result, the number of tactical nuclear weapons in Korea, which had reached 950 by 1967, was reduced to 540 in 1976, and the last remaining 100 in December 1991 was withdrawn to the United States Air Force Base in Colorado. In the end, the security situation in Northeast Asia had been also significantly improved. The United States had withdrawn tactical nuclear weapons from South Korea since September 1991 and had pledged to stop the South Korea–US joint military exercise, Team Spirit training if North Korea accepted inspections. In December 1991, the final

Table 1.1 Discrepancies between North Korea report and IAEA inspection results

	North Korea Report	IAEA Claim
PU volume	90g	A few kg
PU extraction time	Once (1990)	3 times (1989, 1990, 1991) or more
PU extraction source	Damaged spent fuel rods	Spent fuel
Unreported facilities (2 locations)	Military base	Nuclear waste repository

100 remaining were withdrawn to the US Air Force Base in Colorado. North Korea refused to sign the Nuclear Safety Agreement on the grounds that the USFK had nuclear weapons. However, as pressure from the international community intensified, North Korea reluctantly accepted the US proposal, signed a nuclear safeguards agreement, agreed on a joint declaration of denuclearization, and accepted IAEA inspections. The inspections on the nuclear facilities were carried out six times from May 25, 1992 to February 6, 1993. However, in the second inspections of July 1992, two incompatible amounts of plutonium in the report submitted by North Korea and two unrecorded facilities estimated as reprocessed nuclear waste repositories were found as shown in Table 1.1. North Korea and the international organizations again collided around the results of field inspections of nuclear facilities.

The first nuclear crisis in 1993 and the death of Kim Il-sung

The year 1993, when the first North Korean nuclear crisis began, was the period of regime change for both North Korea and the United States. US President Clinton and Kim Jong-il, the son of Kim Il-sung who actually began to rule the North Korean regime in the 1990s, adhered to hardline policies against North Korea and the US, respectively. Then South Korean President Kim Young-sam's North Korean policy (1993.2~1998.2), who was trying to differentiate his brand from former President Roh Tae-woo (1988.2~1993.3) who pursued a northward policy, planned the first North–South summit meeting with President Kim Il-sung in July 1994. However, as Kim Il-sung died suddenly in July 1994, the policy to solve the problem of nuclear and peninsular unification through the summit ended in failure. After experiencing conflicts with Pyongyang in the process of pursuing policies on North Korea, Kim Young-sam abandoned the policy of exchange and cooperation with the regime in accordance with the logic that "blood is thicker than water", and pursued hardline policy toward North Korea. In response to North Korea refusing to inspect the facilities, South Korea and the United States announced the resumption of Team Spirit training in early 1993. Responding to US demands for special inspections, North Korea did not admit that it violated the basic principles of good faith, such as not declaring that they would develop nuclear weapons. The regime, on the other hand, preposterously proclaimed the state of wartime in response to Team Spirit training on March 8, 1993 and surprisingly declared that it would withdraw from the NPT.

In spite of the North Korea's hardline countermeasures such as the withdrawal of the NPT, South Korean President Kim Young-sam, who said that "there is nothing more important than the people", promoted an emotional policy toward North Korea at the early stage of his term. He repatriated the arrested spy "Lee In-mo", who repeatedly criticized South Korea and supported North Korea in prison, to North Korea at Pyongyang's request. However, after that, when North Korea did not stop the brinkmanship tactics, Kim Young-sam criticized North Korea, saying, "We can't shake hands with a country with a nuclear weapon." The United States proposed to build a light-water reactor in North Korea in 1993, two times during the North Korea–US talks, in return for reservations to withdraw from the NPT and the abandonment of the graphite moderated reactor. North Korea and the United States reached a comprehensive agreement on nuclear inspections in February 1994. However, North Korea's uncooperative attitude toward the IAEA inspections and the "Seoul Bombing Remarks" by North Korean representative, Park Young-soo, which heightened the war crisis at the inter-Korean talks for a certain agreement on the exchange of special envoys between the two Koreas, led to rapid tensions between the two Koreas.

At the time, US President Clinton stressed that the US should never allow it, warning that it will take a very firm and tough stance on North Korea's nuclear program. Clinton said North Korea's nuclear development would be a huge nightmare, since he assessed that North Korea had a high risk of using nuclear weapons upon possessing them. President Clinton stressed that North Korea's nuclear development was being accomplished at the toughest time, noting that Iran and Iraq would soon be opposed to the US if they were to succeed in nuclear development. President Clinton feared that even if North Korea showed the possibility of nuclear development, Japan would soon be rearmed. The United States said it would not allow North Korea to develop nuclear weapons from the beginning because the stability of the region would become very dangerous if the nuclear domino phenomenon swiftly spread in Northeast Asia. Clinton strongly warned that "if North Korea tries to use nuclear weapons, they will meet his end." As the United States deployed Patriot missiles in South Korea, and North Korea enforced the extraction of spent fuel rods, the tensions on the Korean Peninsula grew steadily. US security experts claimed that the preemptive attack on nuclear facilities would be necessary. However, according to his autobiography, former President Clinton came to the conclusion that diplomatic negotiations were more necessary than a local preemptive strike because of the enormous casualties of Americans in the possibility of a war.[16] Should the US forces attacked the Yongbyon nuclear facility at that time, the damage was issued by a review report that the deaths of American citizens residing in the Seoul metropolitan area could reach thousands of people within a week due to the counterattack of the North Korean troops' long-range artillery deployed in the demilitarized zone.

The preemptive bombardment plan for the Yongbyon nuclear facility, which the US and South Korean media reported seriously, was a preliminary measure that assumed an emergency situation, not a final decision. On June 15, 1994, former US President Jimmy Carter visited North Korea and met with Kim Il-sung to agree to solve the North Korean nuclear issue diplomatically, so the North Korean nuclear crisis began to change from armed conflict to negotiation phase. South Korean diplomat, Kim Sam-hoon, the ambassador to the nuclear issue, insisted that China had a big influence on North Korea's return to the talks, just as the two Koreas joined the United Nations simultaneously in 1991. Carter's visit to North Korea provided a basic foundation for solving the nuclear issue through diplomatic negotiations in the dimension that he gave North Korea national pride and the cause of returning to the talks. The proposal for an inter-Korean summit between Kim Young-sam and Kim Il-sung was accepted, but it was not concluded due to Kim Il-sung's sudden death on July 8, 1994. Despite the death, North Korea and the United States continued to hold talks on October 21, 1994 in Geneva, and finally adopted a basic agreement to resolve the North Korean nuclear issue.

A former North Korean refugee who fled to South Korea in 1997, Hwang Jang-yop, a former Juche ideological secretary in North Korea, said at a press conference on North Korea's possession of nuclear weapons: "The Soviet Union opposed North Korea's nuclear development in 1985, but the leaders of North Korea, Kim Il-sung and Kim Jong-il, dismissed it, saying that North Korea's nuclear weapons program was already operated in the mid-1980. When I watched that North Korea had withdrawn from the Nuclear Non-Proliferation Treaty in 1992 to avoid the special inspections of the International Atomic Energy Agency, senior officials of the North Korean Workers' Party insisted that North Korea already possessed nuclear weapons. It was already known in North Korea that the regime has already possessed nuclear weapons." North Korea's nuclear possession had become a reality in South Korean society as a result of testimony by North Korea's high-level executives exposing North Korea's nuclear possession. The Soviet opposition to the development of nuclear weapons was the same story that was mentioned in the testimony of Russian officials in 1994. Vladimir

Kumarov, advisor to the Russian National Security Research Institute at the time, said, "North Korea has produced its own launch vehicle to increase the range of missiles. The Soviet Union had also known since 1985 that North Korea had begun developing nuclear weapons, I returned the experts to my home country." North Korea had already completed practical preparations for nuclear tests and some had crude nuclear warheads in the late 1990s, "North Korea had already possessed five nuclear weapons, developed five more nuclear weapons and planned to announce it to the international community in the near future and to deliver it to the United States," said on July 27, 1994, by Kang Myung-do, a North Korean official who arrived in Seoul. A senior teacher at the Kim Il-sung University, Cho Myung-chul, said at a press conference. "North Korea was keen to develop a nuclear warhead and a rocket to mount a nuclear warhead, and soon it would go into mass production. Kim Il-sung thought the only way to overcome a serious economic and food crisis is to complete nuclear weapons as soon as possible. North Korea was not satisfied with developing five nuclear weapons, and if the truth was released, international pressure would make it impossible to further develop nuclear weapons." In response to the aforementioned Kang's claim, the South Korean media suspiciously commented, "It is an unbelievable claim. It is hard to believe, but careful confirmation is needed. It is not possible that North Korea has already possessed five nuclear weapons." The United States and Japan also reacted cautiously. US Secretary of Defense William Perry said in an interview with the US Public Broadcasting Service (PBS) that North Korea possessed nuclear weapons on one or two occasions.

The US Department of State sent a letter to North Korea on June 20, 1994 under the name of Assistant Secretary Robert Galuchi. The contents of the letter were as follows. If North Korea does not reprocess the spent fuel rods at the Yongbyon 5MW reactor and, and at the same time confirms the IAEA's continuing activities and its intention to freeze the nuclear program, the US would stop economic sanctions against North Korea, and resume high-level talks with Pyongyang in three stages. The North Korean Ministry of

Foreign Affairs sent a reply on June 22, 1994, that it would accept the three conditions of the US Department of State under the name of the first deputy head, Kang Suk-joo. This led to high-level talks in Geneva on July 8, 1994. The talk was resumed on August 5 after the announcement of Kim Il-sung's death on July 9. The United States had a general consensus that it would phase out the implementation of the IAEA safeguards and the Joint Declaration on the Denuclearization of the Korean Peninsula. The United States banned North Korea from reloading fuel rods, discarded spent fuel and reprocessing facilities, and suspended and discarded 50MW and 200MW nuclear reactors. The United States had the stance that if North Korea actively participated in denuclearization, it could provide a step-by-step process to improve relations between North Korea and the United States, to provide light-water reactors, mitigate sanctions on North Korea, supply economic cooperation, and guarantee nuclear nonproliferation. Meanwhile, North Korea had a position to exclude subjects such as plutonium extraction and suspicion of nuclear weapons for the first one to two bombs identified by the IAEA in June 1992 as sanctuary. North Korea also requested the US to negotiate only the freezing of its capacity to produce nuclear weapons in the future, support diplomatic relations with North Korea, conclude a peace treaty, and supplement the loss of energy due to nuclear freeze. On October 21, 1994, the United States and North Korea officially signed a joint statement reflecting this position, thus completing the so-called "Geneva Agreement". The Geneva Agreement consists of 13 items in four categories, and the main contents are shown in Table 1.2.

The Geneva Agreement was characterized by North Korea's political and economic rewards for improving relations with the United States, such as the construction of light-water reactors and the supply of heavy fuel oil. North Korea had to abandon plutonium production capacity and fully implement nuclear safety measures. It also meant that North Korea explicitly accepted the special inspections of the IAEA for the first time. Since the light-water reactor takes more than 10 years to construct, it was not a desperate demand from North Korea. However, North Korea linked the construction

Table 1.2 Main contents of the Geneva Agreement

Area	Main Contents
Conversion to light water reactor (Two 1,000MW)	President Clinton provides North Korea with a letter confirming that the United States will fulfill its commitments. The United States and North Korea signed an agreement and signed a light-water reactor contract within six months. • The United States supplies 500,000 tons of heavy oil to North Korea every year until the completion of No. 1 light-water reactor. • North Korea freezes graphite furnaces and reprocessing facilities under IAEA supervision within one month after receipt of the President's letter and disposes of it when the light-water reactor is completed. • North Korea keeps the spent fuel rods drawn in May 1994 until the light-water reactor is completed.
Normalization of relations	The United States will ease economic sanctions on North Korea, including telecommunications, finance, trade and investment, within three months of the Geneva Agreement. • The two sides will set up liaison offices in Pyongyang and Washington and upgrade them to ambassadorial-level relations in accordance with the progress of mutual interest.
Denuclearization of the Korean Peninsula	The United States provides formal guarantees that North Korea is not threatened or used by nuclear weapons. • North Korea will take measures to implement the Joint Declaration on the Denuclearization of the Korean Peninsula. • North Korea begins to engage in inter-Korean dialogue.
NPT return and nuclear safety measures	North Korea remains an NPT member and permits the implementation of the safeguard agreement. • North Korea allows interim and general inspections of IAEA facilities that are not subject to freezing immediately after the light-water reactor contract. • North Korea fully implements the safeguards agreement related to verification of past nuclear materials before delivery of key parts of light-water reactor.

of light-water reactor with the denuclearization measures, so that inspections and verification of plutonium reprocessed in 1989–1991 (at least five years), and the dismantling of additional plutonium capacity was reserved until the completion of the light-water reactor (at least 10 years). As a result, North Korea was able to maintain the utility of the nuclear card during the light-water reactor construction period. According to former IAEA Deputy Secretary General Oli Heinonen, the IAEA's chief of staff from the Geneva Agreement to the six-party talks, the IAEA did not have access to areas other than the plutonium reprocessing facility in Yongbyon, and it was possible to conduct the first nuclear test in October 2006, three years after the collapse of the agreement.[17] In the course of reaching the Geneva Agreement, North Korea presumably used three strategies. First, it is a strategy to "tackle the nuclear issue", which allows the Clinton administration to expect policy results before the November mid-term elections, by accepting the State Department's requirements on June 20, 1994. Second, it is a strategy to "condition the nuclear issue" linking light-water reactor construction to denuclearization measures. Finally, North Korea shall set the process of implementation of the denuclearization agreement to more than 10 years and present a mid- to long-term schedule to make it renegotiate with the next US administration after the Clinton administration (January 1993 to January 2001). It is a strategy to return to the starting point of the nuclear issue by weakening the international solidarity for the implementation of the Clinton administration's agreement.

2000: Geneva Agreement and North Korea LWR project

Even after the dramatic conclusion of the Geneva Agreement between the United States and North Korea in October 1994, the conflict between the two sides continued intermittently and the construction of light-water reactors was often delayed. The Geneva Agreement had a twist in the process, but steadily progressed in 1995, and the Clinton administration promised to support the light-water reactors in accordance with the Geneva Agreement. As the US

Republican Party, which was critical of the Clinton administration's North Korea policy, had taken control of the House and Senate, measures such as supplying 500,000 tons of heavy oil annually to North Korea and lifting sanctions had been delayed. The negotiation phase deteriorated sharply due to suspicions about the underground nuclear weapons development facility detected in Kumchang-ri, North Pyongan Province, North Korea, and Taepodong missile launch in August 1998. The underground cave, which was suspected of nuclear development at Kumchang-ri, was later turned into a composite tunnel. In February 2000, just before the first inter-Korean summit, preparations for light-water reactor construction began in the Sinpo area of South Hamgyong Province. The first inter-Korean summit meeting was held in June 2000, and negotiation and dialogue were active on the Korean Peninsula. US Secretary of State Madeleine Albright travelled to Pyongyang on a four-day visit and met with North Korean leader Kim Jong-il on October 2000.

The situation changed dramatically when the Bush administration was formed in the United States. The Bush administration actively promoted the policy of "anything but Clinton" (ABC), which invalidated the Clinton administration's policy in the field of diplomacy and security. Especially after the terrorist attacks on September 11, 2001, the security environment of the United States changed drastically and the relations with hostile countries became worse. John Bolton said on November 9 that North Korea might have offered weapons to Iraq. Immediately after the September 11 attacks, North Korea was surprised by US hardline policy toward Pyongyang and signed two anti-terrorism agreements. At last, President George W. Bush declared North Korea as "axis of evil" with Iran and Iraq in the New Year's edition of the State of the Union, issued on January 29, 2002. President George W. Bush included North Korea in the target countries and reserved the president's official approval of the Geneva Basic Agreement. In the United States, even if the congressional approval is given in an external aid agreement, the president must final publicly certify that fuel oil can be provided to certain countries. North Korea realized that the international situation was not favorable to the Kim Jong-il regime and proposed unusually a preemptive dialogue with the United States. Washington's hardliners, the Neo-cons, found it ineffective to tackle the North Korean nuclear issue on an action for action basis. They favored a collective agreement on the basis of fundamental changes in the acceptance of the CVID (complete, verifiable and irreversible dismantlement) principle and the human rights issue in the North Korean nuclear discussion.

Pyongyang also began withdrawing seals from its nuclear facilities and loading nuclear fuel rods into its enrichment facilities in front of the IAEA inspectors and declaring withdrawal from the NPT. North Korea also lashed out with military provocations such as launching missiles in the East Sea and attempting to threaten the US reconnaissance aircraft. The US proposed North Korea the six-party talks, because the US preemptive strike was virtually impossible and its sanctions could not keep pace with North Korea's nuclear development, in an urgent situation where North Korea's nuclear reactors actually operated. As the United States transformed existing bilateral talks into multilateral issues, the North Korean Foreign Ministry spokesperson, in a statement, accused the United States of trying to avoid responsibility and intensify international pressure on North Korea. However, in view of the special circumstances of the United States, which had been unfathomable for the war with Iraq and Afghanistan, North Korea advanced its nuclear capabilities and sought negotiations with the United States. North Korea accepted both multilateral and bilateral talks between two countries, and eventually agreed to the six-party talks, despite the fact that the six members of the talks rejected Japan's exclusion. North Korea determined that it was difficult to continue to fight hard against the United States because the development of nuclear weapons had not yet been completed. Since the Kim Il-sung administration, North Korea had long been engaged in the development of nuclear weapons, the fundamental problem with its practical use was that the destructive power of nuclear weapons was asymmetrical compared to existing conventional weapons.

As the United States determined that North Korea's nuclear development would be completed within the next three to four years, nuclear dismantlement through bilateral and multilateral negotiations with North Korea was very necessary. Intelligence officials in Russia and the United States evaluated that North Korea's nuclear development was imminent. In September 2003, the Tokyo newspaper of Japan reported that the KGB had already been aware of the fact that North Korea was completing its nuclear weapons development system around 1990, citing the testimony of Crestinsky from Russia's KGB cadre. He confirmed that the KGB was aware of North Korea's nuclear development. Kirtikov, KGB chairman, submitted to the Central Committee of the Communist Party in 1990, the report that the first nuclear explosive device development in North Korea was completed in Yongbyon, and it is also noticed by this author that North Korea built a plutonium extraction facility in Yongbyon that could be used for nuclear weapons in 1987. The Pentagon had released a photo of satellite taken at the site of the facility as evidence of the announcement. Since the 1980s, North Korea had been using nuclear weapons as a source of nuclear fuel; North Korea had conducted high-level experiments dozens of times and confirmed the performance of nuclear weapons through high-intensity experiments instead of actual nuclear tests before the first nuclear test in 2006.

The six-party talks, the September 19 Joint Statement and the first nuclear test (2003–2007)

The first round of six-party talks aimed at resolving the North Korean nuclear issue was held in Beijing, China from August 27 to August 29, 2003. The multilateral talks, in which the stance of each party was different, were dismissed with mutual slander. Unlike the US, China and Russia defended North Korea, and the objective of denuclearization through international pressure was not achieved. The second round of six-party talks was held in February 2005 and ended without concrete results. The US Republican Party, which had to contest in the presidential election soon, had no choice. The Republican administration strongly tried to apply the Libyan model of giving up the nuclear development by President Muammar

Gaddafi in 2004 to North Korea. At the third round of talks held in June, the United States offered a Libyan-type comprehensive resolution, but North Korea rejected it. North Korea declared nuclear possession officially on February 10, 2005. The United States could no longer afford to neglect the North Korean nuclear issue. The situation began to change as Assistant Secretary Christopher Hill, a negotiator, appeared as a solver. The South Korean Roh Moo-hyun government, which pursued strict reciprocity such as pursuing a special investigation into North Korea at the beginning of the regime, took some appeasement measures, such as suggesting the transmission of electricity to North Korea, and a slight reconciliation atmosphere was created on the Korean Peninsula. In addition, leaders of both Koreas had raised the title of their opponents in order to create atmosphere for negotiation. For example, US Secretary of State Condoleezza Rice called North Korea a sovereign state and President George W. Bush called North Korean leader Kim Jong-il as Mr. Kim Jong-il unlike past protocols. Such an atmosphere of compromise was an answer to the North Korean demand for the withdrawal of President George W. Bush's remarks that North Korea had been the outpost of tyranny as a prerequisite for returning to the six-party talks. Finally, North Korea announced on July 9 that it agreed to resume the six-party talks through Chosun Central TV.

The September 19 Joint Statement was adopted at the fourth round of talks held at the end of several twists and turns. The statement included denuclearization of North Korea that can be verified, US guarantee of security of North Korea, adherence to Joint Declaration of Denuclearization, provision of light-water reactor at proper time, normalization of relations between North Korea and US as well as North Korea and Japan, respect for mutual sovereignty, economic support in energy trade and investment cooperation with the United States, seeking a permanent peace regime, and principles of action for actions that were agreed in the Geneva Convention. However, as Banco Delta Asia Bank (BDA) emerged as a major issue, the statement was not fulfilled on schedule. The US Treasury Department was putting financial sanctions on BDA from January

2006. A North Korean account of US$25 million was frozen at the bank. US sanctions stemmed from suspicions about dollar forgery and money laundering, which were confined to the BDA. However, North Korea suffered serious damage because other banks that had been conscious of the US had stopped financial transactions with North Korea. Subsequently, the United States imposed sanctions on eight North Korean companies. North Korea asked to unfreeze its bank account, but the US demanded that the illegal transactions be abandoned in exchange for the withdrawal of their money from the account. In response to the US freezing its financial accounts, North Korea launched a high-intensity provocation as a brinkmanship tactic. North Korea did not claim to launch a satellite on July 4, 2006, when it launched seven ballistic missiles. In addition, the launch of the Taepodong missile No. 2 was seen as an unfavorable provocation. Resolution 1695 was adopted by the UN Security Council to sanction North Korea's massive launch of missiles. The North's missile launches were banned altogether, including for peaceful purposes. North Korea conducted a first nuclear test on October 9, 2006, in response to pressure from the international community.

The power of the first nuclear test was 0.5 kt, well below the expected 4 kt, which North Korea announced in advance to China, which meant that North Korea's nuclear capability was still rudimentary. It finally succeeded in entering the power stage of "3~4 kt scale" through the second nuclear test in May 2009. Kim Jong-il suggested to the United States on October 11 that he could return to the six-party talks on the grounds that he still needed time to develop nuclear weapons. The US changed its existing principles and agreed to resume the six-party talks through bilateral meetings with North Korea. The result of the fifth round of six-party talks in 2007 was the "Feb 13 agreement". The contents were as follows. North Korea would shut down and seal the Yongbyon nuclear and reprocessing facilities. It would also accept the due diligence of the IAEA. Five countries, like the US, China, Russia, Japan and South Korea shall provide energy assistance to North Korea starting from 50,000 tons of heavy oil within 60 days. All six countries shall agree to make positive steps to promote mutual trust and joint efforts for peace in

Northeast Asia. The parties shall also negotiate in a separate forum appropriate for the permanent peace of the Korean Peninsula. The six countries would form five working groups on: denuclearization of the Korean Peninsula, normalization of North American relations, normalization of North Korean relations, economic and energy cooperation, and peace and security in Northeast Asia.

Through the five working groups, North Korea pursued to make diplomatic relations with other countries and had a plan to seek security guarantees. In early July 2007, North Korea's Yongbyon nuclear facility was shut down. The Yongbyon nuclear reactor was closed on July 15, and the IAEA Director General visited the Yongbyon facility to confirm the shutdown of the reactor. The "Agreement on full reporting of nuclear facilities and disabling of nuclear facilities by the end of the year" was reached in Geneva, Switzerland on September 1. As a result of the six-party talks in October, "October 3 agreement" was announced. The main focus was on the abandonment of facilities for North Korea's nuclear development and the lifting of US economic sanctions against North Korea. North Korea was offered economic benefits instead of abandoning its will to develop nuclear weapons, such as receiving IAEA as well as US and Russian expert inspections. It was a good negotiation between the two sides to exchange denuclearization and economic compensation. North Korea launched its nuclear disabling measures in November and submitted a plan for denuclearization in June 2008. The Obama administration, which was inaugurated in January 2008, had launched a process to remove North Korea from the state of terrorism list. The New York Philharmonic Orchestra of the United States also had new cultural exchanges in Pyongyang in February 2008, playing North Korea's national anthem (*Aegukka*, Patriotic Song) and the American national anthem, the Star Spangled Banner. North Korea bombed a cooling tower, symbol of the Yongbyon nuclear research institute, on June 27, and many foreign journalists and diplomats attended. At that time, the cooling tower bombing of the light-water reactor was intended as a meaningful denuclearization measure as it was shown in a news bulletin 20 minutes after the bombing, even if it was not live for the international community. The bombing of the cooling tower received much interest from the international community, unlike the event in which North Korea bombed the Punggye nuclear test site in Gilju County, North Hamgyong Province on May 24, just before the Singapore Summit in June 2018.

Second nuclear test and declaration of enriched uranium (2008)

When the United States postponed removing North Korea from the list of terrorism-sponsoring countries, North Korea responded by complaining that Washington violated the October 3 agreement on August 26, 2008 and announced that it would consider to restore the Yongbyon nuclear facility. A spokesman for the North Korean Foreign Ministry finally announced on September 19 the restoration of the Yongbyon nuclear facility. The United States announced on October 11 that it would remove North Korea from the state of terrorism list in response to North Korea's demands. South Korea's Lee Myung-bak government stopped purchasing North Korea's nuclear fuel rods because it was twice as expensive as international prices, thus ending a transaction arising from the denuclearization agreement in 2007. Since then, the principle of denuclearization of North Korea, which was emphasized by Kim Il-sung, had disappeared in North Korea and the inter-Korean relations had been further strained. The problem of delaying the removal from the state of terrorism list or the termination of the purchase of fuel rods was a secondary issue in the implementation process of the September 19 Joint Statement and the collapse of the six-party talks. In the process of denuclearization verification, North Korea continued to refuse to report its highly enriched uranium program, and it was a key issue as uncertainty arose over North Korea's willingness to denuclearize. North Korea reported only the plutonium reprocessing program at the Yongbyon reactor, and the conditions were such that the collection of samples at the Yongbyon nuclear facility was unacceptable. Moreover, North

Korea had taken a strong position that it would only be possible to interview inspectors of the facilities reported in writing, in addition to interviews with researchers. This stance was not satisfactory to the participating countries as they demanded unrestricted inspections by IAEA inspectors on unrecognized facilities. Considering that the beginning of the second nuclear crisis was caused by problem over the HEU program, the permission to inspect only the unrecognized and reported facilities under the HEU program was virtually rejected. As a result, the six-party talks in December 2008 ended in failure to adopt the verification protocol. The 9.19 Joint Statement failed to verify the denuclearization process and began to collapse.

North Korea declared the absence of the six-party talks in April 2009 and insisted that South Korea's participation in the PSI (anti-proliferation initiative) training was a declaration of war. On May 25, 2009, North Korea conducted a second nuclear test, declaring that it would start "reprocessing the spent fuel rods at Yongbyon nuclear facility." The atmosphere seemed to be alleviated by a North Korean delegation visiting Seoul at the funeral of President Kim Dae-jung, who died a while later, and former US President Clinton's visit to North Korea for the release of US journalists. However, North Korea eventually succeeded in its own uranium enrichment test. The North Korean Navy attacked the South Korean Navy on the West Sea on November 10, and a North Korean submarine attacked the South Korean warship, Cheonanham with a torpedo, killing 46 military personnel on March 26, 2010. Consequently, the relationship between the two Koreas deteriorated to the worst level. North Korea claimed to have succeeded in its own nuclear fusion in May, and it was revealed in November that there were several hundred centrifuges and uranium enrichment facilities and a 100MW experimental light-water reactor was being built in Yongbyon with the aim of completion in 2012. North Korea bombarded Yeonpyeong Island, raising tensions between the two Koreas on November 23.

Obama administration's "strategic patience" and North Korea's third nuclear test

In the United States, the Obama administration was formed in January 2009. Immediately after its establishment, the United States began to struggle with the North over its long-range missile launch. North Korea launched a long-range rocket at dawn on April 5. This was also the day President Barack Obama planned to make his historic speech in Prague, Czech Republic, entitled "A World without Nuclear Weapons". The United States referred to the North Korean rocket launch as a test firing of an intercontinental ballistic missile (ICBM) and referred it to the violation of UN Security Council resolutions. The UN Security Council adopted a statement of the chairman denouncing North Korea. North Korea responded with a second underground nuclear test on May 25. When the UN Security Council unanimously adopted Resolution 1874 on North Korea in June against North Korea's nuclear test, North Korea officially declared the resumption of reprocessing of plutonium and the development of enriched uranium. Since then, the Obama administration had taken a hardline approach toward North Korea. The Obama administration declared a "strategic patience" policy which would require the biding of time for Pyongyang to denuclearize. "Strategic patience" included the denuclearization of North Korea, the return of the six-party talks, the improvement of relations with South Korea, the persuading of China to take a tough stance on the North Korean nuclear crisis, and the pressure on North Korea through measures such as blocking weapons and sanctions. Kim Jong-il, chief nuclear officer in North Korea, died in December 2011. At that time, there was a sense of hope that things would get better, but it did not take that long to realize that it was hopeless.

Accelerated nuclear development in 2012 by Kim Jong-un: Satellite launches and fourth, fifth, and sixth nuclear tests

With the passing of Kim Jong-il, North Korea's nuclear development will progress even more. On December 12, 2012, North Korea's satellite Kwangmyongseong No. 3 was launched on the Rocket Galaxy No. 3 and Pyongyang announced that it had successfully launched the satellite into orbit. The UN Security Council adopted a resolution condemning the launch of a long-range rocket on January 22, 2013. The next day, North Korea announced a third nuclear test. It was reported to be equivalent to the level of Little Boy dropped over Hiroshima, Japan on August 6, 1945. The Security Council said on January 29 it would adopt an additional resolution to impose sanctions on North Korea. This invoked the UN Chapter 7, stipulating economic and military measures if North Korea were to conduct a third nuclear test. The first UN sanctions against North Korea, adopted in 2006, acted in accordance with the Charter of the United Nations (countermeasures to threats to peace and aggression) and pursuant to clause 41 (economic sanctions). But the UN Security Council's citation of Chapter 7 in the UN Charter suggests the use of military means against North Korea. As a result, military tension was once again present on the Korean Peninsula.

In January 2013, after the launch of the Unha (Galaxy) rocket, intelligence gathered that North Korea was preparing to conduct a nuclear test, and on February 12, the third nuclear test was carried out. An artificial earthquake with a magnitude of 4.9 was detected in Gilju County, North Hamgyong Province. The South Korean Ministry of National Defense estimated that the strength of the nuclear test would be about 6 to 7 kt based on the 4.9 magnitude of the earthquake caused by the nuclear test. It would have increased its destructive power compared to the second nuclear test, which had an explosive force of 2 to 6 kt at 4.5. The destruction of Hiroshima by US atomic bombs in August 1945 was about 15 kt. Cable News Network (CNN) and other media in the world reported the test immediately. The South Korean government and the Japanese government each condemned North Korea for failing to comply with the UN Security Council resolution. The ROK–US Combined Forces Command had upgraded its alertness to North Korea to the second stage by Watch con, and the armed forces around the armistice zone had strengthened their alertness to North Korea. US President Barack Obama had expressed concern and had given orders to keep an eye on the situation.

North Korea's nuclear and missile capabilities had been strengthened while the United States had taken a "strategic patience" policy against North Korea. In December 2012, the Galaxy No. 3 long-range rocket launch experiment was successful, and the third nuclear test was conducted in February 2013. The Galaxy 3 was estimated to have demonstrated satellite launching rockets or North Korea's intercontinental ballistic missile launch technology. North Korea insisted that "the superior performance of our multi-sided nuclear deterrent was physically demonstrated." This suggests that the third nuclear test used HEU rather than plutonium used in the first and second experiments. Since the HEU system is more advantageous than the plutonium-based nuclear warhead for ballistic missiles, it also means that North Korea's nuclear weapons had entered a miniaturization project. North Korea's uranium reserves reached 4 million tons, which is advantageous for securing natural uranium. The purpose of the North Korean nuclear test is estimated as follows. First, Kim Jong-un, who had just been inaugurated, made use of nuclear test for political purposes to strengthen his supportive forces and bring them together as well as resolve the anxiety surrounding his leadership. The second is the purpose of warning that the new regime will become nuclear state. The third is the unspoken pressure to receive support from the South Korean government and a warning message to the United States.

Pyongyang had subsequently conducted nuclear tests three times within two years, beginning with the fourth nuclear test in January 2016 and ending in September 2017 with the sixth nuclear test. International sanctions had been strengthened, but the effects are limited as China and Russia do not actively participate. North Korea succeeded in launching Polaris 1 in 2016, North Korea Polar Code 2 at intermediate range ballistic missile (IRBM) level in 2017, and Hwasong-14 at ICBM level, raising the possibility of a completed nuclear weapon. North Korea claimed to have completed the development of the hydrogen bomb for the ICBM. An earthquake measuring 4.8 on the Richter scale was observed near the Punggye nuclear facility in Ryanggang Province, North Korea, on January 6, 2016 at 10:30 am (South Korea time). Two hours later, North Korea's Central Television announced a government statement saying, "Following the strategic decision of the Korean Workers' Party, the first hydrographic experiment of North Korea was successfully conducted at 10:00 am on January 6." North Korea said in a statement that "this test is the higher level of our nuclear arsenal," and that "the nuclear test was carried out by nuclear-armed nations that even possessed hydrogen." Many experts, however, pointed out that it was hard to believe North Korea's claim as the earthquake magnitude was too weak to be attributed to the hydrogen bomb, which is believed to be tens or hundreds of times stronger than the atomic bomb. The magnitude of the earthquake caused by the fourth experiment was rather small compared to the previous nuclear tests such as the first experiment at 3.9, the second 4.5, and the third 4.9.

Experts' assessment of the success of North Korea's hydrogen experiments was somewhat negative. IHS, a US defense investigation agency, said in a press release, "It is more likely to be false information from North Korea than an explosion of hydrogen bombs. To make a hydrogen bomb, it is necessary to have a solid raw material of lithium deuterated, but it is doubtful whether North Korea has a technical basis for producing such a substance." It is also pointed out that North Korea may have experimented with "amplified fission flares" that have augmented the power of existing atomic bombs. Amplified nuclear fission is a nuclear weapon with explosive power by putting tritium and deuterium or lithium 6 in the center of an atomic bomb surrounded by plutonium or uranium, and usually has a power of 40 to 150 kt or more. North Korea's nuclear test power was 6 kt, so it had been said that even if it was experimented with amplified nuclear fission, it actually failed. Meanwhile, the fourth nuclear test was carried out without warning. It was not the same as the one sent out by the Ministry of Foreign Affairs to announce the nuclear test ahead of the first, second and third nuclear tests. Previous experiments and the launch of a long-range rocket seemed to be a reaction to the international sanctions imposed by the US Banco Delta Asia (BDA) in 2006. But this experiment also did not go through this advanced process. North Korea insists not only on completing the development of hydrogen bombs, but also completing the Electromagnetic Pulse Bomb (EMP) explosion capability of the concept of Nuclear Physics Fusion Electronic Warfare. The weapon can be a serious threat in the future, even though this is not grounded on objective data.

Differences between North Korea and Iran's nuclear negotiations

On July 14, 2015, when the United States concluded a nuclear deal with Iran, the North Korean nuclear issue was again focused on. Chinese Foreign Ministry said after the conclusion of the nuclear negotiations, "the conclusion of the Iranian nuclear deal will serve as an example for dealing with international issues including the nuclear issue on the Korean peninsula." However, the attitudes of North Korea and the United States were cold. The United States said it could only negotiate if North Korea were to show a genuine and credible attitude toward denuclearization. Shortly after the conclusion of the Iranian nuclear negotiations, North Korea also said, "We have no interest in a conversation that involves unilaterally freezing or giving up nuclear weapons." First, the difference between North Korea and Iran is considered. Unlike Iran, North Korea is at an early stage of its nuclear development and its nuclear capabilities are being upgraded. North Korea has been a nuclear power since February 2009, three months before its second nuclear test. In April 2012, North Korea stated that it is a nuclear power in the preamble to the revised Constitution. North Korea is promoting the construction of a nuclear-armed economy through the adoption of the 2013 translational route, making it a top priority that cannot be abandoned. The US also has different methods of countering Iran and North Korea. Many analysts argue that the Obama administration had actively concluded negotiations with Iran because it was expected to play a balancer role in the Middle East, amid the rise of the Islamic State (IS) and the prolonged internal war in Syria and the Yemeni civil war. On the other hand, the North Korean nuclear issue involves the balancing of power of Northeast Asian international politics. China and Russia have been focusing on weakening US influence in Northeast Asia by supporting North Korea. Therefore, the two countries have not been actively participating in the UN sanctions. Because of the limited sanctions, this provides an opportunity for North Korea to undertake a defensive and passive approach toward its denuclearization talks with the United States. Last but not least, there are countries like the UK that act as honest brokers in Iran's nuclear negotiations. But such actors do not exist in the North Korean nuclear negotiations which makes the conclusion of talks difficult.

Chapter 2

North Korea's Nuclear Quest and Complexity

Technological path toward nuclear proliferation

To judge North Korea's nuclear proliferation progress within and across different nuclear status levels, this chapter shall first explain the technical steps required to acquire fissile materials sufficient for a nuclear weapon — from the supply of raw uranium to the finished core of a nuclear weapon. First, a proliferator must acquire a supply of raw uranium to produce fissile materials. The acquisition of raw uranium has often been used as an indicator of potential nuclear weapons interest, since the worldwide market for nuclear power plant fuel is experiencing a glut. Although it did turn out to be incorrect, intelligence that Iraq was seeking uranium in Africa was one of many pieces of information that pointed to a possible nuclear weapons program. Even though in theory many different materials can be used in a nuclear device, in practice two particular isotopes are used: the plutonium-239 (239-Pu) and uranium-235 (235-U). Neither of these isotopes is found separated in abundance naturally; they must be produced from natural uranium, which is usually found with a 235-U concentration of 0.71%; the remainder of the uranium is primarily made of the non-fissile (under most circumstances) isotope 23Su. Natural uranium is found in deposits around the world; as of 2003, the International Atomic Energy Agency

(IAEA) World Distribution of Uranium Deposits Database listed 49 countries with significant deposits. This did not include North Korea's deposits, which are large but uncertain, and are estimated to be between 200 and 300 thousand tons of uranium.

Uranium ore must be extracted from the ground and milled to convert the ore into uranium ore concentrate, or yellowcake (U308). The U308 is then converted to uranium dioxide (U02), using (among other chemical compounds) nitric acid and tri-butyl phosphate (TBP). The latter is part of the PUREX (Plutonium and Uranium Extraction) process used to extract plutonium and uranium from spent fuel; importation of TBP is often seen as an indication of a nuclear program. If a country is using heavy water-reactors (HWRs, see below), the U02 can be used directly as fuel. Otherwise, for either a plutonium-production or a uranium-enrichment program, the UO2 must be first turned into uranium tetrafluoride (UF4) using anhydrous hydrogen fluoride (AHF). Like TBP, imports of large quantities of AHF are often taken as a sign that a country is developing a nuclear program. At this point, the natural UF4 can either be converted into uranium metal (U) to be used as fuel in a graphite-moderated reactor to produce plutonium or turned into uranium hexafluoride (UF6) and enriched.

The plutonium path

A military program that involves plutonium-based weapons needs to pass through several stages. Many or all of the preliminary stages involve activities that are also legitimate in civilian nuclear programs. Uranium must be mined, refined, (sometimes) enriched, and cast into fuel rods. These rods are then irradiated in a reactor; some reactors are more proliferation-prone than others due to the ratio of isotopes of plutonium they produce. The rods are removed and reprocessed to remove the plutonium, which is recovered as an oxide. The oxide can be turned into a metal suitable for casting into pits for warheads. Many of these steps are detectable even at long distances. For example, a reactor's cooling tower (if it has one) will release plumes of steam that are visible from satellites on clear days:

a reprocessing plant will release Krypton-85, a radioactive gas that can be sampled from the air if weather patterns are right. Later, this chapter will cover the basic technical details required to understand and estimate a state's progress toward a plutonium capability. For plutonium-production reactors, natural (0.71%, 235U) uranium is usually used. Natural uranium dioxide (U02) can be used directly as a fuel in HWRs or can be converted into uranium metal for use in graphite-moderated reactors; typically, these can be either cooled with light water-cooled graphite reactors (LWGRs) or with gas (gas-cooled reactors, or GCRs). More exotic reactor types can also be used, but these three types have been used most heavily by proliferators. Heavy water-moderated reactors require much less fuel for the same energy (and plutonium) production due to the tendency of heavy water to absorb fewer neutrons and to slow neutrons more efficiently than graphite by a combined factor of about 7.5. Nonetheless, the abundance of graphite and the scarcity and expense of heavy water have led several countries to use graphite as a moderator.

Let us assume a GCR similar to that constructed by North Korea, which requires about 50 tons of natural uranium metal (U) fuel for a full load. After irradiation, the fuel is left to cool for a few months, and then is reprocessed to recover the produced plutonium. A 25MWt (megawatts of thermal energy) reactor running with a 60% capacity factor would produce about 5kg of plutonium per year. After a cooling-off period of a few months, the fuel can be unloaded from the reactor and reprocessed using the PUREX process, in which compounds similar to those used in uranium conversion (including TBP) are used to separate the plutonium and uranium remaining in the fuel rods from the fission products. If there were no losses in reprocessing, a proliferator could recover about 5kg of plutonium. While the standard figure used for calculating the amount of plutonium required per weapon is around 5kg, 6kg is often used as a more conservative estimate for a weapon design by a new proliferator. The Trinity test and the Nagasaki bomb both used about 6kg of plutonium; a "first weapon" can require up to 8kg.[18] The IAEA has defined a "significant quantity" of plutonium to be 8kg. However, the same design used for Trinity and Nagasaki would still produce a yield of 1kt if half the amount of plutonium were used (3kg). Whether a new nuclear state would be satisfied with a 1kt weapon is another question in view that India and Pakistan claimed yields for their tests well above Western estimates for the actual yield, leading to claims that the devices had "fizzled".

While a 1kt yield is certainly considerable, the desire of the Indian and Pakistani governments to claim higher yields instead of simply claiming the actual lower yield indicates that states may at least initially shoot for larger-yield weapons using more plutonium rather than smaller-yield weapons using less, especially if prestige motivations are stronger than military ones. Another issue with plutonium production is the purity of the plutonium recovered through chemical separation. Along with 239Pu, other isotopes of plutonium are created. "Weapons-grade" plutonium contains 93% or higher 239Pu although this label is somewhat misleading. Due to its higher neutron emission rate, a high concentration of 240Pu and other isotopes makes nuclear weapon design more difficult, since excess neutrons may cause a weapon made of a substantial fraction of isotopes other than 239Pu predetonate. This reduces the yield substantially, perhaps to one or a few kilotons for a bomb, similar to the Nagasaki design using reactor-grade (82% or lower 239Pu) plutonium. This is still a substantial yield, which may be an undesirable characteristic for a new nuclear state, as it does not eliminate the possibility of a state using reactor-grade plutonium. The 25MWt graphite-moderated reactor produces weapons-grade plutonium through a burn up of 1,000MWt and with 50 tons of fuel Under these conditions, the reactor would take 2,000 days at 100% capacity before degrading the plutonium quality to sub-weapons-grade. A 25MWt heavy-water reactor, which only requires about $6\frac{2}{3}$ tons of fuel, would do so after 265 days; however, many HWRs are built so that they can be unloaded while operating. Although small research reactors (10MWt) can be used to produce plutonium, reactors intended for producing weapons-grade plutonium are often much larger

(30–50MW or higher), while power-production reactors generally are 1,000MWt or greater (and are normally referred to by the amount of energy produced, usually around a third of the thermal output e.g., about 1,000 megawatts of electric power, or MWe, for a 3,000MWt reactor). In operation, plutonium-production and power-production reactors operate continuously, while research reactors operate intermittently. In other words, power-production reactors generally are operated over long periods of time, while the core in plutonium-production reactors is changed frequently.

The operation of a plant with a steam tower can be monitored simply by observing the tower via satellite photos, while plants that use rivers or other bodies of water for cooling can be monitored by measuring temperature changes in the water from a sufficiently close distance. Separation can be remotely detected by sensing of 85Kr, a radioactive gas that is produced through fission of 235U and released during the PUREX process. This measure is sufficiently reliable to be used as a secondary check against other estimates of total plutonium production (as it was for estimates of Soviet production during the Cold War). Reprocessing facilities are often large and require much heavier shielding for workers than simple facilities for production of isotopes for medical or industrial use. Additionally, the dissolution of metals in nitric acid results in red-brown fumes potentially observable from a facility.[19]

The uranium path

A military HEU program involves a different set of technologies from a plutonium program. After mining, refining, and conversion to uranium tetrafluoride, the UF4 must be converted to uranium hexafluoride before being enriched in centrifuges (or through other methods), converted back to uranium metal, then cast into pits. Uranium has two main isotopes: 235U, the fissile part, and 238U, a (relatively) non-fissile part. Weapons-grade uranium consists mostly of 238U. Depending on the efficiency of the hundreds that are required, however, they can fit into a relatively small area and so are more difficult to detect than larger facilities such as a large reprocessing plant or a reactor cooling tower. Many centrifuge parts, however, are under export controls, and so much of the information that is discovered about HEU programs comes from the interception of the materials needed for fabrication of centrifuges. The dissolution of A.Q. Khan's nuclear network has also produced a great deal of information. Similar to plutonium programs, a few basic technical details are required to understand and estimate a state's progress toward a uranium capability. After uranium mining, refining, and conversion, the UF4 is combined with fluorine to convert it to UF6 which is a gas at relatively low temperatures (57°C). It can then be enriched using any one of a variety of methods. While early uranium enrichment programs used gas diffusion (GD) and/or electromagnetic separation (EMIS), most modem programs use centrifuge technology due to its lower cost and power requirements. All enrichment methods use the small mass difference between 235U and 238U. Gas diffusion works by passing UF6 through small holes; molecules with 235U pass through these holes at a slightly higher rate than those containing 238U. Centrifuges spin the gas; the heavier 238U molecules tend to gather near the walls of the spinning centrifuge and are discarded. Electromagnetic separation accelerates the molecules in an arc, with the lighter 235U molecules tending to move toward larger radii. Other techniques more rarely used in production of fissile materials (and never proven commercially viable) include aerodynamic enrichment (used by South Africa for its weapons program), laser enrichment, and chemical separation.

In addition to the nuclear weapons states, Iraq pursued a number of technologies including EMIS, chemical separation, gas diffusion, and gas centrifuges; Iran has primarily experimented with laser and centrifuge enrichment technologies; Korea is only known to have centrifuge technologies. Netherlands, Germany, Japan, Argentina and Brazil have enrichment technology; all but the latter two have operating commercial enrichment plants in use for power-production reactor fuel. The standard measure of the ability of an enrichment technology to separate 235U from 238U is the Separative Work Unit (SWU). Calculating the number of SWU needed for a given application depends on the amount and initial enrichment of the feed, the amount and enrichment of the final product, and the enrichment of the depleted uranium and the tails. The higher the initial enrichment, the lower the final enrichment, and the higher the enrichment of the depleted uranium, the fewer SWUs are needed. Assuming an initial enrichment of 6.5 tons of 0.71% 235U, a tails enrichment (called an assay) of 0.3%, and traction of 30kg of 90% 235U, approximately 4,000 SWUs are needed. A given machine is measured in SWUs per year, for example, the P4 centrifuges distributed by the A.Q. Khan network produce about two SWUs per year. For light-water-moderated and cooled power-production reactors the fuel must be ended, often up to 5% 235U. It must be enriched to at least 30% to be reasonably usable in an implosion weapon (requiring 100kg with a tamper),[20] although implosion weapons usually contain uranium enriched to 90%, known as weapons-grade uranium (WGU). The standard figure used for calculating the amount of weapons-grade uranium used per weapon is between 15 and 30kg for an implosion weapon. The IAEA standard for a significant quantity of weapons-grade uranium is 25kg; the Iraqi design required about 18kg, and the solid-core Chinese design transferred to Pakistan and Libya (and likely Iran and North Korea) would require no more than 15kg.

However, 20kg is often used as an estimate, since a new nuclear state might desire higher yield and reliability. For a simpler, gun-type design, about 60kg is required. It is to be noted that South Africa's design was 54kg, while the Hiroshima bomb contained 60kg. Uranium enrichment facilities using gas diffusion are usually quite large, while those employing centrifuges can be relatively small. Detection of these facilities, therefore, depends upon observing imports of certain crucial materials and parts from other countries. For example, high-strength aluminum, maraging steel, or carbon fiber are required for the centrifuge rotors and the vacuum vessel around the rotors; the bearings often use cobalt; and frequency converters are used to drive the rotors at the proper speeds. Detection of the actual facility in operation is very difficult, since centrifuges have low power requirements.

North Korea's motivations for a nuclear program

Understanding why North Korea continues to build up nuclear weapons will help US policymakers to design and develop the most appropriate and effective approach and strategy in dealing with the nuclear crisis. The rationale for the North Korean nuclear program has been hotly debated. On one hand, it is argued that it serves as a defense for the regime. On the other hand, it is argued that the nuclear build-up is for the accumulation of power and to threaten other countries. What are the motives that drive the quest for nuclear weapons? Fear and the quest for power and prestige have been the major causes for the proliferation of nuclear arms.[21] For one, many leaders are highly motivated to develop nuclear weapons because they symbolize power and offer a means of wielding significant influence in the international arena. Nuclear weapons are perceived to be a potent source of military and political power, and with the power vacuum created by the collapse of the Soviet Union, cautious regional rivals seek to obtain nuclear weapons to achieve regional dominance. Alternately, nuclear weapons serve as equalizers in situations in which the leaders of one nation feel militarily inferior to a regional adversary. Nuclear weapons also effectively bestow significant power on sub-national groups struggling for independence, as well as on terrorist groups and nuclear blackmailers. Furthermore, nuclear weapons are viewed as a source of economic control. In cases such as Ukraine and North Korea, nuclear weapons serve as a bargaining chip to gain control of desperately needed hard currency and economic assistance from other countries, especially the US. At the same time, nuclear weapons mean technological prowess and elite status of the declared nuclear weapons states. Others, mostly developing nations, even perceive a correlation between the declared possession of nuclear weapons and a permanent seat on the United Nations Security Council. Nuclear programs also serve as a powerful instrument in the intense struggle for identity and nationalism in ethnic conflicts that have erupted around the world. As status competition is a major motivation in the search for identity, the development of nuclear weapons provides a powerful means of increasing the status of one's group. In this regard, it is perhaps possible to empathize with North Korea, who has been overshadowed by its adversaries (especially the US), its relatively powerful neighbors like Russia, Japan and China, as well as an economically more prosperous South Korea. Arguably, the dominant motivating factor in developing a nuclear program is security.

As illustrated by the US–Soviet confrontation during the Cold War, mutual fears induce strong images of an adversary that is monolithically aggressive, diabolical, and untrustworthy. With the adversaries holding equally negative images of each other, the ability for each side to misperceive the enemy's intent becomes more pervasive. Moreover, while the leaders of each nation may seek weapons for defensive purposes, they will tend to perceive the adversary's weapons as being primarily offensive in character, thus presenting the problem of drawing a tight distinction between defensive and offensive weapons, or to advocate the proliferation of defensive weapons. Moreover, these reciprocal perceptual bases provide dangerous contributions to arms races, and a cruel spiral process of hostile interaction. In conclusion, the regional instabilities and security fears invite enemy imaging, misperceptions, and malignant spiral processes that contribute to the quest for nuclear weapons. In fact, North Korea's motivations for starting (and continuing) its program could come from a number of different sources. A history of being threatened indirectly with nuclear weapons, its long animosity with a nuclear-armed United States and the contemporary conventional superiority of the combined South Korean/US forces give it significant military motivations. North Korea may even believe that a nuclear deterrent is an economically optimal choice; the costs of maintaining its million-man army may be much higher than maintaining a small domestic nuclear infrastructure capable of producing a few nuclear weapons. Its long and partially self-imposed isolation may have led North Korea to seek prestige and social recognition from a nuclear weapons infrastructure. Regardless of its original motivations, the important question is what types of incentives are likely to convince North Korea to give up its nuclear program. The wide range of motives that North Korea has to develop such weapons suggests that there may be many different points of leverage that can be used to help convince North Korea to give up its program. The range of possible motivations and solutions to the North Korean problem suggested by observers is equally broad. Michael Mazarr suggests that North Korea is motivated by security concerns and legitimacy both at home and abroad. He highlights that military and economic sanctions will likely fail, and that a combination of implied sticks and explicit carrots is needed.[22] Selig Harrison argues that economic motivations in particular have come to the forefront and would be the key to successful negotiations.[23] Victor Cha argues for containment-plus-engagement, where engagement is highly conditional, in order to build a case for punishment later.[24] Michael O'Hanlon and Mike Mochizuki advocate a wide-ranging grand bargain with North Korea including all varieties of incentives in exchange for a deal that not only includes nuclear weapons but also conventional forces.[25] A wide range of strategies is consequently advocated by scholars of North Korea. Few, however, suggest that North Korea cannot be dealt with; studies of North Korea's negotiating style find that while North Korea often uses brinkmanship and can make outrageous demands, it acts rationally and can make deals.[26] Domestic politics, and therefore responsibility for the nuclear program, in North Korea is opaque at best. Many observers argue that there are clear splits, however, between military proponents of a nuclear weapons program and members of the foreign ministry who want to use it as a bargaining chip.[27] An exception to this is a few neoconservatives, who argue that military coercion in the form of regime change is indispensable since North Korea is monolithic and implacable.[28]

Economic demand

It is arguable that through the maintenance and cultivation of a nuclear program, North Korea is attempting to achieve a broader goal of unifying North and South Korea. Not only has this assertion taken form through economic and military actions, it was explicitly stated during the regime's creation in 1948, that the primary national goal was not merely state survival and the protection of sovereignty, but victorious unification — or unification through the victory of Communism — over the rival regime in the South. Both sides in the Korean War wanted more than a continuing division of the peninsula, but neither attained its goal. Kim Il-sung and Lee Seung-man each wanted to unite the country under his own leadership. It must be emphasized that the economic superiority of South Korea came about only after the early 1980s. Indeed, throughout the first three decades of the Cold War, the two regimes faced off as relative equals, each buttressed by security guarantees from their great power patrons. Moreover, from the early 1960s to the 1970s, North Korean gross national product (GNP) per capita, as well as its conventional military capabilities rivaled, if not surpassed, that of its southern counterpart. This relative equality enabled each regime to nurture its own particular vision of political unification, which essentially meant domination of one over the other for each side. However, for North Korea, the goal of overthrowing South Korea became unrealistic because of the insurmountable gap of economic developments between the two countries, and, most especially, the outbreak of the Cold War led to the disintegration of the Soviet Union and China as patrons. The nearly 20-fold gap in the gross domestic products of the two countries and the per capita income difference amounting to 23:1 show the economic gap of the two countries. This has also shifted the paradigm of the North Korean Government's core principle from the goal of communization to self-dependency as the ultimate revolutionary goal. Immediate survival for a political regime depends upon its capacity to maintain a functioning economy. In the North Korean case, the state has been experiencing food crisis for more than a decade, and estimates show that a famine in the late 1990s alone resulted in the deaths of almost a million people. North Korea's failure to provide even the most basic conditions for human existence has caused an increase in the black market economy, the spread of foreign particularly US currency, a surge in migration flows across the Chinese border, widespread electricity shortages, and inadequate infrastructure undermining modernization attempts. Despite humanitarian and development assistance which has ameliorated the situation, the country is recently once again on the verge of another famine by international pressure and sanctions.

While conditions have improved somewhat since the peak of the crisis in 1996–97 chronic food shortages remain and are likely to continue. Alarmingly, the United Nations World Food Program (UNWFP) predicts another severe humanitarian crisis, with famine conditions in the coming years. Moreover, with the expenditure preferences of the regime, the North Korean economy is not producing enough output to sustain its population; and population maintenance has become increasingly aid-dependent. Yet, the exposé of a nuclear weapons program based on highly enriched uranium in October 2002, followed by North Korea's subsequent withdrawal from the Non-Proliferation Treaty (NPT), have put continued international assistance in doubt. North Korea desperately needs the economic and diplomatic rewards from the United States, South Korea, China and Japan. According to the available data mostly from the late 1990s, North Korea's major trading partners include China, Japan, and South Korea. Russia, a major trading partner before the collapse of the Soviet Union, was of declining importance a decade ago, and now accounts for less than 3% of North Korea's total merchandise trade which is about the same as Germany. China is by far North Korea's most important economic partner, allowing it to run large trade deficits.

Substantial economic disruption could increase the risk of either a North Korean military response or internal economic collapse, both of which would be detrimental to regional stability. The volume of potential economic leverage is limited because of North Korea's self-imposed isolation, Still, If China, Japan, and South Korea successfully cooperate, the sanctions would cover more than 50% of North Korea's reported trade flows, well above the average in past successful cases (36% in difficult cases). The façade of North Korea's relative autarky is that its trade is not large enough to be of much economic importance to its partners. Concerns about these potential costs were major factors dictating a cautious strategy in the earlier crisis and remain an impediment to gaining the co-operation of key partners. Although North Korea may find a vital security interest in acquiring nuclear weapon, they argue that the regime has an even more convincing interest in securing outside help for its failing economy. Indeed, it is in this argument that the United States and South Korea maintain their long-term bargaining edge, and thus Pyongyang ultimately would have no choice but to trade its nuclear option to secure its economic future. However, if the economic imperative was more significant than the security imperative, one would expect North Korea to have given some indication of the economic and political price it would demand in exchange for agreeing to intrusive inspections. In fact, from the summer to the fall of 1994 when shaping the Agreed Framework in Geneva, North Korea showed that it was willing to cooperate with the United States. Also, North Korea was even keen on accepting intrusive inspections in exchange for massive economic aid and political concessions from the United States in 1994 and in the fall of 2000. Moreover, while evidence strongly suggests that North Korea is firm in its stand to continue with its nuclear weapons program, it does not explain how the country will cope with its faltering economy. Indeed, North Korea's problem is not simply coping with its extant economic crisis but the prospect of dealing with a much more serious crisis if UN sanctions are imposed as well.

Security demand

In order to preserve a regime, North Korea must be able to defend itself. As part of its revolutionary ideological heritage, North Korea claims that its security is threatened, confronted by the increasing superiority of the US military as evidenced by the Gulf War and the Afghanistan conflict and by the potential overwhelming superiority of US Forces emboldened by the successful Iraq conflict and rapidly building advanced National Missile Defense (NMD) technology. Specifically, North Korea justifies its nuclear program as (1) providing a countervailing deterrent against US nuclear threats, which continue to exist in the form of the nuclear umbrella held over South Korea; (2) countering the possibility of a future South Korean bomb (indeed, South Korea's involvement in nuclear activities in the 1970s provided an early incentive for the North's bomb program; (3) deterring South Korea's overwhelming conventional military superiority; (4) compensating for the loss of its nuclear ally, Russia; and (5) ensuring that the North Korean regime is taken seriously as a major player in the region, even though its economy may be in crisis. Indeed, there are different schools of thought on the motivations behind North Korea's nuclear weapons program. On the one hand, those who believe North Korea is a revisionist state argue that the nuclear motivations constitute a serious external threat. Evidence for these claims includes North Korea's initiation of the Korean War, acts of terrorism, forward-deployed military forces, a constitution whereby North Korea is the sole legitimate government for all of Korea, and Korean Workers' Party's bylaws calling for a completion of the revolution in South Korea.

Many analysts further argue that Pyongyang's record of exporting ballistic missiles indicates that North Korea would also be willing to sell nuclear materials, technology, or complete nuclear weapons. On the other hand, a second argument finds that North Korea's nuclear motivations are naturally defensive and designed to deter external threats to the state. Evidence supporting this claim includes the July 4 North–South Joint Communiqué of 1972; the Agreement on Reconciliation, Nonaggression, and Exchanges and Cooperation between North and South Korea of 1991; the Joint Declaration on the Denuclearization of the Korean Peninsula of 1991; the summit meeting of 2000; the Agreed Framework with the US; and reunification proposals that would recognize "Two systems" for North and South Korea. North Korea doubtlessly appreciates that with its weakened economy, its ability to continue the high levels of military expenditure is decreasing daily, and the economic goal shift from communization to self-dependency has led to the debate on the real intentions of their nuclear weapon and bears direct correlation to deterrence. In the discussion of security threats as a motivation for nuclear proliferation, it is important to consider the general strategic uses of nuclear weapons: offensive, defensive, and deterrent. The offensive use of nuclear weapon does not provide an attractive option for North Korea, as it opens the possibility of severely exacerbated tensions with South Korea or Japan, thus forcing regional instability, or the United States, thus creating scenarios that are not viable. Defensively, the use of nuclear weapons is far less enticing, as utilization would thus mean application against an advancing adversary, in order to repel it back to its pre-offensive position. Moreover, nuclear defense strategies are limited in development, for the obvious reason that a nuclear defense means using nuclear weapons within, or near, one's own territory.

Amid the offense/defense debate, North Korea perceives the nuclear deterrent as essential to its defense. However, rather than using a deterrence method to stabilize the balance of power, as is done by the US, North Korea relies on a rationale of existential deterrence, which implies that the mere existence of nuclear forces provides an irreducible risk that an armed conflict might escalate into a nuclear war. This persistent fear of escalation is thus factored into political calculations, and states, as a result tend to be much more cautious and prudent than they otherwise might be. Security for the proliferator is therefore achieved not through assured second-strike capability, but by creating first-strike uncertainty. Indeed, deterrence and security derive from having just enough capabilities to raise uncertainty in the mind of the opponent so that it cannot neutralize with a first strike. According to theorists, existential deterrent doctrines, or the capacity to deter threats to the state's survival, are most likely among proliferating states that are small, limited in resources, and with proximate adversaries. North Korea's well-documented economic difficulties in the 1990s impose severe resource constraints on closing gaps with rival competitors through modernization and a buildup of conventional forces. The self-help imperatives of anarchy also render reliance on allies for security an unattractive proposition or an unfeasible one. Nuclear weapons, therefore, offer the most efficient means by which to optimize security needs, abandon fears, and overcome resource constraints. However, as long as anarchy defines the international condition, superpower protectors could treat alliance security as a private rather than a collective good.

It can also be argued that nuclear weapons are more fungible than conventional forces, in that they remain relevant security assets in most cases, regardless of wholesale changes in future adversaries or contingencies. Indeed, programs that are developed under a veil of secrecy are often done out of existential deterrence, in that increased opacity often generates worst-case assessments that tend to err on the side of caution, hence increasing first-strike uncertainty. Moreover, nuclear arsenals that are small, inaccurate, and counter value-oriented, are usually indicative of a doctrine not based on nuclear conflict or second-strike capabilities. In assessing possible reasons for the adoption of an existential deterrent policy by North Korea, it is possible to cite a number of reasons. Most notably, and of primary concern, one can look to the issues directly related to South Korea, considering first the downfall of the Soviet Union, which served as North Korea's chief Cold War patron against its rival in the South. Second, as a result of its opening of a market economy, China sought diplomatic normalization with South Korea in 1992, disavowing its "as close as lips to teeth" security relationship with the North in the process. Finally, as a final blow, Russia normalized relations with Seoul in September 1990, and declared that it would not honor Soviet Cold War security guarantees to North Korea's defense. Thus, the period from 1989 to 1992, in which Mikhail Gorbachev implemented Glasnost and Perestroika, North Korea was left alone as a rogue state by its major allies. The political, economic, and military imbalance between the North and South provided North Korea an impetus to produce nuclear weapons, for survival and for security. Moreover, the intensification of North Korea's nuclear program provided the only alternative to guarantee North Korea's own style of socialism, and indeed, to ensure the continuation of Kim Il-sung dynasty.

Another issue has been the recurring failure of American and South Korean analysts in accurately perceiving and assessing Pyongyang's behavior. In late 1993, for example, there was an outbreak of media reports of a military buildup in North Korea, tests of new ballistic missiles, a tripling in frequency of fighter training exercises, and the movement of heavy artillery and multiple-rocket launchers closer to the Demilitarized Zone. Unnamed US officials speculated that the buildup was being undertaken because North Korea was planning an invasion of the South. Moreover, the possibility that the North's actions were defensive in nature was not considered. While there is no evidence to date suggesting that the US and South Korea have aggressive designs against North Korea, it is possible to understand the rhetoric as being intended to pressure North Korea to abandon its nuclear program, or to warn it of the costly consequences of military adventurism. Yet these misperceptions were detrimental to existing tensions, as from Pyongyang's perspective, much of the American and South Korean reactionary rhetoric was viewed as threatening, fueling both North Korea's paranoia, and its determination to continue developing a nuclear program at all costs. Although the nuclear proliferation motivations discussed above — political, technological, military and economic powers; struggle for identity; status competition; and security fears — have been discussed separately, they are interrelated in various ways, depending on the social and political context under which they are being examined. Indeed, these pressures in obtaining nuclear weapons are a result of strategic, foreign policy, and internal political and economic factors; and situational variables determine which motives will be active in a particular context and which specific courses of action will be chosen.

Due to the highly secretive nature of North Korea, it is difficult to discern with precise accuracy its motivation for nuclear proliferation. As shown earlier in this section, the North Korean case exemplifies the very high levels of threat and risk associated with nuclear proliferation, and it also raises difficult questions about the most effective means of halting continued proliferation. Although North Korea may see nuclear weapons primarily as a means of deterring attack by the United States and South Korea, it is possible that the state also sees nuclear weapons as a means of achieving greater regional power or as a bargaining chip for extracting concessions from the United States. Whatever the case, the intense desire of North Korea to obtain and develop nuclear weapons heightens security fears and encourages the perception that North Korea needs nuclear weapons to protect itself from known and hostile adversaries.

Chapter 3

After the Fifth and Sixth Nuclear Tests of DPRK, the Situation in Northeast Asia and the US Response

Evaluation of North Korean nuclear test and missile launch, and its intentions

North Korea carried out its fifth nuclear test on September 9, 2016 and boasted of a weapon that is too light and small enough to be mounted atop a ballistic missile, a nightmare scenario for Seoul and Washington — the latter having military bases in the Pacific and on its west coast within Pyongyang's striking range. The latest test produced a more powerful explosive yield than the North's previous detonations, indicating that the country had been making progress in its efforts to build a functional nuclear warhead. It was North Korea's most powerful test ever. After the test, the North's nuclear weapons institute issued a statement saying that the test was successfully conducted for a final check on the explosive power and other characteristics of a "nuclear warhead that has been standardized to be able to be mounted on" its ballistic missiles. The North also argued that the standardization of the nuclear warhead will enable the DPRK (Democratic People's Republic of Korea) to produce at will and as many as it would want a variety of smaller, lighter and diversified nuclear warheads of higher strike power. North Korea conducted its fourth nuclear test on January 6, 2016 which it claimed was the successful detonation of a hydrogen bomb. The North Koreans successfully put a satellite into space on February 7, even as diplomats were negotiating the Resolution 2270.[29] The claim, if true, signified that the isolated regime in Pyongyang had made a major leap in its nuclear weapons capabilities. Pyongyang had conducted nuclear tests on three times occasions in 2006, 2009 and 2013. The North drew international condemnation by conducting its fourth nuclear test on January 6, 2016. That was followed by a camouflaged rocket launch which was regarded by many experts as a disguise for a test of its long-range missile technology. After United Nations Security Council resolution, in defiance of mounting pressure from the international community, North Korea's leader claimed his country had completed the miniaturizing of nuclear warheads and warned of an "all-out offensive" and "pre-emptive" nuclear strikes against Seoul and Washington. North Korean young leader Kim Jong-un vowed a nuclear test "in a short time" as well as tests of several kinds of ballistic rockets capable of carrying nuclear warheads. Kim Jong-un allegedly led a test of a new technology that would allow a ballistic missile armed with a warhead to re-enter the earth's atmosphere, according to North Korea's state-run Korean Central News Agency.

The UN Resolution 2270: A stern message to North Korea

The US and China had reached an agreement to impose tougher sanctions against North Korea in what appeared to be a diplomatic shift by Beijing regarding its intransigent ally. In the past, after previous nuclear tests condemned by the Security Council, China agreed only to ban weapons transfers and limited sanctions against those linked to the nuclear program. The strongest-ever UN sanctions proposed by the United States against North Korea would put a sectorial ban on the export of mineral resources and require mandatory inspection of all cargo leaving and entering North Korea, cutting major sources of hard currency to Pyongyang. Going beyond sanctions in place since 2006, the Security Council passed the UN Resolution 2270 in 2016 which would dramatically tighten sanctions on North Korea following its recent nuclear test and long-range missile launch. A day after Beijing and Washington reached an agreement on a draft resolution, both sides agreed not to accept North Korea as a nuclear-armed state. It would be the strongest set of sanctions imposed by the Security Council in more than two decades. The resolution was reportedly called comprehensive, robust and unyielding. It was a major upgrade, and there could be — provided it goes forward — more pressure points through the strengthening of enforcement mechanism and inclusion of more sectors under the resolution. It was breaking new ground in a whole host of ways. The proposed package of sanctions was stronger than oil and financial sanctions imposed on Iran, which were lifted after a deal to terminate Iran's nuclear development program was reached in 2015. The sectorial ban included the prohibition of the export of coal, iron, gold, titanium and rare earth minerals by North Korea. Several others were unprecedented. For the first time in history, all cargo going in and out of the DPRK would be subjected to mandatory inspection. Unprecedentedly, all small arms and other conventional weapons would be prohibited from being sold to the DPRK. The resolution also covered the imposition of financial sanctions targeting North Korean banks and assets as well as the banning of aviation and rocket fuel supplies to the North.

The recent statistics on trade between China and North Korea, as well as news reports from their borders indicate that the Chinese still allow a booming network of trade and smuggling across their 1,420-km frontier. Beijing's cooperation is instrumental because North Korea depends heavily on China economically. The world is watching to see if China enforces the sanctions. China, North Korea's main trading partner and diplomatic backer, is its main supplier of oil. The point is that sanctions would not alone curtail Pyongyang's nuclear ambitions without "sustained diplomacy". Russia also insisted on easing the ban on aviation fuel exports to allow for North Korean commercial airliners refueling at Russian airports to receive jet fuel so that they can return to Pyongyang. Russia emphasized that the sanctions should not include any provisions that would affect "certain Russian economic interests," namely a project to build a railway connecting North Korea to China and South Korea that would enable delivery of its coal. It is presumed that Beijing prefers keeping a nuclear-armed North Korea afloat as a buffer against the South and the United States to risking the collapse of the North's government with overly severe enforcement of sanctions. China sees living with a communist nuclear-armed state on its border as preferable to the chaos of its collapse. To ensure the communist regime's survival, China is able to control its neighbor by providing enough oil to keep its economy afloat. The alternative is a nightmare for Beijing: a collapsed North Korean regime, millions of refugees fleeing into China, and a unified Korean Peninsula under an American defense treaty. So despite what Chinese analysts describe as the government's distaste for Kim Jong-un and his unpredictable behavior, China's basic calculus on North Korea remains firms. The longstanding fear that punitive economic action would destabilize North Korea makes it unlikely that Beijing would cooperate with the United States on more stringent UN sanctions. The Chinese leadership is questioning why China would work with the United States at the UN after Washington had gone ahead with antimissile system against Chinese wishes.

The system serves to reinforce China's view that its alliance with North Korea is integral part of China's strategic interest in Asia, in consideration of America's treaty allies, Japan and South Korea. The resolutions in March and October 2016 also did not affect tens of thousands of North Koreans employed in factories, construction projects and logging camps in China and the Middle East. The sanctions imposed in March and October had been enforced in only a desultory fashion. If China were to stop the flow of oil, North Korea would face a severe economic crisis in about one year, and then face a choice between keeping its economy going and compromising on its nuclear program. One of China's biggest fears is a collapse of North Korea that would result in a unified Korean Peninsula under an American defense treaty. For that reason, China has tolerated Kim Jong-un's advances in nuclear weapons. Pyongyang had exported a total of US$2.5 billion worth of mineral resources to China in 2017, while importing US$3 billion. Given China's accounting for 90% of North Korea's trade volume, the success of the newest round of sanctions would hinge on China. According to the Korea Trade-Investment Promotion Agency, the North's total trade volume in 2014 stood at US$7.61 billion, exports at US$3.16 billion and imports at US$4.45 billion. Total trade volume with China was US$6.86 billion, exporting US$2.84 billion and importing US$4.02 billion. China reportedly agreed to an embargo on mineral resources even though it risks damaging Chinese business. Whether the proposed new sanctions will succeed in curtailing Pyongyang's nuclear ambitions remains to be seen. Past efforts to halt its nuclear program had not been fully carried out, nor had they prevented North Korea from pursuing a nuclear arsenal. Whether China would follow through on tougher sanctions was also a key question. Significant loopholes remain. North Korea is still able to buy oil and sell its coal and iron ore, as long as the trading commodities are not being used to fund its nuclear weapons program — which would be difficult to prove.

Deterioration of inter-Korean relation

Inter-Korean relations had rapidly deteriorated in the aftermath of North Korea's nuclear test on January 6, 2016 and launch of a long-range missile on February 7. The South Korean government decided to close the operation of the joint complex in the North's border city of Kaesong in response to Pyongyang's recent nuclear test and long-range rocket launch. On February 10, South Korea shut down the jointly run industrial complex after it determined that the money flowing into Pyongyang was being diverted to develop nuclear weapons and intercontinental ballistic missiles. About 54,000 North Korean workers were employed by 124 South Korean firms in production factories in Kaesong. The industrial complex first went into operation in 2004. In a special parliamentary address on February 16, South Korean President Park Geun-hye declared a shift in her focus on North Korea from engagement to pressure. She even talked about "regime collapse", something of a taboo for South Korean leaders in their public remarks. It is the opinion of this author that inter-Korean relations were expected to remain icy throughout the remainder of her term that ended in early 2018. Until the end of the Park administration's tenure, the confrontational mode, rather than dialogue, continued. Military tensions were escalating. All cross-border exchanges had come to a grinding halt. Park's signature policy, inter-Korean Trust-Building Process, was in tatters. Her "unification bonanza" vision was doubtful. "The shutdown of an inter-Korean industrial complex would not affect Pyongyang's nuclear program, as it started before the opening of the zone," the North Korean Central News Agency (KCNA) reported and added the shutdown of the industrial zone was set to drive Kaesong-based South Korean firms to "death". The measure had drawn mixed views on its effects, given the fact that local manufacturers had run production facilities there with the output hovering above US$500 million in 2015.[30] The KCNA, the mouthpiece of Pyongyang, argued its development of nuclear and "space" programs would remain intact after the shutdown, adding that South Korea's plan to cut the funding of such moves by closing the complex would be unsuccessful. In 2013, the industrial zone was also closed due to Pyongyang's protest against a joint military exercise between South Korean and US forces. The two Koreas are still technically in a state of war since the 1950–53 Korean War ended in a truce, not a peace treaty.

New Cold War in Northeast Asia: China, Russia, North Korea versus US, Japan, South Korea

The communist neighbor's back-to-back provocations roiled the security conditions in Northeast Asia, a major spot for rivalry and cooperation between the United States and China. The North's provocations have also complicated South Korean government's diplomacy. It has especially driven a wedge between Seoul and Beijing, upending much of what President Park Geun-hye did between 2012 to 2015. South Korean President Park Geun-hye attended China's key war anniversary event on September 3, 2015, demonstrating her resolve to build a bilateral strategic partnership. Despite her efforts and personal ties with President Xi Jinping, China had been lukewarm toward imposing painful new sanctions on the North in initial stage after the fourth nuclear test in 2016. Beijing had emphasized the need for dialogue instead of a sanctions-only approach. In order to deter and respond to North Korea's nuclear, weapons of mass destruction, and missile threats, the US and South Korea agreed to utilize efforts in every category including South Korea's conventional capabilities and the US's extended deterrence. Both countries agreed with the deployment of the US-led THAAD (Terminal High Altitude Area Defense system) in South Korea. China and Russia were fiercely opposed to South Korea's move to bring the US advanced missile defense system to the Korean Peninsula. During a Reuters interview, Chinese Foreign Minister Wang Yi criticized South Korea and the US for threatening its national security interests. Wang maintained that the coverage of the THAAD missile defense system, especially the monitoring scope of its X-Band radar, would go far beyond the defense needs of the Korean Peninsula. He also argued that by reaching deep into the hinterland of Asia, the THAAD deployment would not only directly damage China's strategic security interests, but also harm the security interests of other countries across the region.[31]

But the South Korean government made it clear that making a decision on whether to deploy a THAAD battery to the peninsula is Seoul's sovereign right, referring to objections regarding the issue voiced by China.[32] Even though Seoul argued that the decision would be made in accordance with national security and interests, and no other conditions are linked to this, the complicated stance has been subtle. The remark was construed as downplaying speculation that Seoul and Washington provoked the THAAD issue to pressure China to join hands with them on producing harsher sanctions against Pyongyang, if Beijing does not want a THAAD battery to be placed on South Korean soil. South Korea's basic position has been that the THAAD issue is not directly linked with Beijing's participation in the UN Security Council for sanctions. China has been opposed to the THAAD deployment on the peninsula out of concerns that its radar could snoop on the country's military activities. The Obama administration's decision to deploy an advanced missile defensive system in South Korea also gave Chinese President Xi less incentive to cooperate with Washington on a North Korea strategy that could aim, for example, to freeze the North's nuclear capacity. China was strongly opposed to North Korea's nuclear weapons and had at the same time a negative policy on the missile defense system in South Korea. Beijing interpreted the THAAD deployment as another American effort to strongly contain China. Even though President Obama said after meeting with Xi in Hangzhou, China, Chinese officials argued that the THAAD radar can detect Chinese missiles on the mainland under its nuclear undermining.

The argument of this author is that Northeast Asia is being gripped by a new Cold War. Concerns are growing over the fallout from the strain in the Seoul–Beijing relationship. The Chinese Ambassador to South Korea, Qiu Guohong said the resolution was "paving a stone for political settlement of the nuclear issue on the Korean Peninsula, signaling a desire for a return to dialogue." Even if a UN Security Council resolution was adopted to punish the North, chances were slim that it would move toward denuclearization. Despite tensions over North Korea's nuclear and missile tests, American scholars considered the issue less important than Middle Eastern problems, a rising China, tensions with Russia and even climate change, a survey showed on February 23, 2016.[33] The survey reflected widespread perceptions that North Korean topic stands low on the US diplomatic priority list and that the Obama administration had little appetite for tackling the problem as it had been preoccupied with Middle Eastern issues, such as Iran's nuclear program and the militant group Islamic State. The United States would not engage in talks with North Korea unless the discussions were focused on denuclearization.

US versus North Korea: Denuclearization and peace agreement

The US had reportedly agreed to hold peace treaty talks with Pyongyang on condition that the discussions also dealt with denuclearization since the beginning of negotiation with North Korea in six-party talks (2003–2007) and four-party talks (1997–1999). Washington insisted that denuclearization had remained core issue in any kind of talks and made it clear that a denuclearized Korean Peninsula should be an overriding priority before peace agreement. It is, however, not clear that the US would engage in concerted discussions with North Korea that did not place an emphasis on denuclearization. The *Wall Street Journal* report said that the US had conditionally agreed to accept the North's offer to hold peace treaty talks, just days before the North's nuclear test, but Pyongyang rejected the counterproposal and went ahead with the fourth nuclear test in January 6, 2016. The strategy was also shared by other parties of the six-party talks, including South Korea and Japan — partners of an ironclad alliance. The US had consistently told Pyongyang that they remained open to authentic and credible negotiations based on the agreement reached with all members of the six-party talks in September 2005.[34] It was not new that North Korea wanted a peace treaty with the US to formally end the Korean War. DPRK for the first time proposed the initiative in 1974. Pyongyang had continued to iterate the argument. The consistent proposal was officially included in the September agreement of 2005. Pyongyang pressed the demand harder in 2016 after Foreign Minister Ri Su Yong made the demand during a speech at the UN General Assembly in October 2015. The US had said the demand was a non-starter with the North pursuing nuclear ambitions. US officials had stressed that the communist regime had gotten the order wrong and should first focus on negotiations to end its nuclear program.

Cash flow into North Korea: China

North Korea was believed to be relying on cash delivery or borrowed-name bank accounts in a bid to avert China's possible financial sanctions. Chinese banks in areas bordering North Korea had begun to freeze accounts held by North Koreans apparently in response to the North's fourth nuclear test and missile launch. The North was thought to directly deliver cash or use borrowed-name bank accounts when engaging in external trade with China. China has been under pressure to join the US-led efforts to slap more stringent sanctions on North Korea. In 2013, the Bank of China closed accounts with North Korea's Foreign Trade Bank, which was accused by the US of helping finance the North's nuclear weapons program. Washington's unilateral financial sanctions hit Pyongyang hard in 2005. The US blacklisted the Macau-based Banco Delta Asia Bank (BDA) for alleged counterfeiting and money laundering by North Korea. The move froze about US$24 million worth of funds in North Korea's accounts at the BDA. This explains the thinking of the US government that financial pressure would remain very important in dealing with nuclear developing countries like North Korea and Iran over the long term. In that sense, strategic communication with China was of importance. Some Chinese banks operating near the border with North Korea had begun frozen bank accounts held by North Koreans, through suspending deposit and transfer services. Among the banks was the Industrial and Commercial Bank of China (ICBC), the country's largest bank. As a result, the Chinese banks were believed to have taken such measures to manage potential risks in advance. Dandong in Liaoning Province, linked to the North Korean city of Sinuiju through a single-track rail bridge, serves as the major conduit for nearly three-quarters of all trade between the two countries. It was also aimed at choking off sources of cash for the regime by sanctioning trade in coal, minerals and precious metals, and blacklisting those helping with Pyongyang's money laundering, counterfeiting, cash smuggling and narcotics trafficking. China-bound exports of North Korea's natural resources had been blocked to improve the efficiency of economic sanctions being ramped up against the reclusive communist country in the wake of its consecutive and provocative actions. Pyongyang's total exports had been shrinking after the fourth nuclear test, mostly affected by a marked drop in overseas sales of its natural resources. The shrinkage in exports was the result of a significant drop in exports of its natural resources. Its natural resources exports continued to decline into the third quarter of last year. Behind the positive growth of the North Korean economy after 2010 was its abundant resources buried under the ground and high-quality labor force, which combined to expand its trade with China. Pyongyang's efforts to secure foreign currencies could hit a snag, should the China-bound exports continue to decline. North Korea's natural resources exports to China rose to an all-time high of US$1.84 billion in 2013 but fell to US$1.52 billion in 2014. During the same period, the ratio of natural resources to its total overseas shipments fell from 63.2% to 53.7%. North Korea is known as being dependent almost entirely on China for its overseas trade. The heavy reliance on China could further increase down the road after South Korea shut down the operation of an inter-Korean industrial complex in the North's border city of Kaesong in apparent retaliation against its recent series of provocative acts.

Cash flow into North Korea: Kaesong Industrial Park

Kim Dae-jung, then South Korean president, held a landmark summit with the North's Kim Jong-il in Pyongyang in 2000. South and North Korea opened the factory park in the North's western border city of Kaesong. South Korea launched the factory park in order to induce positive changes in Pyongyang, though North Korea diverted the money for its nuclear and missile programs as well as for luxury goods and various campaigns to extol the achievements of its ruling family. A controversy was rapidly escalating regarding a claim first made by a government minister on February 2016 that North Korea redirected wages intended for its citizens who worked at the now-closed Kaesong Industrial Complex, for nuclear weapons and missile development. South Korean President Park Geun-hye also stated in her address to the National Assembly that a hefty chunk of wages paid to North Korean workers was funneled to its leadership, hinting that the regime may have used the money to develop weapons. Park added that some ₩616 billion (about US$560 million) have been provided to North Korean workers, including some ₩132 billion in 2012. The president's remark came one day after Unification Minister Hong Yong-pyo retracted his claim that the government had data to prove the North's diversion of funds. If Park's claim was true, it could mean that South Korea had violated a UN Security Council resolution against contributing funds to North Korea's weapons of mass destruction program. In response to the North's third nuclear test in 2013, the UN slapped Resolution 2094 banning the flow of "bulk cash" into North Korea and restricting the financial network of North Korean banks linked to the nation's illegal activities. According to the unification ministry of South Korea, about US$560 million had flowed to the repressive regime via the joint industrial park, with US$120 million alone in 2015. However, profits from the industrial complex accounted for around 1% of North Korea's annual trade revenue. Under the resolution, member states are required to prevent the provision of financial services or monetary transfers of any financial or other assets or resources, including bulk cash that could contribute to funding the North's nuclear or ballistic missile programs. "Most of the dollars we paid are presumed to have been funneled into the Workers' Party responsible for nuclear and missile development," President Park told lawmakers.

The South Korean government shuttered the joint factory in 2016 and that the government had obtained "multiple documents" related to concerns or speculation that its payments to workers from the Kaesong Industrial Park had been used to bankroll the development of nuclear weapons and missiles. But the unification minister went a step further, saying that 70% of the money was misused but did not provide any evidence to support this, citing a need for confidentiality. The issue of money diversion came to the fore in the South after South Korea shuttered the industrial zone in response to North Korea's recent nuclear test and long-range rocket launch. South Korea has said more than 120 of its firms provided around US$560 million in cash to North Korea for the income of North Korean workers at the sprawling zone. South Korea provided the money directly to the North Korean government, instead of its workers, creating a loophole for the diversion of the cash to North

Korea's leadership. Pyongyang had expelled all South Koreans from the joint factory park, putting an end to the last-remaining economic cooperation project between the two Koreas. South Korea wanted to work closely with the United States to force a change in North Korea's behavior so as to curb its nuclear and missile development. US President Obama signed a North Korea sanctions bill that had passed Congress with overwhelming support, saying the legislation would serve the administration's goal of increasing pressure on Pyongyang. The legislation (H.R.757) passed through the Senate and the House on March 2016 in a demonstration of bipartisan support for a tough response to the North's nuclear and missile tests that raised concern that Pyongyang had made progress in efforts to develop nuclear missiles capable of striking the US.[35] The legislation calls for the mandatory blacklisting of those assisting Pyongyang with its nuclear and missile programs, human rights abuses, cyberattacks and other crimes. It was believed to be the strongest sanctions bill ever introduced in Congress against the communist nation. It was the first time that a sanctions bill exclusively targeting North Korea had been passed by both the House and the Senate. Many North Korea sanctions proposals have since been introduced to Congress. The North Korean regime has continued to be isolated until it begins to take steps closer in the direction of not just the United States and South Korea, but even countries like China, with whom the North Korean leadership has a vital relationship.

Cash flow into North Korea: Overseas workers

North Korea has few items to export, other than arms and mineral resources, the shipments of which have become difficult because of international sanctions. This has forced its leadership to resort to sending workers abroad. Russia and China also prefer North Korean workers because they work long hours for low wages under the strict control of supervisors. Jang Song-thaek, Kim Jong-un's uncle and mentor before he was executed in 2013, had been in exclusive charge of labor dispatch. However, the cabinet, military and the party are reportedly competing to take part in the business. North

Korean laborers abroad earn US$100 to US$1,500 a month but get only 10% to 30% of it, with the other 70% to 90% going to the secretariat of the Workers' Party, or Office 39, which is responsible for managing foreign exchange earned by the party, administration and military. This hard cash is used for nuclear and missile projects and buying luxuries for the Kim family and other North Korean leaders. Between 50,000 and 60,000 North Korean overseas workers remit up to US$200 million home a year, twice as much as the 54,000 workers in the now-closed Kaesong Industrial Complex earned. North Korea has reportedly sent up to 60,000 workers to about 50 countries, mainly those that have high demand for construction workers, including 20,000 in Russia, 19,000 in China, 4,000 to 5,000 in Kuwait, 2,000 in the United Arab Emirates and 1,800 in Qatar. Given there are many more who do not fall into the statistics, the actual number may exceed 100,000. Since Kim Jong-un ordered that as many workers as possible should be sent overseas, the number has sharply increased from 20,000 in 2010, and their areas of work have also expanded to dressmaking, logging, health care and even information technology. This means the UN Security Council should include workers' foreign earnings in its targets for sanctions. North Korean authorities are doing all they can to increase labor dispatch but finding it hard because many of their host governments are moving to regulate it, either by canceling and reducing dispatches or preventing the exploitation of workers' income by officials in Pyongyang.

Cash flow into North Korea: Others

Since the North conducted a nuclear test in January 2016 and went ahead with a rocket launch in February, Seoul has instructed its citizens to not patronize the government-affiliated North Korean restaurants that usually pull in a steady stream of curious South Korean travelers — and their precious foreign currency. Some may wonder how having a meal at these restaurants could fund nuclear and missile development costs. But it is estimated that North Korea makes about US$10 million a year from the restaurant business.

There had been about 100 North Korean restaurants when Kim Jong-un came into power in 2012, but there were more than 130 in operation in 2015. In February 2016, the South Korean embassy in Beijing issued an advisory warning to its citizens living in or traveling to China to avoid eating at North Korean restaurants, citing "concerns about safety". "Those who are living in or traveling to China need to refrain from visiting North Korean restaurants or North Korea-related facilities," the statement said. The Park Geun-hye administration had suspended provision of humanitarian aid to the isolated country. It was inevitable to suspend humanitarian assistance as well as overall exchanges that Seoul closed down the inter-Korean industrial complex. The Park Geun-hye administration previously provided financial support to vulnerable citizens in the North through international bodies such as United Nations Children's Fund (UNICEF) and World Health Organization (WHO). Approximately ₩10 billion (US$8.28 million) had been sent each year since Park Geun-hye government was inaugurated in 2013. A series of harsh moves might slow down its nuclear development to some extent, but these tightening measures were not enough for the North to drop the plan. It signified that the government's strong stance on North Korea was regarded as pressing China, the North's major ally, to join the international drive to impose tough sanctions against Pyongyang.

North Korea's fifth nuclear test posed an imminent threat to South Korean security and survival. The remaining question was when — not whether — the North would deploy nuclear weapons in real battles. It is only a matter of time before North Korea increases its nuclear arsenal (now estimated at 20 devices) and figures out how to miniaturize its weapon for delivery by missiles of increasing range and accuracy. There is another risk as well. A cash-strapped North Korea might be tempted to sell nuclear arms to the highest bidder. The chances of further nuclear proliferation have increased the actual use possibility of nuclear weapons. North Korea is expected to obtain nuclear materials to make 100 warheads by 2020 and secure ballistic missile technologies that are sufficient to fire missiles as far as the US mainland. It is time to call a spade a spade. North Korea becomes a nuclear state. It has matched its words with action. If there has been any doubt, its two latest provocations have proved otherwise. North Korea tested what it claimed was a small-scale H-bomb and fired a rocket that can be converted to a long-range missile. So far, South Korea has said it will help the North if it gives up its nuclear development. This is nothing but wishful thinking. Now Seoul and Washington are trying to persuade Beijing to stop protecting its client state and join an effort at the UN to punish the North for its provocative acts. The nations are separately preparing steps against Pyongyang. Seoul, for one, has done what is seen as an extreme measure, having pulled out of the Kaesong Industrial Complex, the 13-year-old last remnant of inter-Korean cooperation. The North has not budged and it would not because it has no other choice. The ruling Kim dynasty knows well that the nuclear weapons and missiles are the key to its survival. Without them, it would collapse. Kim Jong-un cannot afford to open up to the outside world for full economic cooperation because it would cause the public to become disenchanted and rebel against him. The third-generation heir would not have a chance of holding on to power in an "open" North Korea.

His double take of nuclear development and economic development is unrealistic. Since inheriting power from his father, Kim Jong-il, in late 2011, Kim Jong-un has called for accelerating the North's pursuit of long-range missiles and nuclear weapons in defiance of international pressure. Three of the North's five nuclear tests had been conducted under his rule. North Korea is reportedly now able to mount a nuclear warhead on a short-range Scud or medium-range Rodong missile, if not on an ICBM. Therefore, its survival strategy is to portray the US as public enemy No. 1 and give North Koreans an object to hate. This is why the North claims its missiles and nuclear weapons target the US, which is far stronger than the impoverished North. The South is also included on the North's list of imaginary list of foes as a US puppet that needs toppling. North Korean leader Kim Jong-un has called for launching of more satellites as Pyongyang launched a long-range rocket carrying what it claimed was an earth observation. The North's leader offered words of encouragement to scientists, technicians and officials who contributed to the successful launch of its satellite, named Kwangmyongsong-4, and fifth nuclear test at a banquet on August and September 2016, according to the KCNA.[36] Pyongyang had made significant progress in the miniaturization of nuclear warheads. Sixth nuclear test by Pyongyang was looming and came true in September 2017.

As it is beyond doubt that the North will not give up its weapons of mass destruction, it is inevitable for Seoul to make a shift in its bona fide policy toward the North and seek a regime change in Pyongyang. Or, if that is too controversial, Seoul at least should not rule it out. This author thinks that the strongest resolution can be useful as leverage to persuade Pyongyang to return to the bargaining table. No matter how tough on paper, the sanctions will be effective only if they are enforced. There are good reasons to doubt that every country will follow through. The burden falls heavily on China, the North's chief ally in providing food, fuel and political cover. Chinese leaders have long opposed the North's nuclear program. Even though Beijing agreed to the UN Resolution 2270, the country has feared that doing so would destabilize North Korea and send refugees fleeing to China. It took pressure from governments in Washington and Seoul to get China to shift course. Beijing's cooperation is essential to implement a meaningful sanctions resolution, as it is one of five veto-holding permanent members of the UN Security Council and the main provider of food and fuel aid to the impoverished North. Although North Korea has threatened the United States with a nuclear strike, it urged the United States to prepare for diplomatic negotiations, as an alternative to military pressure and unilateral sanctions. Denouncing the latest UN Security Council sanctions as "anachronistic and suicidal", North Korea's top military body requested that the United States end sanctions and work instead toward stabilizing tensions on the Korean Peninsula.[37] Tougher sanctions will not by themselves end this long-term threat. At some point, six-party countries will have to find a way to revive negotiation with North Korea to shut down, or at least curb, its nuclear program. Final chance of denuclearization remains on the Korean Peninsula. This author again hopes that Pyongyang benchmark the Teheran model of the Middle East. The six-party countries including US, Japan and South Korea have options, but none are particularly attractive. As for negotiations, there is little if any reason to be confident that North Korea would give up what it considers to be its best guarantee of survival. In fact, it has often used negotiations to buy time for further advances in its nuclear and missile capabilities.

Another option is to continue with a version of the current policy of extensive sanctions. The problem is that sanctions will not be potent enough to force North Korea to give up its nuclear and missile programs. This is partly because China, fearing large refugee inflows and a unified Korea in America's strategic orbit should North Korea collapse, would most likely continue to ensure that its communist neighbor gets the fuel and food it needs. As a result, it makes more sense to focus on diplomacy with China. The US, after consulting closely with South Korea and Japan, should meet with Chinese officials to discuss what a unified Korea would look like, so that some Chinese concerns could be met. For example, a unified country could be non-nuclear, and any remaining US military forces on the Korean Peninsula could be fewer and farther south than they are now. It is of course possible or even probable that such assurances would not lead to any meaningful diminution in Chinese support for North Korea. In that case, the US would have three more options. One would be to live with a North Korea in possession of missiles that could bring nuclear bombs to US soil. The policy would become one of defense (deploying additional anti-missile systems) and deterrence, with North Korea understanding that any use or spread of nuclear weapons would lead to the end of the regime and possibly nuclear retaliation. Cyber weapons might also be employed to obstruct and impede the progress of North Korea's program. The second option would be a conventional military attack, targeting North Korean nuclear and missile capabilities. This would be a classic preventive strike. The danger is that such a strike might not achieve all objectives and instead trigger either a conventional military attack on South Korea (where nearly 30,000 US troops are based) or even a nuclear attack from the North. Needless to say, Japan and South Korea would have to be prepared to support any US military response before it could be undertaken. The third option would be to launch a surgical strike, only if intelligence can show North Korea putting its missiles on alert and readying them for imminent use. This would be a classic pre-emptive strike. The danger here is that the intelligence might not be sufficiently clear — or come early enough. Three options would be unlikely to solve the crisis. Therefore, diplomatic negotiation is very useful and discerning, suggesting the concrete bargaining deals include satisfactory economic aids and complete denuclearization process. It depends finally on Kim Jong-un's decision, in particular to decide on final, fully verified denuclearization (FFVD) and fulfill the dream of wealthy country like Vietnam in the style of grand bargaining.

Chapter 4

The US Denuclearization Policy toward North Korea: Trump's Choices — Diplomacy and Military Options

North Korea claimed success in testing a hydrogen bomb

North Korea's sixth nuclear test in September 2017 fundamentally changed the international political and security environment of the Korean Peninsula and Northeast Asia. Following the fourth and fifth nuclear bomb test in 2016, North Korea declared its success in the hydrogen bomb test. North Korea's nuclear armament is nearing actual deployment due to its sixth nuclear test. The ballistic missiles (IRBM and ICBM) launched into the Pacific before and after the nuclear test were intended to show off the possibility of attacks on the US mainland as well as South Korea and Japan. Military tension on the Korean Peninsula is also escalating as the possibility of North Korea attacking the US mainland has raised.[38] North Korea's nuclear and missile threats have turned into a more complex regional security issue that disrupts the Korean Peninsula as well as the Non-Proliferation Treaty (NPT), rather than a conflict between the US and North Korea or South Korea, Japan and North Korea.[39] In particular, discussions are accelerating whether the sixth nuclear test had exceeded the red line of US security or functioned as a game changer.[40] As a result, international efforts to curb North Korea's nuclear threat are accelerating, but the differences in the implementation of the sanctions have not produced any tangible results. The international community is making efforts on sanctions against North Korea, focusing on non-military aspects, mainly on resolution adopted by the United Nations Security Council. However, it is uncertain whether the resolution on sanctions against North Korea will be firmly implemented as planned due to the passive stance of China and Russia, which are permanent members of the Security Council. Both countries say that North Korea's nuclear armament is against the principle of denuclearization of Northeast Asia, but they are taking a position that they have accepted as a balance of power. Since the Obama administration's announcement of "Pivot to Asia" policy[41] in 2012, the US–Japan alliance has played an important role in deterring China's expansion. China's basic position is that North Korea's nuclear weapons are acting as a breakwater for the continental United States amid military confrontation between the US–Japan alliance and the North Korea–China alliance. In particular, China believes that the status quo policy and North Korea's nuclear-holding strategy can serve as a counterbalance without conflict on the Korean Peninsula.[42] Also, China considers that North Korea's nuclear weapons are the last bastion to prevent the collapse of the North due to international pressure. On the other hand, even if sanctions are implemented according to the Security Council's resolution, it is uncertain whether North Korea, which gives priority to its regime's survival, can give up its nuclear program.[43]

North Korea's sixth nuclear test has emerged as a detonator that hinders peace and stability in Northeast Asia. North Korean leader Kim Jong-un mentioned the modernization of strategic forces and the reinforcement of military power when the Hwasong-12 launched on August 30, 2017. His remarks suggested that the future military provocations could be extended to the

Pacific including Guam as well as to the Korean Peninsula and its surrounding areas like Japan. In fact, if a provocation occurs near the territorial waters of Guam or near the territorial waters near Japan, it is inevitable for Japan to take a hardline approach against Pyongyang. The North Korean government has formed a serious confrontation between the US and North Korea by referring to the Pacific Ocean as the target site of missile launches. In July 2017, North Korea conducted a drill to deploy the missile at the missile test stage with a 45-degree launch, rather than a high-angle launch. Even though the sixth nuclear test took place a year after the fifth nuclear test, North Korea claimed that it had almost succeeded in conducting a hydrogen bomb test for ICBMs. It is possible for experts to assess that the North has reached the level of "achievement of great work" along with the test of a normal launch of the Hwasong-14. After the sixth nuclear test, North Korea will no longer be the object of nuclear dismantlement. North Korea hoped to be the main advocate of denuclearization of the world.[44] Given the confrontational structure of the five countries versus North Korea, the preexisting six-party talks is not easy to replicate for future multilateral talks. North Korea's demands and comments will weigh more than they did in the past. The argument of a nuclear power state is different from that of a conventional weapons state. The US government's efforts to denuclearize North Korea will be concrete and expedited. If North Korea is officially recognized as the country that possesses nuclear weapons, the nuclear dominoes of Northeast Asia, including Japan and Taiwan as well as South Korea, will be inevitably spread. Therefore, North Korea's denuclearization is one of top priority issues for US diplomacy in the 21st century. It is inevitable that the Trump administration's North Korea policy will be changed fundamentally with the sixth nuclear test. Chapter 4 examines security situations surrounding the North Korean nuclear standoff in Northeast Asia and analyze how dramatically the Trump administration's policy on North Korea's denuclearization in the Korean Peninsula had changed before and after the sixth nuclear test.

North Korean nuclear and security situation in Northeast Asia: Crisis and cooperation

Multi-layered and complex Northeast Asian situation: Rise of a new Cold War structure

While North Korea played a passive role in the Northeast Asian international order in the 20th century, with the advent of the 21st century, the North is focusing on playing an active role in the international community. Since the serious consideration of the 1994 local surgical strike on the Yongbyon nuclear complex, the US had continued negotiations with North Korea through the Geneva Agreement. However, since the George W. Bush administration's "Axis of Evil" policy in 2002, relations between the two countries have been a series of conflicts. In the sixth round of talks on September 19, 2006, the Joint Statement was announced to try to resolve the issue through negotiations but it failed to overcome the mutual serious distrust. North Korea has conducted nuclear tests on six occasions since 2006, raising its voice as a major player in the Northeast Asian international order. In particular, Kim Jong-un, the third-generation leader who came to power on December 30, 2011, has urged North Korea to strengthen its offensive military power. His military provocation is based on the judgment that only nuclear weapons and ballistic missiles will protect the North Korean regime and raise its global status in the Northeast Asian international order.[45] North Korea has seen no meaningful progress coming from both conservative and progressive South Korean governments since 2008, and has also observed that the US and China would not accommodate as it wishes. The Abe administration's conservative swing in Japan is also a burden on North Korea. Kim Jong-un has recognized the stark reality that North Korea is not perceived as a normal country by the international community and seeks every opportunity to break it down. The North Korean leadership has also judged on the essentiality to recover from the Cold War structure between South Korea, China, the US and Japan by escaping the frame of being pressurized by the five members during the previous six-party talks. Pyongyang has believed that accelerating nuclear and missile development and inducing military tension on the Korean Peninsula would result in enhancing its interests from the realignment of the political structure in Northeast Asia. It has been established as an "alienation strategy" in which tension on the Korean Peninsula can lead to an armed buildup in South Korea, the US, and Japan, which can simultaneously cause a backlash from China. In fact, North Korea criticized the South Korea–U.S. joint maritime exercise on October 12, 2016 as a military provocation that could destabilize the Korean Peninsula and escalate into worst crisis.[46]

The deployment of the THAAD (Terminal High Altitude Area Defense) system is partly attributable to the entrapment of South Korea and the US as well as to North Korea's skillful inducement. Pyongyang provoked China to react by speeding up nuclear and missile provocations and causing the acceleration of THAAD deployment on the Korean Peninsula under the pretext of the South Korea–US joint drill. This led to China's long-standing demand for South Korea to withdraw the THAAD system from the Korean Peninsula. Amid China's conflict with South Korea, the former had concurrent conflict with Pyongyang due to Kim Jong-un's nuclear provocation. Regarding North Korea's possible violation of the denuclearization on the Korean Peninsula, it caused Seoul to be antagonistic with Pyongyang. Last but not least, the North sought a new honeymoon relationship with Russia because of the partial estrangement of relations with China.[47] Kim Jong-un's military provocations resulted in the formation of the order of a new cold war on the Korean Peninsula.

China's equilibrium policy on the Korean Peninsula

The period 2016–17 was a time when regional balance of power was constantly moving away and returning to the new order. US President Barack Obama's visit to Hiroshima on May 27, 2016 and the lightning meeting between Chinese President Xi Jinping and North Korean diplomatic minister Ri Su-yong on June 2, 2016 were the peculiar diplomatic actions that straightforwardly exhibit the balance of power in Northeast Asia. If one thinks that there is no correlation between the chain contacts of Northeast Asian leaders with a difference of seven days, it may be that he/she has not understood the balance of power theory of international politics yet or does not understand the foreign policy of each country. China has been strengthening its cooperation with North Korea in response to the strengthening of the alliance between the US and Japan since the declaration of the US's "Pivot to Asia" policy in 2012. China regards its relationship with North Korea as a "lips and teeth" relationship. The meeting between Xi and South Korean Prime Minister Hwang Kyo-ahn in June 2016 was part of a diplomatic effort to block South Korea's deployment of THAAD on the Korean Peninsula. China judged that South Korea's decision to deploy the THAAD system was an attempt to bring down the balance of power in Northeast Asia. In response, Xi pushed for a policy to restore the balance of power in Northeast Asia within a short period of time by showing off the friendly relationship between North Korea and China. In December 2016, Japanese Prime Minister Shinzo Abe visited Pearl Harbor in Hawaii as a return visit for Obama's visit to Hiroshima and strengthened the US–Japan alliance by downplaying the history of the outbreak of World War II.

In the 23rd ASEAN Regional Forum (ARF) held in Vientiane, Laos in July 2016, Chinese Foreign Minister Wang Yi and North Korean Foreign Minister Ri Yong-ho held a meeting of foreign ministers between the two countries in two years. North Korea urged China to respond by claiming that the THAAD deployment would be included in the missile defense system of the US that can neutralize China's response toward US interceptor missile system. China, which sympathized with North Korea's claim, naturally formed a new Cold War zone with the presence of THAAD. Aside from North Korea's sixth nuclear test, China has simultaneously pushed for the resumption of international talks on resolving the North Korean nuclear issue and the participation in sanctions against North Korea. China focused on clarifying the dialogue agreement between US Secretary of State John Kerry and Chinese Foreign Minister Wang that was made in February 2016. Wu Dawei, China's chief delegate to the six-party talks, stressed that the six-party talks should resume as soon as possible at a 1.5-track seminar in ARF Workshop on Management of Marine Hazards in the Asia-Pacific in Beijing on June 2016.[48] At the seminar, North Korean representative Choi Sun-hee rejected China's efforts to resolve the issue by returning to the six-party talks, claiming that the six-party talks had ended.[49] Aside from the final denuclearization of North Korea, the US–North Korea relationship needs to be reconciled, the North Korea–China relationship should also be tuned, and the issue of whether to return to the six-party talks in the first place has to be addressed.[50] North Korea has formed its desired international political structure in Northeast Asia through nuclear and missile provocations. The year 2017 was the period when the US and China were partly working together to reorganize the structure of pressure on North Korea. At the US–China summit in April 2017, the US emphasized China's role in resolving the North Korean issue. The US assessment of "Chinese role theory" is still ongoing. If the US believes that China's role theory has reached its limit, it will turn to the direct and tough sanctions against North Korea through bilateral route. An instance is when China was pressured by the US to join sanctions on North Korea upon President Donald Trump's visit to China in November 2017.

North Korea's strategy to escape from isolation

North Korea made use of South Korea's decision to deploy THAAD on July 8, 2016 and the temporary deployment of THAAD on September 5, 2016 as a golden opportunity to escape international isolation. With eight sanctions in operation, including the UN resolutions 2270 (March 3, 2016), 2371 (August 5, 2017), and 2375 (September 12, 2017), North Korea has focused on restoring its traditional relations with China. China's implementation of the Security Council resolutions is limited. The international cooperation for the sanctions against North Korea is insufficient due to China's dilemma between the sanctions and the THAAD deployment. Since the deployment of THAAD, China's participation in the sanctions against North Korea has become restricted. North Korea has tried to escape isolation by acting as an active player in the international order of Northeast Asia. During the campaigning of the 2016 US presidential election, North Korea expressed its goodwill toward Republican presidential candidate Trump who made provocative remarks on Kim Jong-un, rather than Democratic presidential candidate Hillary Clinton, who was highly likely to be consistent with strategic patience.[51] North Korea judged that Trump's policy of pursuing change in an unconventional way rather than the Democratic Party's administration of strategic patience would be more positive in overcoming the current situation.[52] On the other hand, as with the George W. Bush administration's September 11 countermeasure, fears of a preemptive strike still exists in North Korea. So the US pursued two-sided strategies, including continuing dialogue with the North at the same time. Since President Trump took office on January 20, 2017, North Korea has a preconceived plan to seek nuclear disarmament talks with the US to scrap part of its nuclear weapons, not to negotiate nuclear renunciation. In this process, the North judged that completing its nuclear weapons rather than halting its nuclear development would be advantageous in resuming negotiations with the US. In the second half of 2017, North Korea used both its sixth nuclear test and a long-range missile launch as basis for the strategy of military provocation.

Evaluation of the Trump administration's Korean Peninsula policy prior to the sixth nuclear test

Trump and the Republican Party's isolationist diplomatic principles

President Trump's foreign policy is based on isolationism that emerged in the US in the 1930s. During the First World War and the Great Depression in the 1930s, the United States declared its policy of concentrating only on domestic governance without any further intervention in international affairs. The Republican Party then pursued foreign policy based on isolationism. Trump's "America First" policy is based on the growing burden of traditional alliances like the North Atlantic Treaty Organization (NATO), Japan and South Korea, and his foreign policy, which requires a reduction of huge budget, is inevitable to trouble local and international politics. "The US can no longer be a police force in the world," Trump said. He also said the US would stop making high-cost, low-efficiency budget investments and approaches, focusing instead on a cost-benefit analysis in maintaining the alliance. The pragmatism of the US national interest is an important criterion for diplomatic judgment. Trump has no choice but to focus on creating jobs and filling the wallets of white middle- and low-income people who supported him in the Rust Belt region of the US. The related budget is being financed through the reduction of US defense spending, increased defense cost of allies and the surplus from protectionism in trade with China and other countries like Japan and South Korea. In particular, Trump prioritizes negotiations in the process of realigning foreign relations with three groups — allies, non-affiliates and adversaries. President Trump, who needs economic results in a short period of time, is focusing on pursuing practical interests in negotiations with his allies rather than negotiations with non-aligned or hostile countries, which are difficult to negotiate with. Trump is more interested in "money-making" such as increasing the share of US military spending in South Korea, Japan and NATO, or renegotiation of the free trade agreement (FTA) between South Korea and US. In the process, it is inevitable to revise policies on hostile countries that are known historically as a security threat to the US.[53]

North Korea policy without a discussion: Between intervention and disapproval

Trump, who has been a successful businessman, has only a dichotomy in terms of diplomacy. The unconventional leader, who sided with his business experience through the framework of negotiations that he gave least to his counterpart and received maximum from the partner, has showed the nature of a "shrewd business man" in foreign policies. The Trump administration attempted to seek an exploration of an unknown person while dealing with the world's only reclusive leader, Kim Jong-un, who declared his country as a nuclear state in May 2016. However, both leaders do not pursue long-term dialogue in which they can grasp the intentions of others who have little chance of profit. Trump's standard of value judgment in the diplomatic field is only a general perception that the US's national interest is a priority. The regional foreign policy is becoming visible in the process of the establishment of a diplomatic lineup. Trump does not come up with a landmark solution if he believes that the Korean Peninsula issue is difficult to make profitability in terms of cost and benefits analysis. "If Kim visits the US, he will negotiate over a hamburger at the conference table (June 15, 2016)." "The US is willing to talk to Kim Jong-un. There is no problem in talking with him (May 17, 2016)." Trump's remarks were aimed at preempting issues and managing his image during the election period. Such media-promoting remarks have been of little use since taking office. North Korea has been seen as an "axis of evil" country since the George W. Bush administration. North Korea has conducted six nuclear tests. The direction of the policy toward North Korea is being discussed with limited military solutions amid the dominance of diplomatic solutions. In the process of appointing a person in charge of diplomatic agendas for the first year of Trump's tenure, it is difficult for security advisors to produce productive results on the North Korean nuclear issue. It is also possible that US just focuses on its "status quo" policy, which maintains the Obama administration's sanctions on North Korea and pressure policy, unless North Korea crosses the red line of installing nuclear warheads on ICBM. However, since there are various variables in using military solutions, even Trump himself cannot predict the end of his North Korea policy.

Trump has argued for China's role as the latter has real influence over North Korea, in order to control the North, rather than directly controlling the North. It held detailed discussions at the first US–China summit in April 2017. Trump has hoped that China is positively cooperating to join the sanctions. Specific demands were expected at the US–China summit in Beijing in November, 2017.[54] So far, the US has been having a difficult time coming up with innovative solutions due to the structural nature of US–China relations and US–North Korea relations.[55] Trump has continued to point out the incumbent administration's failure in its North Korea policy and stressed the need for a change. However, it is not enough to consider the side effects of the drastic change in US policy toward North Korea. If North Korea decides that its nuclear and missile capabilities have become more advanced and that US military solutions are not feasible, the North Korea would try to benchmark the Pakistan nuclear model. While the goal is realistic, it is inevitable for the Trump administration to clarify its denuclearization policy because the means to curb the goal are very limited. In particular, it is not easy to apply creative nuclear dismantlement models such as Iranian-style nuclear bargaining models[56] to North Korea — a declared nuclear state. In the end, the US is expected to be at a crossroads between nuclear disarmament negotiations and pressing for nuclear renunciation.[57] Then US President Obama made a "leap day agreement" with North Korea on February 29, 2012, but the agreement was not implemented because of serious distrust between Washington and Pyongyang. The Obama administration had used strategic patience to focus on UN sanctions whenever North Korea conducted a nuclear test or launched a missile. Trump has not turned to a strategic neglect policy that disregards the request of North Korea's dialogue with the US, not using preemptive force, which costs huge amounts of money if initial negotiations fail to go smoothly. Pragmatic hawkish figures, such as those from military sources who are confident about the US national power and military power, and hardliners who worked in the George W. Bush administration, had been appointed as defense minister, national security adviser, and Central Intelligence Agency (CIA) director in the first security lineup. They were skeptical about the results of short-term negotiations with dictatorships like North Korea. The idea of negotiating with dictatorships has created hostility, even within the US Congress. The US House of Representatives Foreign Affairs Committee collectively dealt with the resolutions on March 29, 2017.[58] In an unusual move, the US Congress passed all three bills and resolutions related to North Korea in one day. The H.R.

1644 was passed quickly, only eight days after it was proposed on March 21, 2017. This reflects the anti-North Korean atmosphere in the US Congress.

Evaluation of United Nations Security Council's Resolution 2371 and 2375

The UN Security Council Resolution 2371 was adopted unanimously after North Korea launched two ballistic missiles (June 4 and 28, 2017). The resolution blocked the Kim Jong-un administration from exporting minerals and fisheries products, considered as North Korea's main sources of cash flow. Although it failed to completely cut oil supplies to the North, the resolution could reduce the North's annual exports by 30%, or US$1 billion. The sanctions had reduced North Korea's foreign currency imports by about US$400 million in coal exports, US$250 million in iron and iron ore, US$100 million in lead and lead ore, and US$200 million in seafood. It had also a US$750-million export-cutting effect on mineral resources alone. Mining accounted for 12.6% of the North Korean economy. North Korea's real gross domestic product (GDP) grew 3.9% in 2017 compared with the previous year, with the mining industry growing at 8.4%.[59] Until now, the North's military has tried to compensate for the lack of foreign exchange imports due to restrictions on coal exports. Many fishermen were killed due to excessive fishing as they did not have sufficient equipment in order to achieve their target. North Korea's foreign exchange earnings had been reduced with the new sanctions banning all kinds of fish products from North Korea. Whenever international sanctions are strengthened, North Korea has increased its export of fishery products to China and Russia.

The sanctions also banned additional investments in new and existing joint ventures with North Korea. The measure had made it impossible for Chinese companies to invest in North Korea, targeting North Korean minerals and marine products. It is also to be noted that nine individuals and four organizations from North Korea were added to the list of sanctions against the North, subjecting them to overseas travel restriction and asset freeze. Precise sanctions were imposed by the addition of the Mansudae Foreign Development Company Group, due to its involvement in the export of North Korean workers and large-scale sculptures to Africa and South Asia. Since the first nuclear test in 2006, the UN Security Council has adopted seven resolutions, including 1718 (2006), 1874 (2009), 2087 and 2094 (2013), 2270 and 2321 (2016), and 2356 (2017). Resolution 2371 was the eighth resolution on sanctions against North Korea. The US draft Resolution 2371 focused on dealing a blow to North Korea's exports. The UN Security Council reached a swift agreement on Resolution 2371 within only 33 days after North Korea's ICBM launch. Sanctions were prepared in a very short period of time compared to 82 days spent on sanctions after the fifth nuclear test.[60] China has opposed to the suspension of crude oil for fear of possible collapse of the North Korean regime. If oil is not supplied to North Korea, not only the North's military but also its factories will stop, shaking the foundation of the regime. Currently, China is responsible for more than 90% of the oil supply to North Korea. China supplies a total of 1 million tons of crude oil to North Korea every year; half in the form of aid, and half in the form of commercial transactions. Russia and Iran are also supplying some of their crude oil to North Korea. Russia's opposition to the ban is attributable to its export of crude oil to North Korea. In the end, unless China and Russia close their oil pipelines which supply oil to North Korea, the North's economy has its own way.

According to a study conducted by the Korea Trade-Investment Promotion Agency (KOTRA), North Korea's top export item to China in the first half of 2017 was clothing excluding textiles. The second, third, and fourth places were coal, iron ore, and fishery products, while the fifth place was clothing, including textiles.[61] In the end, the limitation of the 2371 sanctions is that North Korea's top export item to China has been closely connected for the North Korean people's livelihood. Chinese companies use low-wage workers in North Korea to do forestry work. As the number of North Korean workers in China, Russia, Eastern Europe and the Middle East totals around 100,000, the effect of sanctions might be limited if the North continues to send workers who are the continuous sources of funds.[62] Therefore, the US had also focused on individual sanctions separately from the Security Council resolution. Following the US House of Representatives on July 27, 2017, the Senate passed a package of sanctions against North Korea, Russia, and Iran, which contained a complete blockade of North Korea's oil imports.[63] The US had received considerable concessions from China and Russia in other areas by involving credit card companies to reduce supplying oil toward North Korea. However, the reason why China agreed on the agreement in a short period of time was that the North Korean regime can be maintained despite the resolution. In the end, most of the respondents said the sanctions were not fatal.[64] The 2371 sanctions have a long-term negative impact[65] on the shattered North Korean economy, but this measure is not enough for the North to give up its nuclear program. From past record, it was expected that the resolution would put a lot of pressure on North Korea, but would not bring it down to the negotiating table.

After the sixth nuclear test, the UN Security Council was expected to draw up a final sanctions resolution, but failed to implement it. It was uncertain whether economic sanctions against North Korea would suffice to fatally strike its economy. Even when the US proposed to block the supply of crude oil by non-military means, it cautiously predicted the inflection point of the North Korean nuclear issue. The UN Security Council resolution, which was originally circulated by the US, included a suspension of exports of crude oil and oil products to North Korea, a ban on exports of clothing and textile products — a means of earning foreign currency — and a ban on the export of foreign workers. It also included sanctions on Kim Jong-un and his younger sister Kim Yo-jong. However, due to the opposition from China and Russia, all the substances were left out. Both countries were determined to protect North Korea. The ban on oil and natural gas, which drew the most attention, was compounded by a phased ban. Refined petroleum products were limited to 2 million barrels (260,000 tons) per year, while oil exports had also been frozen to the current level. At the center of the resolution on sanctions against North Korea was whether China would join in the blocking of oil supply to the North. After talking with President Xi on the phone in the aftermath of the sixth nuclear test, President Trump said on Twitter that the Chinese leader wanted to do something. There were no specific details on what was said, but it was clear that something would mean blocking the supply of crude oil to the North. Cutting off oil supplies was the last economic measure to bring North Korea to the stage of denuclearization talks. Due to China's opposition in lieu that its oil supply is the lifeline of North Korea's economy and military industry, the UN Security Council did not include the supply of crude oil in the resolutions until the fifth nuclear test was carried out. If North Korea is on the brink of collapse, China will lose its strategic buffer zone. China's "Two-Korea policies in Korean Peninsula" is bound to be at a standstill. Even after the sixth nuclear test, China did not revise its previous policy. Will North Korea stop its nuclear ambitions because of the UN Security Council's sanctions, which it presented as a stopgap measure? The answer has not been so until now. If US expects Kim Jong-un to stop his military provocations by blocking the import of US$1 billion in cash and 30% of crude oil, this will be evidence that the Western world has failed to grasp the characteristics of North Korean regime. Kim Jong-un, who declared that the hydrogen bomb test was a result of tightening his belt and paying for his blood, continues his "My Way style" provocation.[66]

The theoretical background of the Trump administration's foreign policy

Three theoretical backgrounds can be deduced regarding the change of President Trump's North Korea policy after the sixth nuclear test. President Trump is showing a different diplomatic attitude from the conventional US president. The theoretical reasons for predicting President Trump's diplomatic behavior are Unpredictable Theory, Madman Theory and Offensive Realism. Based on businessman behavior, Trump has pursued policies by mixing three theories.

Unpredictable Theory, Madman Theory and Offensive Realism

During his presidential campaign in 2016, Trump argued that the US should become an unpredictable country. This means that he will not let the other party know about his plan in advance, but will wrap himself up as a mysterious person so that other countries and ordinary persons do not recognize the exact intention of his action and policy, thus preventing the other country or person from responding in advance.[67] For the sake of its own interests, the government can push any policy that goes beyond the existing normative aspects of foreign policy.[68] The Madman Theory is that he seeks to make concessions through suspicions that his opponent may not be bluffing through his "brinkmanship". It originated from the foreign policy of former President Richard M. Nixon. It is to create fear in the other person by recognizing himself as an unpredictable and reckless lunatic. This could lead to a favorable negotiation situation.[69] H.R. Haldman, who served as the chief presidential secretary during the Nixon administration, referred to Nixon's extreme behavior as a "Madman Theory".[70] The theory was made public by American thinker and historian Arthur M. Schlesinger (1917–2007). He reported the direction of policy toward Latin America to the new president, John F. Kennedy, citing Cuban threats.[71] The Nixon administration also used this theory as a strategy to force North Vietnam to come out of peace negotiations to end the Vietnam War.[72] President Trump is also using crazy strategies in part, whether he intended or not. In particular, he rules out the step-by-step and systematic discussion process of the US foreign policy. Trump's 140-character tweets suggest the direction of foreign policy, which is difficult to trace in the history of the White House. For example, the policy of the Secretary of State, Rex Tillerson, who was on a foreign tour to negotiate, was abruptly denied by a tweet.

John J. Mearsheimer, a professor at the University of Chicago, presented "Offensive Realism" that transcends classical realism and neo-realism in his book and empirically proved his theory by citing historical examples. Offensive Realism belongs to the theory of realism in that it is not norm or morality but power and national interest that governs relations of nations. However, it is different from classical realism in that countries seek power not from human instincts but from an international system of anarchy, which is different from neo-realism in that countries are not satisfied with maintaining balance of power and are seeking enormous power to overwhelm other nations. Mearsheimer said, "Even if we have nuclear weapons, we cannot launch a preemptive strike because if we allow nuclear strikes, we will destroy each other." That is why the nuclear state is trying to gain a "nuclear superiority". A nuclear superiority is when a nuclear monopoly is unilaterally available without retaliating by the other party, or when a nuclear opponent is used to neutralize an opponent. No matter who begins a nuclear attack, it is in the state of being subjected to a follow-up retaliation attack, namely, the "mutually assured destruction (MAD)". Mearsheimer said, "In the Cold War era, conventional wars were possible locally, but they never occurred in a nuclear war."[73] Trump has pursued his policy based on the theory that the US should protect the superiority of nuclear weapons as well as conventional weapons against the backdrop of strong military forces.

Prospects on the changes of the US policy toward Korean Peninsula

The sixth nuclear test fundamentally changed the security landscape of Northeast Asia. In terms of technology, it will take time until North Korea deploys intercontinental ballistic missiles in the actual conflict that can strategically threaten the United States, but in terms of international politics, North Korea's nuclear and missile programs have already been treated as real threats.[74] Since Kim Jong-un took office in 2012, the US believes that North Korea's military threat has been stronger and more serious than expected.[75] North Korea's military provocations have been very intensive since its fourth nuclear test in January 2016. The fact that Kim Jong-un conducted four nuclear tests and fired 70 ballistic missiles after taking power in 2012 indicates that the military technology has exceeded the basic level and finally reached the stage of deployment.

The speed of technological development is beyond the threshold. The US has considered four to five scenarios to resolve the North Korean nuclear crisis.[76] The basic framework of the scenario is divided into following three categories. Plan A: Continuing sanctions and denuclearization, Plan B: diplomatic negotiations and denuclearization and Plan C: military options and denuclearization. This book analyzes the effects and pros and cons of the three scenarios and predicts future options

Plan A: Continuing sanctions and denuclearization

Washington's top policy on North Korea's nuclear weapons is denuclearization through maximum sanction and pressure. Trump apparently believes that the US should apply the Iranian-style economic sanctions to North Korea to correctly start negotiations on denuclearization. The US has proposed to block the supply of crude oil to North Korea as a non-military measure to prevent North Korea from running an additional nuclear test after its sixth nuclear test. Cutting off oil supplies to North Korea is in the same vein as the Iranian-style nuclear solution that German Chancellor Angela Merkel mentioned. The situation worsened when hardliners led by Iranian President Mahmoud Ahmadinejad took power in 2005, although the West and Iran negotiated over the nuclear issue. The UN Security Council adopted a resolution to sanction Iran several times, but it has not worked as intended. The US Congress passed the Iran Sanctions Act in June 2010, which contained a secondary boycott clause that prohibited third countries from trading with their US partners on oil imports. It strengthened sanctions against financial institutions such as the Central Bank of Iran and banned dollar transactions. Due to the suspension of crude oil payment and the fall in the revaluation of the Iranian currency rial, severe economic difficulties followed, and the public's sentiment in Iran worsened. In the 2013 general elections, economy-oriented President Hassan Rouhani, who pledged to lift sanctions through nuclear negotiations, was elected by an overwhelming majority. In the final round of negotiations, the US agreed to lift sanctions on Iran instead of inspecting Iran's nuclear facilities and restricting its nuclear development programs. Secondary boycott is a new concept established by the US sanctions toward Iran. The US has seriously reviewed its secondary boycott card, which imposes unexceptionally tough sanctions on companies from third countries that have traded with North Korea if China and Russia oppose the plan to block crude oil from North Korea or if sanctions are insufficient. China and Russia are opposed to adding sanctions to the North, excluding the ban on textile exports. The two countries are sticking to a two-way solution to stop North Korea's nuclear and missile provocations and to reduce the South Korea–US joint military drills.[77] The decision to propose the UN resolution immediately shows that the US is obstinate. If it is rejected, it could emerge as the cause of a secondary boycott.

The international community is also putting pressure on North Korea for its nuclear tests and missile development. Portugal stopped its 42-year diplomatic relations with North Korea, and Mexico, Peru, Spain, Kuwait and Italy also expelled North Korean ambassadors. After North Korea's sixth nuclear test and ballistic missile provocation, more than 20 countries had cut diplomatic or economic ties with the North. The fact that neutral countries, including Mexico, are imposing their own sanctions indicates that the international community feels the huge threat from North Korea's provocations. The US has planned to apply the Iran-style denuclearization method, which was concluded in July 2015.[78] Since the sixth nuclear test, the US Treasury Department has slapped sanctions on 10 North Korean banks and 26 individuals. The US has also tried to impose additional sanctions on organizations and individuals in other countries that deal with them. North Korean banks that have been subject to sanctions have effectively been expelled from the international financial network.[79] Unlike Iran, which accounts trade for a large portion of its national income, however, North Korea has the characteristics of an isolated economic system that has just less than total trade amount of US$5 billion.[80] It is called "Robinson Crusoe" economy whereby a style of self-reliance is ubiquitous on an island. The US had already expelled North Korea from the international financial network, but the US is still considering implementing a secondary boycott.[81] China's backlash and worsening US–China relations are a major burden to the US. The US is at a crossroads between US–China relations and North Korea's nuclear and missile development. Still, the US has not definitely put pressure on China. The secondary boycott is still burdensome for the US, even though there are the inevitable and lasting conflicts of trade between both countries. Economic interdependence between the US and China may hurt US businesses, and China is also worried about strong opposition.[82] There is a limit to the fact that the sanctions are applied perfectly to North Korea.

Plan B: Diplomatic negotiations and denuclearization

The second scenario is the diplomatic dialogue between North Korea and the United States. The US policy toward North Korea is based on an assumption that it will inevitably serve as a dependent variable in the context of the US–China relationship. Although North Korea's nuclear and missile threats are an urgent matter, it is not a pressing and important issue that is serious enough to surpass the US–China relations and it is not easy for the US to implement a secondary boycott, hurting bilateral cooperation and interdependencies. In addition to the North Korean issue, the South China Sea and the US–China trade relations are more important issues, and chances are high that the US shifts its position from the North Korean issue to cooperation rather than collision. The purpose and criteria of the current dialogue between the US and North Korea have been to a considerable extent different. Through dialogue, North Korea has suggested recognition of its status as a nuclear power, and the US has proposed a freeze to test North Korea's additional nuclear weapon as a precondition for dialogue. It is uncertain whether the Trump administration succeeds to keep the principle in negotiation with North Korea. The US operated a channel between Choi Sun-hee, representing the Foreign Ministry of North Korea and the director of the US Central Intelligence Agency Gina Haspel, which oversees North Korea's negotiations with the US.[83] In addition, the Swedish Embassy in Pyongyang or the North Korean Embassy in Beijing were operated through secret channels.[84]

The Trump administration's strategy for negotiating North Korea has been one of ambiguity and non-certifiable. There are moves to seek dialogue with the North, but they are often flexible depending on the sincerity of the North. The US wants North Korea to give up its nuclear weapons and missiles, but the North must complete its nuclear-equipped ICBM to ensure regime security. US President Trump told Secretary of State Rex Tillerson that negotiations with North Korea were a waste of time.[85] Since Tillerson, who visited China, met with Chinese President Xi on the previous day, there were two or three channels open with North Korea. "I can talk to them," Tillerson said after a day of hinting that he was trying to make behind-the-scenes contacts with North Korea. It was the first time since the inauguration of the Trump administration that the US had made direct contact with North Korea over the North Korean nuclear issue.[86] However, the president's immediate reversal of the secretary of state's remarks can be understandable in only three existing theories. After President Trump mentioned the suspension of negotiations, US State Department spokesman Heather Nauert also stressed that the diplomatic channel was open but would not be open forever. It could be interpreted that revealing differences between President Trump and Secretary of State Tillerson was aimed at dividing roles. It was a tactic to receive the North's concessions in the future through playing the role of Tillerson's "good cop" and Trump's "bad cop".[87] Another interpretation was that Trump had no intention of negotiating with North Korea. He mentioned negotiations with North Korea, but this was nothing more than a diplomatic gesture.

In the past, US Republican administrations were reluctant to talk to North Korea because of their opposition to the dictatorship. The George H.W. Bush administration had induced the South and North Korea to declare a nuclear-free Korean Peninsula instead of a direct dialogue due to North Korea's nuclear development. Even during the George W. Bush administration, the US paradoxically remained indifferent to China's use of the six-party talks as well as direct dialogue between Washington and Pyongyang. Through the North Korea–US dialogue, the US had been pushing for a nuclear freeze before achieving a complete, verifiable and irreversible denuclearization (CVID) of North Korea or at least formally reaching a nuclear state. North Korea had effectively demanded recognition of its status as a nuclear power as a condition for dialogue with the US. With the two countries not meeting the terms for resuming dialogue, the United States saw the possibility of productive dialogue very low. Amid this stalemate, some in the United States voiced opinions that the US had no choice but to allow North Korea's nuclear program.[88] However, if the US recognizes its nuclear possession, there is a high possibility of a "nuclear domino" phenomenon across Northeast Asia, as public opinion on nuclear armament would increase in South Korea and Japan as well. First of all, recognition of North Korea's status as a nuclear power is at least an option that is not *officially* possible and acceptable. As soon as the US recognizes its status as a nuclear power, it could undermine the alliance by stimulating Japan and South Korea's willingness to develop nuclear weapons, shaking the foundation of the US Asian policy.

Plan C: Military options

If the US sanctions against North Korea fail to curb its nuclear development, it inevitably shifts its focus from diplomatic solutions to military solutions. The US Congress and the administration in Washington have given a skeptical response about preventing North Korea from possessing nuclear weapons and long-range missile technology with only economic sanctions. If strong economic resources such as the US secondary boycott do not actually work due to China's non-cooperation, the US conciliatory gestures on North Korea are likely to change through the sprawling negative mood in Washington. North Korea has been standing up against the UN sanctions by launching nuclear and missile tests since the first nuclear test in 2006. North Korea is known to have up to 60 nuclear weapons already. It is also known that it has cyber warfare capabilities and stockpiles large amounts of biological, chemical and biological weapons. The miniaturization of nuclear warheads and completion of ICBM, which are at the range of the US mainland, are "red lines" for the US.[89] If the US takes actual military action, the goal will be to eliminate nuclear weapons and missiles. Preemptive strike is carried out to proactively attack the threat of other party in order to remove the risk in advance. The operational execution of preventive strikes does not have a significant benefit in terms of the cause of the attack and cost-effectiveness.[90] Since US's attack on its nuclear and missile bases across the country will cause serious damage to the Seoul metropolitan area due to the North's retaliatory counterattack, the strike is the last option and possible only when enemy threats and attacks are imminent.[91] In May 1994, a local attack on the Yongbyon nuclear facility was considered, but eventually it changed its direction to diplomatic negotiations. At that time, South Korean President Kim Young-sam focused on persuading US President Bill Clinton that a military clash on the Korean Peninsula would essentially require the South Korean leader's decision and permission.[92] As North Korean leader Kim Il-sung's proposal for negotiations and second damage from the armed attack were mixed, the US attempted to resolve the issue with the diplomacy of Geneva Agreed Framework in October 1994. The danger of a direct strike on North Korea was ironically the driving force for both the North and the United States to negotiate.[93] Considering the side effects of all scenarios, such as redeployment of tactical B61 and the F-22 Raptors, the world's strongest stealth fighter, and the killing operation toward Kim Jong-un, it is hard to think of a military option that can fully protect Seoul from North Korea's retaliation. In order to strengthen the response of the South Korea–US alliance, however, both countries have announced that they increase the deployment of strategic assets and are pressuring North Korea militarily.

The US military has several military operations, including limited air strikes on major military facilities in North Korea. In particular, the ROK–US Combined Forces Command's *Operation Plan 5015* includes a plan to launch a strike while preventing North Korea from attacking the South Korea. The plan is to destroy telecommunication and radar facilities first by using stealth fighter jets, and then to launch strategic bombers to deal with the situation immediately. However, unless the mainland of the US is attacked directly, it will be difficult for the scenario to become a reality. North Korea has a large amount of weapons of mass destruction (WMD), including various biological and chemical weapons and more than 1,000 ballistic missiles. Some 300 to 400 long-range artillery pieces are deployed near the inter-Korean Military Demarcation Line (MDL). The distance to Seoul is only 50km. It is estimated that more than 6,000 to 7,000 missiles can be fired in an hour, and that even if half of them are intercepted or disabled, 5–7% will destroy Seoul. There are also predictions that if North Korea uses nuclear weapons, more serious damage will be expected.[94] If the US decides to launch a military action, it should begin by evacuating more than 200,000 US citizens and their families in South Korea. However, this could cause Pyongyang to take the initiative by recognizing signs of a preemptive strike. In fact, it is not easy for the US forces to intercept North Korean missiles in the air by the missile defense (MD) system. Failure of air-to-air interceptors could hurt the credibility of the US MD system. Non-kinetic weapons such as laser, Electromagnetic Pulse Bomb (EMP), microwave, and acoustic weapons are also options.[95] It has also been considered to strengthen deterrence against North Korea by strengthening existing extended deterrence capabilities. At the end of 2016, Center for a New American Security announced a new US arms buildup strategy called the "third offset strategy". The report stated that South Korea should participate in strategies to maintain its military superiority through advanced military forces such as unmanned aerial vehicles and unmanned aerial vehicles.

North Korean Foreign Minister Ri declared that North Korea could respond to President Trump's declaration of war against Pyongyang by the definition of a self-defense right, even if the US strategic bomber does not cross the airspace.[96] On the other hand, the US government refuted that there was no declaration of war against North Korea, saying that it would exercise all options to defend the US mainland and its allies. The tension between the US and North Korea had intensified as the US opened up the possibility of further armed protest. North Korea's Foreign Minister Ri Yong-ho referred to Trump as a mentally ill man with mixed memories and a commander bringing pain to Americans. In a previous speech at the UN General Assembly, Trump called Kim Jong-un "Rocket Man", and later mocked him as "Little Rocket Man" by using the word "Little" to belittle a young person. Foreign Minister Ri also claimed that Trump declared war on the North Korean government again by saying, "It won't last long," and stressed, "The UN Charter recognizes the right to self-defense of individual countries." He mentioned Article 51 of the UN Charter, which defines the logical right to individual self-defense. The articles say that a country of self-defense can use force to defend itself in the event of attacks from another country. This seemed to be aimed at blaming the US by announcing that North Korea's possible military action in the future would be an inevitable response to the US's illegal preemptive strike. The two sides, which had been engaged in fierce verbal warfare, had started to build justification with the possibility of military clashes in mind.[97] Foreign Minister Ri mentioned the natural right to self-defense, which could prolong the US–North Korea conflict.[98] In addition, the tension on the Korean Peninsula had heightened due to Trump's Twitter remarks, prompting a flurry of measures to prevent the second Korean War in the US.[99]

Implications and feasibility of scenarios

The three scenarios of the Trump administration for denuclearization of North Korea have their advantages and disadvantages. There are hot debates on the feasibilities of the scenarios. Plan A is a scenario in which North Korea reaches denuclearization through negotiations by yielding to international sanctions against the North. It is a model of deterrence and containment. Japan and Israel's nuclear response strategies have implications. The goal set by the Japanese government is deterrence and defense. In the case of Israel, it is suppression, defense and attack.[100] Plan B is a scenario in which the two sides conduct denuclearization negotiations in an even relationship. Achieving the goal of denuclearization through peaceful diplomatic negotiations requires the least cost. It is unclear, however, whether the North, which declared a nuclear power, will accept diplomatic negotiations aimed at denuclearization, not freezing. Iran, which has not conducted a nuclear test, has been in constant conflict since the agreement was reached. President Trump criticized the Iran nuclear deal made by Obama administration in July 2017 as incorrect and incomplete in 2018. It is not clear for North Korea which declared its nuclear possession with ICBM to give up the weapons, even though the US agrees to North Korea's demands, including the signing of a peace treaty between the US and the withdrawal of US troops in South Korea. North Korea's demands are incompatible with the US's East Asian policy. The usefulness of US Forces in South Korea during the G2 era will not be reduced in a fast speed, even though Trump talked of the possibility that US Forces can be withdrawn from Korean Peninsula without the financial support from the South Korean government in paying for the stationing of troops. Plan C is a solution to denuclearization by military means, in which negotiations and economic sanctions have failed to produce effective results as shown in Table 4.1.[101] It is the last resort to review if the US and North Korea have failed to reach a denuclearization agreement, and the North's actual deployment of nuclear weapons and missiles have reached a serious threat

Table 4.1 Future scenarios of North Korea denuclearization

Scenario	Performance	Strong and Weak Point, Feasibility	Preference	
			US	North Korea
Plan A: Maximum sanctions	O	Low cost, Low feasibility	O	×
Plan B: Diplomatic negotiation	×	The lengthy process and risk of Pakistan model	△	O
Plan C: Military option	O	Serious damage and denuclearization	×	×

Note: The circle means "good result", the cross means "no result". The circle means "like", the cross means "dislike", and the triangle signifies "like in a short time and dislike in long time" under the "Preference" column, and also implies "no concrete deal consuming time", considering the standard of "Performance".

to both South Korea and the US.[102] President Trump said on Twitter that his predecessors and their governments had talked to North Korea denuclearization for 25 years, and that a lot of agreements had been reached and a lot of money had been paid, but they had not worked. He criticized that the agreement was damaged by North Korea even before the ink dried up, making US negotiators less than competent. It is true that the Trump administration's "maximum pressure" card on North Korea has begun to partially make China's participation in sanction against North Korea. However, considering the situation where there is little chance for North Korea to surrender, the military option seems to be putting weight on the side.

As President Trump mentioned, the North Korean nuclear issue has not been resolved since the first North Korean nuclear crisis in 1994. President Trump's decision to resolve the issue is based on the fact that North Korea's nuclear weapons program is crossing the red line of US security in a very close and visible area. The US plans to strengthen cyber-attacks and psychological warfare to topple the Kim Jong-un regime, but the operation has been futile until now. In fact, the US Forces plans to deploy the Grey Eagle, an unmanned aircraft capable of attacking North Korean missile facilities in the near future. What is important is that there is growing public support in the United States for military action against North Korea, as North Korea threats have been increasing.[103] The North Korean sixth nuclear test in 2017 presented a serious security problem and led to the adoption of the eighth resolution by the UN Security Council.[104] It also exposed the limitations on the effectiveness of the previous UN Security Council resolutions. If the US sees the sanctions as insufficient, it will take its own independent measures, including unexceptional secondary boycott toward Chinese companies dealing with North Korea. If this still does not work, one cannot rule out the possibility of resorting to military force. However, it does not mean that the US definitely wages a war with North Korea. Diplomatic sources in Washington are critical of the Trump administration's foreign affairs and security officials' comments that they can depend on non-diplomatic measures. In particular, former White House National Security Adviser H.R. McMaster told MSNBC on August 5, 2017 that the US should provide all options for a "preventive war". The atmosphere was going wild, mentioning the possibility of limited war. This was the first time that the White House security control tower mentioned the possibility of war. US Ambassador to the United Nations Nikki Haley also warned of the possibility of US military action on October 5, 2016 when the resolution on sanctions against North Korea was passed. According to the Cable News Network (CNN) and other media, Haley warned, "Even if the resolution was passed, we will not mistake that we have solved the North Korean problem and will take all necessary steps to protect the US and its allies."

A "preventive war" is a concept of attacking in advance to prevent an all-out war when the enemy's power becomes stronger at a time when the war is not imminent. This includes the war in Iraq. The Trump administration's military option has been interpreted as a "preemptive strike" to target related facilities in the belief that North Korea's nuclear and missile provocations are imminent. After all, the CIA and other intelligence agencies decided that it was almost impossible to exactly select and remove North Korea's weapons facilities, thus redefining the nature of military options. McMaster stressed that President Trump was clearly determined to prevent North Korea's nuclear weapons even through the act of war. President Trump represented a clear stance on the war. In other words, President Trump said, "If North Korea has nuclear weapons that can threaten the US, it cannot be tolerated from the president's perspective." On the other hand, North Korea claimed that it completely opposed the UN Security Council's resolution to impose sanctions on the North on August 7, 2017. The North's central news agency KCNA reported by the name of DPRK government. It read as follows: The UN Security Council's anti-Republican resolution fabricated by the US and hostile forces is seen as a violent violation toward North Korea's sovereignty and is completely repelling it. North Korea's official response came a day after the UN Security Council adopted the Resolution 2371 on North Korea. It is noteworthy that the announcement was issued in the form and level of a "government" statement, which is more formal than a foreign ministry statement. In the end, North Korea had declared a direct response to international sanctions against the North, signaling a variety of provocations including the launch of ICBMs. North Korea had also expressed its intention to respond to the new sanctions with a provocation. The statement noted that under the circumstances of the United States making a full-fledged provocation against North Korea in all areas of politics, economy and military, it would be inevitable for the North's military and people armed with the firm will and determination to deal with the US by stern retaliation. It has been uncertain whether the Kim Jong-un regime, which has continued to make provocations including eight missile launches, would change its behavior with the UN Security Council sanctions. President Trump's visit to South Korea, China and Japan in November 2017 was the first turning point in the North Korean nuclear crisis. The summit between President Trump, who stressed the North Korean nuclear issue through China, and Chinese President Xi, who emphasized China's dream after the 19th Chinese Communist Party Congress, was an important international political event that can predict the possibility of a scenario of Plan A, B and C in the future of the North Korean nuclear crisis.

Chapter 5

Diplomatic Negotiation between US and DPRK: Summit

How do the negotiations between the North and the US leaders work: Who is the real winner?

The first talk between President Donald Trump and Chairperson Kim Jong-un in Singapore on June 12, 2018 that fundamentally shook established frame in the international politics of Northeast Asia will be recorded in history as one of examples of the US president's fruitless talk at the summit. It will be treated as a subject of research in the US diplomatic community as a representative example of *High Expectations and Low Performance.* It is rare for a US president to show such a precarious or double tongue attitude in summits with foreign leaders. Comparing pre- and post-summit statements is meaningless in diplomatic talks. The only thing recorded in history is the Joint Agreement itself. The behind-the-scenes story during the talks is only to be presented in memoirs of national leaders or ministers. President Trump has to understand that what is more difficult than business transactions may be nuclear arms trade. The agreement itself to end 70 years of hostility and form a new relationship between North Korea and the US was no less than a surreal sci-fi film scene, but its content was far less than expected. Especially, the scene where the US president stayed alone after the talks to explain the outcome and meaning of the summit was enough to remind of a coach of a World Cup soccer team who makes a lengthy excuse on the causes of total defeat. In particular, many doubt that Trump could really understand the essence of the North Korean issue or the North Korean nuclear issue. The public announcement on the reduction of the ROK–US joint military exercise and the withdrawal of the US Forces from South Korea rather than the fundamental nuclear dismantlement in the denuclearization deal is tantamount to losing the game after passing the ball from the outside. In order to understand the 2018 North Korea–United States summit, which is regarded as a "century diplomatic incident", President Trump's perception of nuclear war and interpretation of his irregular business transactions for the past 40 years are essential. It is almost impossible for the experts to exactly understand his denuclearization deal with North Korea which was criticized by the US mainstream media based solely on his 17-month reign at the White House. Two variables are essential to understand President Trump's flamboyant nuclear renunciation musical which played with Kim Jong-un. One is the casino business and the other is the experience of the New York Military Academy, which Trump entered at the age of 13 in 1959. In accordance with his parents' wishes to correct his "rough and defiant" behavior, Trump completed his high school course at the academy. He said he always felt like he was in the army during his school life, adding that he underwent more military training than many young men who went to the army.

The existential fear of war that Trump experienced

Trump experienced the fear of conscription while watching the terror of a nuclear war following the Cuban missile crisis in 1962 when he was 3rd grade in the academy. Military academy periodically conducted drills to escape to underground air-raid shelter after issuing evacuation alerts. Everyone listened tight at President John F. Kennedy's radio address that if the Soviet Union did not withdraw its missiles from Cuba, a war would break out. Rumors pressured students that would be first drafted in case of war. The evacuation training at a military school, which experienced in mid-teen years as an adolescent boy, was enough to instill fear of a nuclear war to Trump. This experience gave him the impression that war is a fear itself but special incident that he must participate in. Trump was fascinated by General Douglas MacArthur, who strongly claimed to bomb Manchuria during the Korean War in his military school days. When General MacArthur died in 1964, he joined a student group to express his condolence. It was based on the judgment that General MacArthur was the only savior who could win a dangerous war. General MacArthur, who impressed deeply on Trump's high school day, was the most respected figure in his teenage years. During the presidential election, he chanted MacArthur and criticized his opponents. However, Trump had been suspended for four times since 1964 during the Vietnam War, citing his college study and ankle injury. The reason that Trump tried to compromise at the last minute over North Korea's nuclear weaponry (which the three former presidents had left as strategic patience) with maximum pressure rather than military options lies in the existential fear of war. Without understanding the Cuban missile crisis experience through military school training and 40-year-old ultra-realistic business transactions, it is impossible to find the *Rosetta Stone* on how Trump will resolve the denuclearization game with Kim Jong-un. The Egyptian hieroglyphs would not have been decoded without the basalt inscription found in the Rosetta Village in Alexandria, Egypt in 1799. Casino businesses are high-return and high-risk trade.

The highlight of Trump's profitable item as a businessman who enjoys trading rather than money is the casino business. He confessed that he would have no moral resistance to gambling. The reason is that opposition to gambling is hypocritical. Trump unconventionally thought that if casino business is illegal, the New York Stock Market is also the world's largest gambling house. The only thing that distinguishes the New York Stock Market from ordinary gambling venues is that gamblers carry leather bags in blue striped suits. Trump's opinion is that if the law permits a gambling place called the *Stock Market* where huge amounts of money are traded, betting on blackjack and roulette games should be allowed. His perception of casinos symbolizes that he does not have the average thinking about the world. Therefore, it is highly realistic to argue that while South Korea–US relations will be weakened, North Korea–US relations will go with warm breeze and achieve breakthroughs such as a peace agreement in the course of North Korea's denuclearization. For Trump, there is no dichotomous thinking of *North Korea is evil, South Korea is goodness.* While North Korea can serve as a favorable factor to consolidate his fragile domestic politics, South Korea is just a rich country that can help fill the US pockets with dollars by reducing the US Forces in Korean Peninsula and combined training. His past visits to Seoul to deal with the Trump Tower project may have contributed to his judgment.

The incarnation of anomaly and makeshift

For Trump, who had taken over casino construction in Atlantic City and casino hotel operated by Hilton Hotel Group, calculated that the Singapore Summit, which was reported fiercely by some 3,000 foreign journalists worldwide, was a lucrative business. He thought the unprecedented summit deserved spotlight itself regardless of its fruits. Had it not been for the casino business in his life, he would have left the North Korean nuclear issue to the State Department with proper periodic pressure and strategic patience like former presidents Bill Clinton, George W. Bush and Barack Obama. Casino businesses are hard to push unless they are trading like people who go to casinos again and again. Due to the nature of the casino business, it is difficult for a businessman to push for a manufacturer. It should accurately understand the process of obtaining a permit for casino business in a certain area and purchase land in an expected region at reasonable prices in the midst of economic recession. He has also to find a surefire supply of budget or banks that will trust and lend him large amounts of money. If he purchases a target area at a low price in the shortest period, he should use cunning and wise local media and politicians to effectively carry out public relation (PR). After all, the casino business needs a super sense of art and ability in the business sector.

Before and after the Singapore Summit, the stock price of South Korean casino companies *GKL* and *Paradise* had been strong. The news that North Korea asked the US to invest in the casino business in Wonsan, a port city of North Korea, had had a positive impact on investor sentiment. President Trump probably asked his son to weigh his investment. In the past, however, Trump was the final candidate to take control of the Australian casino business, the second largest in the world, but finally gave up bidding because the place was a 24-hour flight from New York. It was in 1975 when Trump first realized that the casino business was making money. He finally finished construction in May 1984, 10 years after planning to build a casino in Atlantic City. A site visit was scheduled for the board of partner Holiday Group ahead of the final project approval. As the construction was sluggish unexpectedly, Trump mobilized all bulldozers and dump trucks near the two-acre site a week before to mislead board members visiting the site. Heavy machinery was turned on to show board members that construction was going on quickly. He even dug up dirt at one of the construction sites and filled it with other places. The director got the impression that the scene was rather strange than suspicious. As a result, investment by Holiday Group had been approved. It was a classic example of anomaly and makeshift. Trump had a wild imagination of taking over a large casino hotel, which was started by hotel conglomerate Hilton in 1984. He succeeded in acquiring the casino hotel, which was unlikely to be realized, by borrowing US$320 million in just a year. Hilton started construction but failed to get the city board's casino permit. As the cost snowballed, Trump sought the loophole. He got casino permit and finally earned US$226 million in just one year in 1986. He set high goals and chose to step up to close a deal. Two talents of smartness and instinct as a *broker* were master-key to the success of the deal. As he said, even if someone is a gifted person with an IQ of 170 he cannot make a successful deal without a broker instinct. And he saw it through. Trump confessed that his success was possible because he trusted his sense of self and made bold investments. Trump showed an excellent sense of interactions with his counterpart. He analyzed the exact SWOT (Strengths,

Weaknesses, Opportunities, and Threats) against Hilton's owner Barron and set the best time, and then made the deal a success.

More practical to accept reality than to break the summit

In 1975, Trump suggested that he wanted to buy a 11-story building in Manhattan, but building owner, Genesco, rejected his offer because of no plausible performance in the past. After being rejected, he sent dozens of letters to Genesco. In the end, the letter became to pump out of closing the deal. The reason why Trump declared the resumption of the talks by letter from Kim Jong-un after declaring the cancel of first summit was probably because of his experience of successful communication through his letter. Later, the building became the Trump Tower that was famous for selling a peculiar fantasy made on the site. He introduced virtual reality into real estate business earlier. The way in which Trump induced investment by using virtual scenarios that do not exist in reality was revealed in his self-fulfilling press conference held after the summit. The "fantastic" wording by Trump after the meeting with Kim was an expression of virtual reality thinking that it could be a big hit in the future, even though it was a result of insufficient negotiations. This was also the result of self-confidence and camouflage tactic taken by his life. Of course, not all Trump's casino businesses were successful. When the economic recession made it difficult for him to repay his loan, he suffered a bankruptcy crisis in 1991. He financed a billion dollars for the construction of his third casino, the Trump Taj Mahal. He took out additional loans but could not stand the increase in debt. Trump filed for bankruptcy, and also was on the verge of personal bankruptcy. Eventually, he settled his debts by selling off his property. The June 12 agreement between the US and North Korea is like a Christian who was always shouting for *Hallelujah* before the festivities but ended up zipping up one's lips on Christmas Day. Evaporation of the term CVID (complete, verifiable and irreversible denuclearization) in the agreement at the Singapore Summit was similar to the way in which bankruptcy solved the financial problem. His double poker face statement that could not include CVID due to a lack of time was based on his judgment that accepting reality would be more practical than breaking the summit. Trump, businessman style politician, overlooked the fact that negotiations with communism cannot succeed without a firm resolution waging war with brinkmanship strategy of former president Kennedy in response to Cuban missile crisis.

Kim Jong-un's childhood environment was very different from his father, Kim Jong-il. He had a fierce power struggle with his half-brothers like Kim Pyong-il and Kim Young-il and his younger father Kim Young-joo. He grew up with an obsession that should attract Kim Il-sung's interest. Kim Jong-il strongly felt to display his potential leadership of the next generation is superior to that of his half-brothers to Kim Il-sung. In 1947, when Kim Jong-il was six years old, his younger brother drowned. Two years later, his mother Kim Jong-sook died in 1949. After reaching adulthood, he sought his own survival despite the jealousy of his half-brother and stepmother Kim Sung-ae. Kim Jong-il armed with prudence and vigilance carefully managed sly old politicians who had an attitude of treacherous obedience with carrots and sticks. Kim Jong-un, however, had not experienced rough struggle for the hegemony since a young age. He was in Kim Jong-il's absolute love and inherited disciplines of kingship. Kenji Fujimoto, a chef attached to Kim Jong-il, testified that Kim Jong-un was a snob and had a strong desire to win since he was young unlike his older brother Kim Jong-chul. Kim Jong-un liked basketball, so he often called basketball players in his official residence and shared the team with Kim Jong-chul. After the game, Kim Jong-un pointed out faults to his players in informal language. "After the basketball game, his brother Jong-chul only said three words: 'We had a hard time.' 'You did great job.' 'Dismiss!'" On the other hand, Kim Jong-un criticized on the players' faults. All of them were 22 or 23 years old. But he yelled out loud to the older players by saying, "The style is how you work out and can't get score, understand?" Fujimoto recalled.

While studying in Switzerland, Jong-chul and Jong-un celebrated in Pyongyang the North Korean national holidays, especially Kim

Jong-il and Kim Il-sung's birthday (February 16, April 15), the anniversary of the DPRK regime (September 9), and the anniversary of the Workers' Party (October 10). Once they returned home, they stayed in Pyongyang for about two months. Kim Jong-il expressed special interest in his third son, Jong-un because his second son Jong-chul seemed like a girl since his childhood. Kim Jong-il gave Jong-un a big birthday party every year. However, Kim Jung-chul had to share a birthday party on the same day, saying that his birthday was similar to that of his youngest daughter Kim Yo-jong. Kim Jong-un hated to lose to someone else and had a highly competitive spirit. When his classmates made fun of him for watching *Pokémon* while studying in Switzerland, he threw books and tried to fight his classmates. Kim Jong-il's aides once called Kim Jong-chul and Kim Jong-un "Big Captain Comrade" and "Little Captain Comrade", respectively. When Kim Jong-un heard that his aunt called him a "Little Captain Comrade", he nitpicked, "Why am I a *little* captain comrade?" After this event, Kim Jong-un's title changed to "Captain Comrade" or "Kim Captain Comrade" without the modifier "little". He also had a rude and rough manner, such as throwing beads on his brother's face when he was angry or kicking Kim Il-sung's deputy secretary who was over 60 years old and making fun of him as a "Humpty-Dumpty". Kim Jong-un's record when studying in middle and high school of Switzerland was mediocre, but his judgment was fast and he was so quick on the uptake. As the Chief of the National Security Strategy Research Institute under the National Intelligence Service, this author calculated social IQ based on Kim Jong-un's conversation with relatives lived in Osaka, Japan during childhoods and classmates at the Swiss school. The analysis suggests that Kim Jong-un quickly understood, responded appropriately to questions as he communicated with others, had a high understanding of the issues, and provided a proper logic for his argument. The negotiating style between Trump who has sense-dependent, impromptu character and Kim Jong-un who has brute force, daredevil character were worlds apart. Let us evaluate the Singapore Summit based on their characters, ambitions, goals, trade skills and results. When analyzing the characters of the two leaders from the perspective of

SWOT (Strengths, Weaknesses, Opportunities, and Threats), the strength of the two is that they have a strong, adventurous temperament. In particular, if someone refuses his favor and starts a fight, he does not mind fighting. During the competition to get the opportunity of casino business in Hilton Hotel, Trump attempted to reach an agreement by every kind of ways and means, but the other filed a US$5 million lawsuit. He finally won the suit by mobilizing the strongest lawyer. If the other party puts pressure on the negotiation process, he pays back strongly. North Korean vice minister, Kim Kye-gwan and Choi Sun-hee's criticism against the US were overwhelmed by Trump's cancellation of the summit and barely restored it by sending letters to him.

Betting on the principle of not retreating from the core interest

Kim Jong-un, however, also showed his determination to stick to stepwise and simultaneous solutions in the process of denuclearization. Kim firmly maintained his stance not only during the three summits with China's President Xi Jinping held in Beijing and Dalian, but also during Mike Pompeo's two visits to North Korea and North Korean negotiation representative Kim Yong-chol's visit to the White House. Kim Jong-un played an unpredictable match against John Bolton and Pompeo's CVID (complete, verifiable and irreversible dismantlement of nuclear weapons) swords with the CVIG (complete, verifiable, irreversible guarantee of his regime) shield by putting up Kim Yong-chol. In short, Kim Jong-un penetrated the weakness of the superpower of the US by maintaining his basic fundamental position that North Korea could not definitely accept the US request like reporting, verification and inspection of nuclear weapons and facilities. The US lineup in the North Korean Ministry of Foreign Affairs, which had accumulated know-how for 70 years in North Korea's diplomacy, risked their lives to the situation of retreating from the core interest, as Thae Yong-ho, a former North Korean diplomat defected to Seoul in 2016, noted in his book published in 2018.[105]

The criterion for distinguishing between core and marginal profits is whether the variable acts as a minus in the existence of the North Korean regime. North Korean authority has never allowed Westerners to verify the entire area of inspection that swirls around North Korea even if war breaks out because of concern about the loss of core profits. Kim Jong-un confirmed a phased and simultaneous denuclearization at the three summits with Xi. If this principle was shaken in the meeting with Trump, it would undermine the dignity of Xi as well as Kim Jong-un. If the US failed to read the significance of the agreement made by the Chinese emperor and the North Korean supreme leader in advance, it would be a washout of US diplomacy. US Secretary of State Pompeo said that US should pay attention to follow-up negotiations after the Singapore Summit while visiting South Korea and Japan to clarify the timing and meaning of denuclearization. But this was just repenting of missing a chance. Rather, it is much more realistic to understand that CVID denuclearization has entered a long-term war. Julian Zelizer, a professor of history at Princeton University and CNN political analyst, suggested four things to keep in mind before Trump's North Korea–US Summit. The priority was "Patience". It meant that the US should be patient because it was rare to resolve the long-standing tension through a single talk and reach a final agreement. Zelizer presented one example of disarmament negotiations between US President Ronald Reagan and Soviet Communist Party chief Mikhail Gorbachev. When they met three times between 1985 and 1987, they were able to successfully negotiate at the third round of talks as a result of not losing patience. Trump has shown his patience faithfully in negotiating with Kim Jong-un. If the second and third rounds of talks achieve denuclearization, Trump's choice would be right. However, it is still uncertain whether Kim Jong-un who is the third-generation dictator of North Korea would become Gorbachev who was the last romantic communist who successfully led the reform and opening of the Soviet Union. Kim's policy can also be evaluated in the same way that Gorbachev established in the past.

Another advantage of Kim is that Pyongyang is one step ahead of Washington in the time race. If the negotiations between an at most four- or eight-year-term leader and a lifetime dictator who is not relinquishing in the near future, it will be advantageous to the leader who can afford a long war. Trump's Big Deal strategy based on at least 10 years of long-term battle in the casino business worked as a weakness at the Singapore Summit owing to the time limits of his term. As Trump put it, "time limit" is the biggest weakness in business transactions. The absence of watches, mirrors and windows at the casino signifies that gamblers are not conscious of time. In other words, the game will end only when the winner and loser are finally decided. Trump's biggest weakness is that he needs a breakthrough from the threat of domestic politics due to the impending mid-term elections and presidential election in 2020. Trump said that if you are "desperate" when you negotiate, the opponent can smell blood. Paradoxically, the mid-term elections after just four months away served as a shackle for him. In particular, the movements of a special counsel team led by Robert Mueller who had stepped up to prosecute the related Trump–Russia collusion were quite serious and threatening for Trump. It was very fortunate for Kim Jong-un that the special prosecutor's blade was getting sharpened ahead of the November election. If Trump lost his power due to his mid-term defeat, he could not be ruled out the impeachment scenario. Trump's domestic politics is a weakness or threat factor in denuclearization negotiations.

Trial and error through irregular negotiating structure

It was the worst scenario for Kim Jong-un to return to Pyongyang without the Singapore Summit because he failed to make progress in the preparatory talks. He decided that summit definitely might be very lucrative and helpful to level up the status of his regime. He fully devoted to the accomplishment of the summit. The regime had concentrated the propaganda for the result of summit that was the first big event in the contact history of both countries since the Korean War (1950–53). Pyongyang was making headlines in the government organ, *Rodong* newspaper of North Korea with dozens of photos of Kim Jong-un's talks with US president in Singapore. North Korean society celebrated a perfect victory and propagated that the US president praised their leader. North Korean people were thrilled to see the summit as a tremendous achievement of the great leader, and they were just waiting for the day when sanctions and pressures would be lifted. The situation of continuing sanctions and pressure would be nightmarish for North Korea since the North Korean media repeatedly emphasized the win of the nation and defeat of the US. The top leader Kim Jong-un unprecedentedly held a summit with not only South Korean President Moon Jae-in but also the leaders of the G2 countries in less than a year. It signified the scrupulous victory of North Korean diplomacy. The pressure to achieve a win was a weak factor for Pyongyang since Kim was worried that Trump would leave the venue if he was not satisfied with his performance in advance.

But it was just unfounded fears. As the US fully accepted North Korea's stance struck at the talks between Kim Yong-chol and Pompeo early on the day of the summit, the summit ended unceasingly earlier than scheduled. Trump's comment that he could recognize the other person's intentions in just one minute was nothing but an empty talk. The Singapore Summit, in which all the key points were not put together in advance, was concluded early in the morning during an hour and a half session of extemporaneous talks between assistant chiefs of staff for intelligence. There were too many empty promises for Trump to leave the venue without a denuclearization agreement with North Korea after immediate receipt of invitations for summits brought by South Korean special envoys Chung Eui-yong. The US should have played a non-zero-sum game that balances out the possibility of postponing the summit if both parties did not reach a productive agreement during the previous meeting between North Korean Vice Minister Choi and US representative Sung Kim in Panmunjom, a border town between South and North Korea. Trump should have left Singapore without an announcement of the agreement in accordance with a principle written in his book *The Art of the Deal.* It is expected that the top-down process and style of the first deal confirm the framework of the overall negotiation between two countries. The second summit held in Hanoi on February 2019 had a similar roadmap as the top-down style of the first summit. The second summit resulted in "no deal" which is better than bad deal as both leaders could not reach an agreement. Failed summit means that ministerial level talks would not be able to produce any agreement. It seems difficult for Trump to break the pattern of this trade and deal. Rather, Trump is likely to offer an irregular negotiation plan to reduce defense costs and induce denuclearization of North Korea through the withdrawal of USFK, a safeguard for international politics in Northeast Asia. It means there is no way to rule out the possibility of another risky deal to recoup criticism of his failure to negotiate. Both North Korea and the US have ambitions and goals, but they each have different dreams. Trump's initial goal was to implement CVID in one shot deal. Especially if they would bring at least 50% of the past nuclear weapons manufactured through inspection and verification to Oak Ridge National Laboratory in the US before the mid-term elections in November, the scenario would have been considered successful. The world's attention would be focused on the policy direction from the US and North Korea as both leaders unconventionally created the process of removing nuclear weapons. In short, the visible progress in denuclearization has not been sufficient and necessary condition in evaluating Trump as a great leader until now.

However, Kim Jong-un's strategy is as far from Trump's intention as the distance between Pyongyang and Washington. North Korea is a poor country and therefore, Kim Jong-un does not have a private plane capable of flying 4,500km back and forth in order to have a summit in Washington, so he needs to rent a plane from a neighboring country and board it. However, his negotiation goals do not fall behind those of the US. Rather, his mettle and viewpoint are on top of Trump's head. The presidents of South Korea, the US, China and Russia, and even the prime minister of Japan have been applying for a summit with Kim Jong-un. It is a big miscalculation and misconception, if Washington judges that Pyongyang will forget that nuclear weapons made by tightening belts are the reason for such reality and being. Pyongyang's plausible goal, of course, is to negotiate nuclear disarmament by bartering regime security and economic support. No matter how high the level of denuclearization is, about 50% of all nuclear weapons and materials are expected as the Maginot Line that Pyongyang accepts. North Korea considers that the term CVID is not available in denuclearization negotiation. North Korea has repeatedly mentioned in its diplomatic meetings as Kim Yong-chol versus Mike Pompeo and Choe Sun-hee versus Sung Kim that the unilateral demands that denuclearization be completed during the next two years of Trump's term are not subject to negotiations. If the US does not understand the fact that what is unacceptable in the working-level talks is the same negative position at the summit table, the US has failed to fully understand the North's negotiation strategy. In any case, more than 3,000 journalists around the world were provided with enough press photos and the two sides agreed in Singapore that future talks could lead to a second and third round of summits. Therefore, Trump's intention is incomplete, but he has won half of the game. Trump's view of success in the summit is very different from those of experts. He has reserved several years of storytelling to cover up the special prosecutor Mueller's indictment in domestic politics, so public relations marketing on the summit with North Korea will be more important for the future than contents of the agreement. However, the White House's efforts to persuade the US Congress will inevitably suffer in local politics given that the House of Representatives has controlled by the Democratic Party since mid-term elections in November 2018. As the present Trump administration criticizes the previous Clinton and Obama administration's negotiations with North Korea, it will not be easy for Trump to persuade the Democratic Party with their low diplomatic scores after the mid-term elections in November 2018.

On the other hand, Kim Jong-un clearly told the international community that "declaration to end the Korean War, and peace treaty with US, and then establish diplomatic ties" are the final road map of Pyongyang. It will be a complete, verifiable and irreversible victory (CVIV) of North Korea, if final or partial target comes true in the near future. Things have changed dramatically since the Singapore Summit. Even though UN Resolution 2375 was unanimously adopted in September 2017 after the sixth nuclear test of North Korea, such sanctions that blocked oil imports are partly nominal, despite of the US declaration that it would maintain sanctions. Skilled blacksmiths accurately capture the timing of striking while the iron is hot. If blacksmith misses this moment, the iron does not form the shape one wants. After the Singapore Summit, denuclearization through sanctions and pressure has been difficult to operate for a certain period of time. Right after the summit, China quickly turned to easing sanctions. Trump's initial prospects and expectations that this summit would be a "Big Deal" with the strongest nuclear agreement ended with ambiguity. Although the US used the word "strong pressure" before the summit, one had no choice but to call this summit as a *the-get-to-know-you* stage or starting point of a long-term *process* of denuclearization. In particular, the US withdrew from Iran's nuclear agreement (the Joint Comprehensive Plan of Action) before the negotiations with North Korea, but Trump showed a contradictory attitude by settling negotiations with North Korea. The result of the Singapore Summit had been reportedly inferior to the Iran nuclear agreement. Since even the word "verification", which was stated in the Joint Statement of the fourth round of the Six-Party Talks in Beijing on September 19, 2005, was not included in the negotiations, it has been uncertain whether the denuclearization talks may be advanced smoothly in the future. The procedures for reporting, inspection and verification are the general sequence of denuclearization. In particular, leaders from each country will rush to Pyongyang to learn how to negotiate with Trump. A book called *How to Fight with Trump: Kim Jong-un's Secret Method* may be expected to be published soon. It is highly likely that this book will become a bestseller that surpasses Trump's *The Art of the Deal.* As *The New York Times* put it, this may a turbulent era that *unconventional* powerful people rapidly change the stream of history into an unknown direction. If a man loses one's mind, he could be swept away by the waves and disappear without a trace.

The reality of the North Korean nuclear weapons and its price of transaction and compensation

The United States says, "Yongbyon nuclear is not as expensive as North Korea thinks."

Since the Hanoi talks between the United States and North Korea ended with a "no deal", competition for initiatives to sustain future negotiations among South Korea, North Korea, and the US leaders has been in full swing. President Trump opened the door first. The third round of summit talks between North Korea and the US will not be feasible in the near future without the drastic change of their basic position and the summit between the United States and North Korea depends on the policy change of Kim Jong-un and Trump. South Korean President Moon said on April 12, 2019 in Washington that South Korea will hold an inter-Korean summit soon. Kim Jong-un, the chairman of the North Korean state secretary, made the following remarks at the opening address of the Supreme People's Assembly in Pyongyang on the same day. "If the US wants to hold a third summit meeting with the right attitude and a methodology to share with us, we are willing to do one more. The deadline is until the end of the year." He also rejected the US demand for a big deal because he does not give in to the sanctions and pressures of the United States and is not interested in US calculations. Kim Jong-un had expectedly another summit with Russian President Vladimir Putin in Vladivostok, a far eastern city of Russia on April 26, 2019. He tried to seek political and economic supports from Putin in order to confront US's pressure and sanctions in the long term.

There may be two reasons why the Hanoi Summit could not produce an agreement. One is the scope of sanctions against North Korea. The other is the definition of the range and type of nuclear weapons and facilities that North Korea possesses. At the end of the Hanoi talks, President Trump left Hanoi telling Kim Jong-un that "You are not ready for a deal." The statement is an unreported anecdote about the Hanoi meeting that was first unveiled by President Trump at the annual Spring Meeting of the Republican National Committee (RNC) in early March 2019. Trump has a good relationship with Kim Jong-un, but said, "It is the first time for anyone to talk to him like this and leave." The expression of "preparedness" is the level of diplomatic incompetence that should not be done at the summit. Trump thought that Kim Jong-un was not going to get a big deal in the denuclearization talks. Trump, a former seasoned business man, dislikes going behind in negotiations or deals. It is a matter of pride of shopkeepers. Trump had described the basic philosophy of negotiation and deal in his book, *The Techniques of Trading*. "I do not trade because of money. There is a lot of money for me. Much more money than I need. I do business for the transaction itself. Trading is a kind of art to me. Some people have beautiful paintings on the canvas and others have good poetry. But I like to trade something. If the deal is bigger, my interest also will be higher. I feel the fun of life through transactions. Deal to me is an art."

Did Kim Jong-un, who was in the second round of deal with the US president expressed the transaction as the best art, came to Hanoi on a 65-hour train journey to reach particular goal of denuclearization negotiations? What were the final results of the negotiations that Kim Jong-un originally thought? What was not prepared for Kim Jong-un? Veterans of North Korea's negotiations with the United States, such as Vice Chairman of the Commission Kim Young-chol, Foreign Vice-Minister Choi Sun-hee, and the Special Representative for North Korea Kim Hyuk-cheol desperately prepared the summit. The Special Representative of the US State Department Steven Vegan, Secretary of State Mike Pompeo and National Security Adviser John Bolton of the United States also prepared hard at least three months before the second summit. There may be two reasons why President Trump said Kim Jong-un was "not ready" after the summit, even though the top staffs of both sides met many times at the negotiating table during three months of preliminary negotiations. It is possible that North Korean negotiating staff or Kim Jong-un misjudged or both Kim Jong-un and the working group miscalculated.

Trump's miscalculation and Kim Jong-un's misjudgments

If the first Singapore Summit was the product of Trump's miscalculation, the second Hanoi Summit may be the result of a misjudgment made by Kim Jong-un. If Kim Jong-un had prepared a scenario to sign a small deal document that would improvise Trump "lounging and cheating" and exchange Yongbyon nuclear facilities with the lifting of maximum sanction against North Korea at a one-on-one meeting with Trump, excluding hawkish negotiator Bolton and Pompeo, who were quick to notice, North Korean negotiation line with the United States in Pyongyang must be seen as overlooking the classiness and multiplicity of international and local politics in Washington. South Korean President Moon, who went all out to the North Korean nuclear issue, ran to Washington aside from everything including a big event commemorating the 100th anniversary of the provisional Korean government prepared a year ago. The heart of the visit was to ask the United States to lower the level of denuclearization of North Korea. The South Korean government is focusing on persuading the reservation of Washington's big deal by using various English phrases such as "good enough deal" and "early harvest". The point is that although the agreement on the denuclearization roadmap is comprehensive, it is possible to give rewards to North Korea such as mitigation of the sanctions by stepwise denuclearization. But unfortunately, the only actual talk time between President Moon and President Trump in Washington were only two minutes, except for remarks for the media. It has been reported that it had not led to any effective conversation that would change Trump's position. President Trump appreciated South Korea's arms purchasing. President Moon concluded the 7th US–Korea summit meeting, saying that South Korea will soon hold a fourth inter-Korean summit. The summit between alliances revealed that even though both countries work together, they each have different aims and views. After all, as with the meeting in Hanoi, the summit between South Korea and the US was also "no deal" in Washington. The only special note is that President Moon delivered Trump the position that he would push for the inter-Korean summit soon after the first anniversary of the April 27 summit. It is unclear, however, whether it will be possible for the two sides of "no deal" to hold a "sooner" summit. It is uncertain whether Kim Jong-un, who has recently strengthened his power as a substantial head of state in

North Korea, will be interested in the inter-Korean summit, which lacks substantial economic benefits. In particular, Kim Jong-un said in his address to the Supreme People's Assembly held in April 2019, that "the president of South Korea should not act as a broad mediator or facilitator, but as a member of the nation, with a sane mind." He said, furthermore, that President Moon should make a decision to demonstrate his sincerity not by words, but by practical actions. Kim Jong-un's accusation forewarns that the North Korean policy of President Moon, that has been pursuing the mediator since 2017, is soon to foresee a future failure or success.

How much is the value of Yongbyon nuclear issue?

The key difference between Washington's big deal and Seoul's "good enough deal" and "early harvesting" is not the implementation of denuclearization but the scope of denuclearization in North Korea. *Reuters* reported the details of the denuclearization of North Korea requested by Trump at the end of March. The title is "a piece of paper, Trump called on Kim to hand over all kinds of nuclear weapons." The document that Trump had given to Kim Jong-un includes "the complete dismantling of North Korea's nuclear facilities, chemical and biological programs, ballistic missiles and other related facilities, including the shipping off nuclear weapons and nuclear material to the United States." It also includes "comprehensive reporting on the nuclear program, full access to US and international inspectors, related activities and construction of new facilities, removal of all nuclear facilities, and a shift to commercial activities for all nuclear program scientists and engineers". At the same time, the Seoul branch of the Japanese *Yomiuri* newspaper reported that President Trump presented a draft of five agreements at the second round of the North Korea–US summit in Hanoi, Vietnam, at the end of February. According to reports, a rough agreement was reached at the stage of consultation between the Special Representative of the US State Department Steven Vegan and the Special Representative for North Korea Kim Hyuk-cheol about the three rewards from the five drafts and the discovery of the bodies of the dead US soldiers, however, there was no breakthrough in the scope and implementation of denuclearization. When President Trump presented a draft of five terms in English and Korean language, Kim negatively responded by saying, "it is difficult to accept the US claims that only demand unilateral denuclearization."

Trump is in a strong position to implement the denuclearization policy proposed in the draft in the next summit. A similar argument was raised by Chinese experts that serious disagreements over the extent of denuclearization led to the breakdown of the talks. Jiang Zheng, a professor at the Center for International Strategic Studies under the Chinese Communist Party, at the North Korea Forum in Beijing on March 24, 2019 insisted that Chairman Kim Jong-un was shocked when he received a new list of North Korean nuclear facilities that the US had never disclosed to North Korea. On the list of new nuclear facilities, the professor interpreted that the US demanded North Korea to dismantle all secret underground facilities related to North Korea's nuclear weapons. "Kim would have been shocked because he felt that the United States was not in agreement with what he had expected, not because US knew his underground nuclear facilities," he stressed. In order to diagnose the authenticity of these observations and assertions, it is important to understand the proportion of nuclear weapons in Yongbyon and the degree of threat. In other words, if the value of Yongbyon is accurately calculated, it is possible to determine the appropriate compensation. The complex is a sacred place and a source of North Korea's nuclear development. The Yongbyon Nuclear Research Institute, which is the core of the Nuclear Research Complex, was built in 1962 west of Yongbyon, North Pyongan Province, about 100km north of Pyongyang. The nuclear facility is a huge complex consisting of 400 buildings, including nuclear reactors and research institutes. In the administrative system, it belongs to the General Directorate of Nuclear Power, which is a direct under-commissioned organization. There are 10 research institutes including uranium resource development, nuclear physics, radiochemistry, nuclear materials, nuclear power, isotope utilization, and neutron physics. The area may be 25km^2.

The reprocessing facility for extracting plutonium from spent nuclear fuel has been in operation since 1989. In addition to the research facilities, the nuclear research complex includes raw materials and equipment plants for the production of scientific equipment and laboratories, a uranium enrichment plant, a nuclear fuel reprocessing plant, and an explosion experiment plant. The Yongbyon nuclear research complex has about 3,000 researchers who had been trained in the Soviet Union and China. The Guryoung River running through the outer area of Yongbyon passes through the research center and water is used to cool the adjacent reactor. North Korea has used some plutonium in its six nuclear tests, but now holds at least 50kg of plutonium in Yongbyon. Since South Korea has a small amount of uranium deposited in Okcheon and Jincheon in North Chungcheong Province, civilian use such as nuclear power plant operation depends on foreign imports such as the US and China. However, the Japanese government estimated that more than 4 million tons of uranium was buried in North Korea during the Japanese colonial period. At that time, Japan also set up a secret nuclear development plan in light of the abundance of nuclear materials in North Korea.

Where are nuclear weapons hidden in North Korea?

Before and after the Hanoi Summit, the areas where the United States has categorized as North Korea's concealed nuclear facilities are the regions of Bungang and Gangsun. The United States has not been able to figure out the exact North Korean uranium output per year. Therefore, it is struggling to detect uranium hexafluoride production facilities that are the raw materials of enriched uranium. Former International Atomic Energy Agency Assistant Secretary Olli Heinonen observed that North Korea had hidden secret uranium enrichment facilities throughout the country. He warned that if North Korea shut down its nuclear facilities in Yongbyon, it could continue to develop nuclear weapons elsewhere. He argued that because the gas centrifuge-based enrichment technology used by North Korea does not require much electricity, the facility cannot be distinguished from any other industrial complex or even a store.

It is very difficult for foreign countries to detect the gas centrifuge facilities that North Korea has everywhere. Another nuclear expert, David Albright, director of the Institute for Science and International Security, pointed out that North Korea is producing deuterides lithium, a raw material for hydrogen bombs, outside Yongbyon. Even though North Korea voluntarily dismantles its nuclear facilities in Yongbyon, North Korea will not only be able to produce hydrogen bombs, but will also have the capacity to manufacture two or three nuclear weapons annually in a uranium enrichment facility equipped with gas centrifuges. The United States has rejected North Korea's request to exchange the lifting of sanctions against North Korea with the dismantlement of Yongbyon site because the US intelligence agencies have already figured out another hidden facilities.

Immediately after the Hanoi Summit, President Trump said, "We know everything about North Korea. Although foreign countries do not know North Korea precisely, the US government is aware of North Korea's nuclear facilities other than Yongbyon." Trump told reporters at a news conference that the nuclear facilities outside Yongbyon are "uranium enrichment facilities". Secretary of State Pompeo, who attended the press conference, said that besides the Yongbyon nuclear facility, there is also a very large nuclear facility. It may be unclear where North Korea's nuclear facilities are mentioned by President Trump. The US media reported that Gangsun was a new uranium enrichment facility outside Yongbyon at the time of the first summit in Singapore in 2018. US media quoted a report by the Institute of Science and International Security (ISIS) and an analysis of the Defense Intelligence Agency (DIA) as saying that North Korea is secretly operating a uranium enrichment facility at Gangsun and it is twice as big as Yongbyon. The content of the press coverage is consistent with Pompeo's statement, "a very large nuclear facility." The Center for Nonproliferation Research at the Middlebury Institute for International Studies analyzed the satellite images taken since 2001 and named the location of the nuclear reactor as the Cheonrima District in Nampo City, South Pyongan Province. It was announced in April 2002 that it was the first building to be found here, which was vacant until 2001. It might be an underground nuclear facility that has not been reported so far, given the president's comments that North Korea seemed surprised. US intelligence officials have suspected that North Korea has been secretly operating an underground nuclear facility. Jeffrey Lewis, director of the Nonproliferation Research Center, pointed to the location of the vessel, saying in an interview with Voice of America (VOA) in July 2018, "The Bungang is not an underground nuclear facility. There is a possibility that there are more underground third facilities underground."

The third nuclear facility, designated by the United States in Hanoi, is reportedly located in the northwest of the existing Yongbyon nuclear complex. North Korea has built a uranium enrichment plant in the basement, fearing that it would be detected outside. The new facility is an area that has not been mentioned in the media, but it is adjacent to Yongbyon and is divided into sections. Until now, the scale of enrichment and the actual existence of uranium enrichment facilities in the bulk steel have not been clarified. Siegfried Hecker, who looked directly at North Korea's nuclear facilities in 2010, estimated that there would be about 2,000 centrifuges at Yongbyon's nuclear facility, which US intelligence authorities believe North Korea will be operating at about 10,000 or more.

North Korea will have 100 nuclear warheads by 2020

Highly enriched uranium (HEU), such as plutonium, used as the core material for nuclear bombs, was also extracted from Yongbyon. The value of Yongbyon depends on the point of view. "If North Korea makes a bold decision like the permanent dismantling of Yongbyon nuclear, South Korea will be able to resume the operation of Gaeseong Industrial Complex and the tour of Mt. Geumgang. If North Korea permanently dismantles its nuclear facilities in Yongbyon, it deserves enough compensation for mitigation," said Moon Chung-in, a special adviser to the Unification, Foreign Affairs and National Security. It may be a position that the price of Yongbyon is at least 80% or more of the North Korean nuclear weapon.

However, since nuclear materials are manufactured in a strictly confidential manner, Yongbyon is no longer a secret facility and is only a backward and publicized nuclear manufacturing facility. North Korea has demanded that the United States free up five civilian-related UN sanctions adopted after 2016 because it will abolish the entirety of Yongbyon in the presence of foreign experts. The key points that North Korea demanded to be lifted are prohibition of overseas branches of banks, restrictions on imports of oil and refined products from North Korea, and prohibition of export of coal, iron, lead, and marine products to North Korea. North Korea hopes to exchange the lifting of sanctions and the dismantling of Yongbyon nuclear weapons. It is the exact value of Yongbyon that North Korea intransigently thinks. However, the US said, "The sanctions that North Korea has asked us to solve are about 90% of the total sanctions against North Korea. Yongbyon is not that expensive."

The South Korean and US intelligence authorities are judging North Korea as having more than 30 nuclear facilities. One of them is the Gangsun nuclear complex, which is 16km away from Pyongyang. In addition, Hamhung Refining Plant, Shinpo Nuclear Power Plant, and Uranium Mine, southwest of Sariwon, are also of interest. There are about 20 missile bases throughout North Korea. There are many intercontinental ballistic missile (ICBM) bases in the borders of North Korea and China, medium-range missile bases on the east coast, and short-range missile bases on the north of the truce line on the Korean Peninsula.

At the end of 2018, all the think tanks of the United States identified nuclear and missile bases, such as Sakganmol and Galgol. In the bunker near the base, missiles at each intersection are hidden. The missile assembly plant, such as the Pyongyang-based Sanuomodong Armory Plant, should also be subject to denuclearization. North Korea has been reportedly estimated to possess 15 to 60 nuclear warheads. In January 2019, US military command in Japan released on its homepage that North Korea has nuclear weapons from at least 15 and up to 60. The high variance in estimates suggests that foreign intelligence agencies have not figured out the exact number of nuclear warheads that North Korea possesses.

North Korea announced in March 2016 that it succeeded in the miniaturization of nuclear warheads. The US Land Research Institute predicted in January 2019 that North Korea would have up to 100 nuclear warheads by 2020. The North Korean nuclear program consists of past, present and future nuclear weapons. A nuclear warhead is a past nuclear weapon that has already been manufactured and hidden in a secret place. The Yongbyon nuclear facility is just a facility that produces the uranium and plutonium needed to manufacture nuclear weapons, both current and future nuclear weapons. A nuclear warhead, a nuclear weapon of the past, becomes a powerful nuclear missile when it combines with a missile. The threat of nuclear weapons already manufactured is several times bigger than the facilities of Yongbyon. It is doubtful how much North Korea has hidden a nuclear warhead, and whether North Korea will openly disclose it. In conclusion, the greatest hurdle to negotiate the denuclearization of North Korea may be the nuclear warhead, and the nuclear infrastructure of Yongbyon is the next problem. At a news conference after Hanoi Summit, US Secretary of State Pompeo also emphasized the dismantlement of nuclear warheads and made clear the US goal of denuclearization. He said that nuclear weapons and nuclear facilities should be clearly included in the denuclearization lists. The lists should include past, present and future nuclear weapons and facilities. Various missiles must also be specified in the lists.

One of the evidences that the United States can detect North Korean nuclear facilities and equipment is reportedly electricity. It takes a lot of electricity to continue rotating the centrifuge. The United States has tracked North Korea's electricity-intensive North Korea areas and found a nuclear facility outside Yongbyon where North Korea kept it hidden. The United States has been able to see every corner of North Korea thanks to US technical intelligence and immense human wealth. The key is intelligence satellites. The power of satellites is tremendous, and the know-how of US intelligence analysts also played a decisive role to detect hidden places. They found clues that North Korea imported high-strength aluminum from Russia in the 2000s. High-strength aluminum is used to make centrifuges to enrich uranium. At that time, the import volume was about 6,000, but in 2010, North Korea revealed about 2,000 centrifuges at Yongbyon. It was judged that there were about 4,000 centrifuges elsewhere. North Korea's foreign minister Ri Yong-ho told reporters at a press conference after the Hanoi Summit that the target of the denuclearization talks includes all nuclear material production facilities, including plutonium and uranium in Yongbyon district. However, he did not specify the concrete places. In addition to the nuclear facilities of Yongbyon, the United States also demanded the dismantling of unannounced uranium enrichment facilities of Gangsun in the vicinity of Pyongyang, but North Korea denied its existence. Pyongyang has vaguely interpreted the definition of the Yongbyon nuclear facility and received as much compensation from the United States as possible, but it is simultaneously also pursuing a Pakistani nuclear-based strategy to retain existing nuclear warheads, as well as facilities such as Gangsun and Bungang. Although the Hanoi Summit has collapsed unexpectedly, the extent of denuclearization and the easing of sanctions are a couple of the biggest obstacles to the denuclearization negotiations in the future. It will be a key issue in the next third summit talks. The Yongbyon nuclear facility, which is also visible on Google Maps, faces a moment of truth that hides all or part of the denuclearization target. South Korean President Moon visited Washington to deliver his position of small deal to the White House, regarding the Yongbyon nuclear facility as a significant part of it, and stress the importance of road map for denuclearization. The South Korean president, who has to play a mediator role between Washington and Pyongyang, will be sidelined by both Washington and Pyongyang if he is not clear what the denuclearization target is.

In conclusion, the argument that the Yongbyon nuclear facilities may be at least 80% of the total North Korean nuclear program is presumably "exaggerated" judging on the basis of various kinds of information, and when the information analysis is combined, the proportion of Yongbyon may be estimated to be at maximum 50%. It is certain that Yongbyon is one of the most important facilities in the production of North Korean nuclear weapons. Only Yongbyon nuclear dismantlement is a necessary condition for North Korea's nuclear dismantlement, not a sufficient condition. In the end, the denuclearization scope of North Korea should include the closing of Yongbyon and the remaining 50%. For the complete and proven denuclearization of North Korea, reporting and external verification of all nuclear facilities is essential. It is better to do summit than otherwise, but it is not magic. If the leaders of the United States and North Korea do not clarify the scope and targets of denuclearization and compensation in advance and hold summit meetings again, the distrust from both parties will be exacerbated and overshadowed the achievement of the first and second summits.

Economic sanctions and North Korea's negative economic growth

Because of the blockade of the United States, North Korea has been hit hard by the supply shortage of oil and foreign currency

North Korea is turning toward the strategy of eliminating the economic crisis from the existing strategy of security guarantee as a cost of denuclearization. After the Hanoi Summit in Vietnam, there has been a ping-pong game that proves the truth between the United States and North Korea. The themes have been the subject of denuclearization and the range of the lifting of sanctions against North Korea. Among them, there has been a fierce criticism of the opposition between North Korea and the US over the scope of lifting of sanctions. It may be the sensitive issue of who is responsible for the breakdown. The main theme of the day when the US and North Korea conducted violent press propaganda on February 28, 2019 was the scope of lifting the UN sanctions against North Korea since 2016. Asked whether he was responsible for the breakdown of the negotiations, US President Trump said, "Kim Jong-un wanted to lift sanctions against North Korea, and we wanted to dismantle a large part of the North's nuclear facilities. We can't lift sanctions against North Korea." North Korea's Foreign Minister Ri said, "We made a feasible proposal and did not ask for the lifting of all sanctions. We demanded partial sanctions." Ri's allegations ran counter to President Trump's remarks. Trump said at a press conference after the talks broke down, "basically, they wanted the sanctions lifted in their entirety." Ri said, "If the United States lifts some parts of the United Nations sanctions that give the damage to the civilian economy, it makes especially people's lives difficult, we will dismantle all nuclear material production facilities in Yongbyon, including plutonium and uranium. It is completely discarded permanently by collaboration of US and North Korean experts. What we have asked for is not full-blown sanctions, but some of the eleven sanctions, specifically 5 items of the 11 sanctions, which were resolved during 2016 to 2017." A senior US State Department official refuted on March 1, 2019 that North Korea requested a lifting of all sanctions exchange for the dismantling of the Yongbyon nuclear facility, except for sanctions on weapons. "I think they are parsing words," he said, referring to North Korea's claim on partial lifting the sanctions.

North Korea's late-night press conference on February 28, 2019 paradoxically proves that sanctions against North Korea have been fatal to the North Korean people's economy. Kim Jong-un would have been informed that the regime can survive if the sanctions are lifted first rather than the reinforcements of nuclear weapons. It would have been unclear whether it would be possible for Kim Jong-un to take power over the next 10 years without mitigating sanctions on North Korea. When Kim Jong-un studied in Switzerland during high school, he saw a lot of goods in the store and compared Pyongyang department store's poor shelf, and lamented, "Why is my country so poor?" An anthology can be found in the writings of Kim Jong-il's Japanese chef, Kenji Fujimoto, who watched Kim Jong-un as a teenager. Kim Jong-un had realized in the eighth year of its rule that one of the causes of poverty facing Pyongyang has been the international sanctions against North Korea.

Is North Korea's request to lift some of its sanctions a sign of serious damage?

The international community's sanctions on North Korea are largely divided into sanctions imposed by the UN Security Council, and sanctions imposed by the US administration on the basis of US law. There are two types of US sanctions against North Korea: "legislative legislation through parliamentary legislation" and "administrative order" in which the US president takes the necessary action according to the powers delegated by relevant laws. First, let us examine the history and effects of US sanctions against North Korea. US sanctions against North Korea date back to the outbreak of the Korean War in 1950. North Korea was designated a hostile country from the US shortly after June 25, 1950, and financial and trade transactions were suspended by the Treasury and the Department of Commerce. In November 1987, North Korea was designated as a state sponsor of terrorism in the following year due to the Korean Airline bombing by North Korean agents and had received various sanctions for 20 years. The US President George W. Bush excluded North Korea from the list of terrorist sponsors in 2008. President Trump reassigned North Korea as a terrorist sponsor after nine years because of the death of American university student Otto F. Warmbier in November 2017 and the assassination of his half-brother Kim Jong-nam in Malaysia in February 2017.

Since then, the US Treasury Department and the Department of Commerce have repeatedly imposed administrative sanctions on North Korea, putting pressure on the level of an economic blockade. The past US administration imposed 470 sanctions against North Korea. More than half of these were done during the Trump administration. Trump's claim that the highest level of sanctions against North Korea has brought North Korea into negotiations is not a boast. Many sanctions prove his argument is based on sufficient evidence. All the sanctions are interlinked, and they put a tight net. Next, let us review the actual situation of the UN Security Council sanctions against North Korea that Kim Jong-un requested President Trump to be lifted. The Security Council had decided 11 sanctions on North Korea since the declaration of the withdrawal of the North Korea from the Non-Proliferation Treaty (NPT) in March 1993. Six of these were resolved in 2016–2017. The rest of the sanctions, except for the June 2017 sanctions imposed on specific institutions and individuals involved in illegal arms trade, appear to be "five UN sanctions" mentioned by Minister Ri in a late-night press conference. It is important to note that the nature of UN sanctions before and after 2016 is fundamentally different. Before 2016, sanctions were mostly partial non-economic sanctions that restricted military supplies and luxury items such as missile parts. However, sanctions after 2016, when the North Korean nuclear test and missile tests became international issues, were economic sanctions that blocked cash inflows into North Korea.

UN Security Council Resolution 1695 adopted in July 2006, recommended for North Korea to suspend its nuclear weapons and missiles, prohibited development of weapons of mass destruction (WMD), froze funds, and banned technology transfer. In Resolution 1718 issued in October of that year, it decided to implement sanctions against North Korea and form a sanctions committee. It was a level of recommendation to urge North Korea to refrain from military provocations. It was the fourth nuclear test of North Korea in January 2016 that the draft resolution firmly tightened the North Korean economy. The resolution began to concentrate on the North Korean economy as well as the civilian economy. In March 2016, the Security Council unanimously adopted a new Resolution 2270 on North Korea that responded to North Korea's fourth nuclear test and rocket launch. The adoption was only 57 days since Pyongyang conducted its fourth nuclear test on January 6, 2016. If the existing resolutions were focused on North Korea's weapons of mass destruction, Resolution 2270 contained measures to hurt the North Korean economy, including major mineral exports, sanctions on ships and aircraft, and the suppression of foreign financial control. US Ambassador to the United Nations Samantha Jane Power said it was "the strongest sanctions of the past 20 years." The Resolution 2321, adopted after the fifth nuclear test in September of that year, blocked the export of coal, the main export item of North Korea. By introducing a ceiling cap on coal exports, North Korea's foreign currency imports have been hit by more than US$700 million annually, and 20% of North Korea's total exports have been reduced. The Mansudae creative company was denied access to US$100 million in foreign currency imports because of the prohibition on the sale of statues in Africa and some Southeast Asian countries. The number of financial accounts that North Korean diplomatic missions could open was limited to one. It also removed the rule of "exception for livelihood".

Since the start of the Trump Administration in 2017, four resolutions have been adopted successively. North Korea's ICBM test launch and the sixth nuclear test in September 2017 were at its peak. In Resolution 2371 after the launch of the missile announced in August 2017, the export of seafood was banned, which was estimated to be the largest window of foreign currency income in North Korea, and the new transmission of overseas workers. A decline in revenues of US$300 million a year is expected due to the reduction of 100,000 North Korean workers in Russia, China and the Middle East. Resolution 2375, which passed in September of that year, included the first commodity sanctions, and freeze crude and refined oil products to 4 million barrels and 2 million barrels a year, respectively. Limiting the supply of crude oil, which is perceived as a 'lifeline' of North Korea, to 4 million barrels per year, created an emergency for North Korea to supply energy. The United States emphasized that North Korea has been avoiding sanctions by transferring crude oil or refined oil from the sea to illegal transfers between ships. After the launch of the Hwasong-15 on December 23, 2017, Resolution 2000 was adopted just before Christmas which set a limit of 500,000 barrels of refinery feedstock supply and required reporting of UN member states' supply of crude oil to North Korea. The resolution called for repatriation of North Korean overseas workers who were already sent to foreign countries within 24 months. It also banned the export of foodstuffs, timber, ships and agricultural products. Finally, confessions that North Korea were suffering from sanctions began to appear in North Korean documents.

In his article entitled "Organized Political Business for Making the Manifestation of the Hostile Powers of the Hostile Party" in the December issue of *Workers*, the agency magazine of the North Korean Workers' Party in December 2017, the chairman of Gyeongheung Leadership Bureau of Labor Party No. 39, Lee Chol-ho frankly confessed serious damage by sanctions. He explained that the sanctions had caused the foreign currency shortage of Labor Party No. 39 and negatively affected the economy. The sanctions had also caused a gas station to shut down due to restrictions on oil supply. President Trump estimated that North Korea's export amount dropped to one-twelfth because of UN sanctions against the United States. In its report on North Korean economic sanctions released in February 2019, the Korea Institute for International Economic Policy predicted that if the last penalty, Resolution 2397, were to be fully operational, North Korea's exports would decrease by more than 90% before the sanctions. North Korea's foreign reserves, estimated at around US$5 billion, are inevitably exhausted if export-related sanctions are fully in effect. The shortage of foreign currencies makes it harder to import goods, and it is in a vicious circle that paralyzes domestic consumption and production. The sanction effectively blocked 90% of North Korean cash flow by completely blocking foreign currency earning points. UN officials estimate that North Korea's ban on coal, iron ore and fishery products would make a yearly cut of US$1 billion. One billion dollars is one-third of North Korea's annual exports, estimated at US$3 billion. If the sanctions continue, it will not be possible to rule out the eventuality of a foreign exchange crisis due to the depletion of foreign reserves within three years.

There is water in North Korea's coal mine

The North Korean economy may be analyzed as a quadruple economy. The size of the second economy, which operates the most important military sector, accounts for about 35% of the entire North Korean economy. The next is the court economy, which is the economic foundation of Kim's ruling politics. The portion may be at 25%. Third, the national economy pursued by the Cabinet ministries of economy occupies about 20%. Finally, the underground economy, which is called "Jangmadang", the base of people's ordinary life, is estimated to be around 20%. The most pressing part of sanctions is the court economy and the military economy. The resources of the court economy and the military economy are composed of revenues from various trading companies, remittances from overseas workers, the sales of weapons and drugs, counterfeiting, the profit from the Kaesong Industrial Complex worth US$100 million annually as of February 2016, and the annual revenue of US$50 million from the Mt. Kumgang tour. At least US$1 billion in royal economy may be the fund for Kim Jong-un's family's imports of luxury goods, gifts on various anniversaries, and the cost of special construction. The UN resolution against North Korea, which was intensively adopted in 2016 and 2017, had been strengthened to undermine North Korean economy. Whenever a new sanction was adopted, it was said to be "the strongest ever". The North Korean economy has no choice but is being forced to face a serious disaster by a series of sanctions. The resolutions were adopted every time whenever a North Korean nuclear test or a heavy-ballistic missile test was conducted. With the tightening of the network, North Korea began to use its strategy to demand the lifting of the sanctions, which would solve the economic crisis rather than the security concerns as the cost of denuclearization in negotiations with the United States. The UN sanctions have seriously hurt Pyongyang's leadership much more than the strategic assets of US air forces taking off from Guam. The pre-2016 sanctions were "direct sanctions" to block procurement of parts needed for nuclear and missile development. Since the fourth nuclear test, however, Resolution 2270 has focused on "indirect sanctions" in a way that puts pressure on the economy by blocking cash imports. The effect has begun to emerge from indirect sanctions that block funds from many sources. The Hanoi talks have paradoxically shown that the consequences of indirect sanctions are tough. In fact, at the previous North Korea–US talks, North Korea had to overcome concerns about withdrawal of US forces from the US through the declaration of the end of the Korean War and the peace regime. The fact that the fundamentals of the North Korean economy are being shaken has been confirmed in domestic and overseas research reports and defectors' testimonies. The output of coal, which is the main product of the North Korean economy, is decreasing as the expression "water comes up in the coal mine." Although North Korea is struggling to turn the coal for export into an internal electric power plant due to the shortage of its exports by sanctions on North Korea, the local price of coal in North Korea is only one-tenth of the exports price, and therefore, the coal mine job of workers is disappearing. Steel production, which is promoted by North Korea as "industrial rice", has also been hampered by the discontinuation of Chinese coke imports. As imports of apparel and fishery products, which are subject to UN sanctions against North Korea, are also stopped, the transport industry and related wholesalers result in serious damages.

The Korea Development Institute (KDI) assessed in *North Korean Economic Review* published in February 2019 that North Korean economy has shrunk enough to say that trade with China has collapsed due to strengthened sanctions against North Korea. North Korea's trade volume, which reached US$6.36 billion in 2014, dropped to US$2.44 billion in 2018. In a report released by the Korea Institute for International Economic Policy in February 2019, the real negative effects of UN sanctions against North Korea were 35%, 35% and 30%, respectively, in the trade, foreign exchange and market sectors. North Korea's economic growth in 2017, when sanctions were fully implemented, fell 3.5% compared to the year 2016 when sanctions were limited. The economic growth rate of 2018 officially announced by the Bank of Korea in June 2019 may be expected to be negative 5% compared to 2017. In conclusion, it is a diagnosis that North Korea's economy is staggering with full sanctions.

Iranian economy sinks due to "secondary boycott" sanctions

Iran has bitterly experienced the typical ripple effects of US economic sanctions. The economic sanctions against Iran over the past 13 years have completely ruined Iran's economy, which consists the fourth largest oil reserves and the second largest gas reserves. The enormous amount of energy buried in the underground was also useless because it could not be exported. Iran is facing sanctions again after President Trump declared the Iranian nuclear agreement is incomplete. Iranian President Hassan Rouhani stressed in a ceremony marking the 40th anniversary of the revolution in Tehran Azadi Square on February 11, 2019 that America is a public enemy. Iranian people are suffering from economic difficulties and surely will overcome them by their solidarity. The Iranian nuclear talks, which the Obama administration has signed with Britain, China, France, Germany and Russia in 2015, have been destroyed since the Trump administration began. As sanctions are restored, the Tehran economy is blowing cold again. Iran is busy trying to find a new way out of the United States that withdraws from the Iranian nuclear agreement (Joint Comprehensive Plan of Action/JCPOA) and restores sanctions. However, the Trump government is increasing the pressure on Iran even after the sanctions are restored. The UN Security Council sanctions against Iran that enriched uranium for nuclear development and reprocessed nuclear materials dates back to Resolution 1696 adopted in 2006. It had since been adopted seven times until Resolution 2049 in 2012. The US Congress passed the "comprehensive sanctions law" in 2010, mandating that all countries dealing with Iran be punished with economic retaliation. What is noteworthy in the US sanctions against North Korea is the secondary boycott. According to the secondary boycott, the United States may sanction individuals, corporations, and financial institutions of third countries that deal with the sanctionee by freezing or depriving the third party's assets or rights in the United States. Third countries cannot rashly participate in trade. The key to sanctions against Iran has been the blockade of oil exports, the lifeline of Iranian economy. Because of the second-party sanctions, Iran's oil exports to four countries, China, India, Japan and South Korea, became difficult. The Obama administration's exports of crude oil have been eased, but the Trump administration has made it difficult to export even a small amount. After a total of 12 years of economic sanctions, the Iranian government signed a denuclearization agreement in 2015. However, President Trump has restored Iranian sanctions by accepting the request of Jewish son-in law Jared Kushner, who said the Iranian nuclear negotiations were incomplete. In November 2019, the US Treasury Department imposed sanctions on two Iranian electronic wallet accounts that helped

Iranian hackers to exchange their criminal interests in virtual currencies for Iranian rial. Brian Hook, the US State Department's special envoy for policy, said in an interview with NHK in early Japan in early 2019 that he would not extend the sanctions exemption of oil exports that was temporarily applied to eight countries, including South Korea and Japan. Now it is time for North Korea to choose whether to confront the full range of sanctions or to accept a big deal of US final, fully verified denuclearization (FFVD). Implicit cooperation of China is essential for North Korea's economic strategy of "Muddle through" scenario while facing international sanctions by means of military provocation such as restoring missile base in Dong Chang-ri.

Specific economic relationship between North Korea and China

A smuggling trade between North Korea and China is a loophole of sanctions against North Korea. This author visits the Dandong City, China at least once a year and attempt to identify the specific economic relationship between North Korea and China. Despite President Trump's sanctions against North Korea, the relationship between the two countries has been completely normalized, due to three summits between Kim Jong-un and Xi Jinping, which began in 2018. Dandong, a border city between North Korea and China, connects Sinuiju in North Korea and various forms of trade take place. Eight-ton trucks loaded much freight with plate of North Korea's "North Pyongan" pass through Dandong Customs and enter the Sinuiju via Friendship Bridge in the Yalu River. The cargoes are covered with plastic, so it is difficult for outsiders to recognize what products are on the trucks. But it is easy to see from North Korean sources in Dandong that restricted items such as refined oil are shipped. It is an open secret that a large Chinese dump truck goes to North Korea carrying iron ore and rare earths. It is a violation of UN Security Council Resolution 2371. The marine products that are prohibited in UN sanctions were also carried out by "ship-to-ship exchange method", in which vessels contact each other at sea. This author's acquaintance whom he met at Dandong in October 2018, replied by quoting a Chinese proverb and refuted his claim that some of the trade between China and North Korea have violated UN resolutions. "If the policy is settled at the upper level, the ordinary people will come up with measures." It means that the ordinary people cannot guarantee their survival if they follow the policy decided by the upper level in a big country like China. There are reportedly more than 10,000 people involved in the trade between North Korea and China, and they argue that it is necessary to survive by avoiding sanctions rather than starving to death without trade.

Since the Joseon Dynasty of Korea (1392–1910), Dandong and Sinuiju were the single economic zones coexisting in the Yalu River. Now Dandong is developing into the top 10 port cities in China, but from the 1950s to the 1960s, it survived by relying on Sinuiju's economic support and trade. In the era of China's upheaval such as the Great Movement of the People (1958–1960), the cooperative farm system, the People's Government System and the Cultural Revolution (1966–1976), Dandong people were dependent on Sinuiju's materials trade and support. It is hard for Chinese authorities to openly violate various sanctions because of the secondary boycott provision. Despite the three summit talks between North and South Korea, in the wake of the US–China trade war, President Xi would not make a decision that would make Trump's North Korean policy uncomfortable.

Kim Jong-un has the strategy of withstanding US maximum pressure in the long term

With the Hanoi talks, the United States clearly understood the Achilles' heel of the North Korean regime. It is not easy for Trump to have a bad deal in order to break through the domestic politics, which has been disgusted by the hearing of a 10-year family lawyer, Michael Cohen. The United States would have considered that the real reason North Korea came to the denuclearization talks is because of sanctions. There is now a consensus among the ruling and opposition parties in Washington that the United States has no means other than sanctions to carry out the full real denuclearization of North

Korea. Thus, President Trump will be severely limited in his attempts to utilize the North Korean problem as part of his campaign for re-election in November 2020. In the end, Pyongyang's negotiating tactic that makes use of Trump's political intention, whereby the issue of North Korea may be one of the hot topics of the re-election campaign, should be revised in the future.

If North Korea recognizes that there is a mainstream like President Trump in the United States, while also acknowledging other versions of political power, it will be a worthwhile achievement of the Hanoi talks. Instead, the staff of the North Korean Foreign Ministry misjudged the decision structure of the US leader and submitted a false report to Kim Jong-un. In some parts of South Korea, there is an allegation that US should negotiate with North Korea again under the "snapback" measures, which will resume sanctions immediately when the country does not denuclearize after the relaxation of sanctions. However, the two countries have tried to make a big deal in top-down style, but they have failed. It is difficult to avoid the accusation that the snapback neglects the fact that both sides are sharply confronted with the scope of mitigation and denuclearization. North Korea's negotiating strategy to lift sanctions with only Yongbyon nuclear facilities, which is only half of the total North Korean nuclear weapons, should be reorganized, including plans to dismantle other areas such as Gangsun. Kim Jong-un returned to Pyongyang after a 130-hour round-trip train journey and announced a related message of self-reliant economic policy in the Labor Party's propaganda. The *Rodong Newspaper* unusually reported the unexpected "no deal" result of Hanoi Summit and announced the strategy for the mid-to-long-term self-independent survival.

Following China, Russia is a country that Korea has requested to cooperate in solving the economic difficulties. North Korea asked Russia to grant 100,000 tons of flour in January 2019, and Russia agreed to provide 50,000 tons of flour to North Korea. Kim Jong-un recently ordered the Ministry of Foreign Affairs to send documents to international organizations that North Korea's food situation is seriously difficult. Chairman Kim Jong-un visited Russia for the first time in April 2019 and held a bilateral summit with President Putin, suggesting various kind of cooperation. First of all, Kim Jong-un explained that the core reason for the breakdown of the Hanoi negotiations was due to unreasonable pressures from the United States and called for Russia to violate the UN Security Council sanctions on North Korea. The North Korean foreign ministry considers that they can nullify UN sanctions if Russia incrementally violates UN sanctions. North Korea will focus on resolving the serious economic difficulties through close economic cooperation with Russia. For example, it is expected that North Korea's coal will be converted into Russian production, which will promote illegal transshipment on the high seas.

There are three scenarios for the North Korean economy in the future

First is the "Optimistic forecast" scenario. The sanctions are strong enough that it was the key agenda of the summit between the United States and North Korea, but not enough to disrupt the North Korean regime. North Korea has already accumulated know-how to overcome the worst economic crisis through the hardships during 1995 to 1998. In particular, know-how to endure international sanctions may be at its top level. The North Korean economy has been emphasizing self-reliance as an isolated "island economy" in the style of Robinson Crusoe, similar to a remote regime unlike Cuba or Vietnam in the past. However, in the cases of Cuba and Vietnam, they could not endure sanctions. Unlike Iran, Cuba, and Vietnam, which had been fully subject to US sanctions in the past, North Korea's reliance on foreign trade is so low. Therefore, it is unlikely that the North Korean regime will make positive political decisions such as reforms and openings or denuclearization scenarios due to UN sanctions. In particular, inflation, like Venezuela, is unlikely to occur due to efficient control toward human and material resources. There is a high possibility that soaring price will be disappeared due to shrinking food rationing and black market surveillance. If UN sanctions continue for more than three years in

2019–2021, the fundamentals of the economy will be seriously shaken and the political unrest in the long term will spread.

The second is the "Muddle through" scenario. Although the UN is not a fatal blow to the North Korean economy, it cannot but be hit at all. It is inevitable that the economy will be shrinking due to the decline and discontinuation of various foreign exchange incomes and the negative growth will continue. However, the North Korean authorities are able to effectively manage the crisis by a thorough command economy. It is not impossible to improve the economy, albeit with slight contraction, by fine tuning economic policy. Therefore, although the North Korean economy is going down, it will moderately respond to the UN sanctions in the scenario of "Muddle through". It may be the most realistic scenario at present. However, it is necessary to perform dynamic analysis that changes its effect over time. The dynamic effect of the sanctions will depend on how long it will last in the future. If the sanctions last for three years and more, the "Muddle through" scenario will turn into a pessimistic scenario.

The last is the "Pessimistic bankrupt" scenario. As the mobilization economy, which collectively draws out the available human and material resources of North Korea, has become prolonged, it has encountered the limitations of supply. New economic sanctions that are different in quality from the past are being implemented, and as time goes by, the situation of North Korea's economy will become unbearable. Among the 11 UN Security Council sanctions, the five sanctions that North Korea asked to be lifted are quite aggressive sanctions that directly strike the North Korean economy. This is a serious economic implication that North Korea experiences for the first time since the establishment of the regime, and it will require considerable energy for the North Korean regime to respond the sanctions that were never experienced in the past. The US sanctions against Vietnam during the decade after the collapse of non-communist South Vietnam in 1975 and the sanctions against Iran over the subsequent three years since 2012 were so enough strong that they are estimated to be more threatening than military pressure. It is likely that North Korea will have to deal with economic bankruptcy before it worries about its regime security. In particular, if the UN sanctions will be tightened, and the monitoring of illegal shipment and smuggling be exhaustively checked, the North Korean economy may be stifled and the pessimism of the economic crisis will spread. US President Trump said, "North Korea is suffering extremely economically. No additional sanctions are needed at this time." His unusual expression means that the United States is confident of the effectiveness of sanctions against North Korea. Especially, if the sanctions continue for more than three years, the pessimistic scenario will gain strength. The pessimistic scenario is bound to be linked to the crisis of the North Korean regime.

Chapter 6

Denuclearization and Financial Issues

Nuclear disarmament is a joint work of human desire and financial aid

After the North Korea–US summit in Singapore on June 12, 2018, the high-level talk between US Secretary of State Mike Pompeo and North Korean counterpart Kim Yong-chol were held in Pyongyang. North Korea protested the US request by using the harsh expression "robber". North Korean authorities that expected a *nice* gift from the US could not accept a friendly meeting between North Korean leader Kim Jong-un and a US delegate who had arrived in Pyongyang in empty hands, as the calm reality. Pyongyang which expects to declare an official end to the Korean War, ease sanctions against them, and even want to get economic compensation has a long way to go with Washington which is continuously pressuring North Korea with CVID (complete, verifiable and irreversible denuclearization) wrapped in new word FFVD (final, fully verified denuclearization). Both sides expect to unilaterally receive nice gifts from each other rather than exchanging them. Especially, the US government has no comment on money issue such as the cost of repatriation of corpses of US soldiers died in North Korea during the Korean War. It might be enough to make Pyongyang feel uncomfortable. The ultimate solution to North Korea's denuclearization might be money. When Thae Yong-ho who is a former North Korean deputy ambassador to the United Kingdom contacted Israel under the direction of DPRK Ministry of Foreign Affairs in 1991, he described in his book *Password of the Third Floor Secretariat: A Memoir by Tae Young-ho* that North Korea demanded US$1 billion in response to the Arab countries' demand for the dismantlement of missiles. Regardless of whether it is true or not, North Korean nuclear weapons are a tool for guaranteeing the regime. On the other hand, however, it is possible to infer that the missiles might be a means to earn foreign currency. The costs of denuclearization can be divided into *initial, medium* and *late costs* based on stages and processes. Initial costs are the direct cost of dismantling nuclear facilities, weapons and intercontinental ballistic missile (ICBM) during the first stage of denuclearization. Medium-term costs are equivalent to *carrot* as an incentive in return to denuclearization. These costs will be used to construct light-water nuclear reactors for energy aid, provide heavy oil and switch jobs for North Korean nuclear physics scientists as denuclearization progresses more than 20%. The US has to put dollars in North Korea's wallets to let the soldiers put down their guns. Late stage costs include financial aid to live on or the reduction of government bonds. First of all, it takes a lot of money to dismantle rusted nuclear weapons, materials, and missiles which are means of transporting nuclear weapons.[106]

The subject of North Korean version of "Nunn–Lugar Program"

Former US Defense Secretary William Perry described in his book *My Journey at the Nuclear Brink* (2015) that the process of bridge between Congress and the administration to finance the removal of nuclear weapons left in new independent countries such as Ukraine after the Soviet Union was disbanded. Perry led the process of dismantling 80 ICBMs and 800 nuclear warheads.[107] For two years since 1994, Perry had visited a nuclear weapons base four times and had dismantled weapons in four stages. First, he removed nuclear warhead and pulled out fissile material. Second, he removed and disassembled missiles and used them as scrap metal. Third, he destroyed the hangar. Finally, he converted missile lot into agricultural land. Two years later, the missile base, which called for death, turned into a sunflower field that Ukrainian farmers considered it as a cash crop. The local farmers took pictures of sunflowers and sent them to Perry with a letter of appreciation, and Perry then returned to his professorship at Stanford University after finishing his ministerial job. Since then, the dismantlement of ICBMs by Kazakhstan and Belarus was really going well with the US financial support. The dismantlement of the Soviet Union's nuclear weapons and ICBMs was a special achievement combining the desire for human peace and the US financial support.

The Nunn–Lugar program, led by US senators Sam Nunn (Democratic Party) and Richard Lugar (Republican Party) in 1991, provided financial aid and equipment to former Soviet republics when they dismantled their nuclear weapons. The official name is CTR (Cooperative Threat Reduction). The US had prepared a US$1.6 billion government budget under this program to eliminate thousands of nuclear weapons in Russia, Ukraine and others. The cost of occupational training for scientists and related technicians was also included. A total of US$600 million was invested in Ukraine, including US$337.5 million in eliminating nuclear and nuclear materials, US$386.6 million in its nuclear control program, and US$263 million in converting nuclear forces into private jobs. The US spent US$180 million on converting some 4,500 Ukrainian nuclear scientists and engineers into private jobs. It would cost at least US$20 billion to dismantle at least 20 nuclear weapons in North Korea and to train 10,000 engineers and related personnel. US Congressman Nunn, who served as a dedicated coordinator between the administration and Congress in the process of procuring the denuclearization budget, made the following speech at Russian nuclear disarmament on October 18, 1996. "I've been in favor of buying missiles, bombers and submarines. That's because I thought they were all necessary for national defense. But the best I've ever agreed on was the budget that allowed us to work together to dismantle the weapons of mass destruction."

The North Korean version of the Nunn–Lugar program requires considerable funding. At the same time, President Donald Trump's attempt to induce Kim Jong-un to denuclearize should be backed by a hefty security. In order to realize a rose-tinted blueprint of Pyongyang, which Mike Pompeo presented to Kim Yong-chol who was a chief of North Korean United Front Department at the end of May 2018, minimum seed money will be necessary. During the banquet, the US State Department released a photo of Kim Yong-chol looking out the window, adding that the spectacular Manhattan skyline represented a bright future for North Korea. Pompeo's face looking at New York's skyline filled with the pride of their numerous and splendid landmarks. His expression seemed to imply that all kind of this could be North Korea's in case of successful denuclearization. New York's skyline will be a rosy future of Pyongyang, the most obvious carrot therapy for North Korea to carry out denuclearization. When this author visited Pyongyang in 2005, he observed Pyongyang's night view at a 45-story rotating observatory restaurant on the top floor of the Koryo Hotel. The night of Pyongyang was dark as he looked from the observation deck, which spins slowly once an hour. In response to this author's comments that the streets were dark at night, an official who works in North Korean Cabinet-affiliated organization responsible for private economic cooperation explained, "The lack of electricity production at Bukchang thermal power plant that supplies electricity to downtown Pyongyang." North Korean largest thermoelectric power plant "Bukchang thermal power plant" located in Bukchang County, North Pyongan Province, had a production capacity of 1.6 million kilowatts, but production was limited to 500,000 kilowatts due to faulty and old facilities. For North Korea, the night view of Manhattan in New York may be a tempting virtual reality vision. How to open up Western moneybags will be of the utmost interest to North Korea.

Consequences of "condominium alliance", one of the pragmatic alliance types

As Kim Jong-un already claimed, North Korea cannot afford to give up nuclear weapons without any financial consideration, as it has long tightened its economic belt and made nuclear weapons. At the summit with Trump, Kim Jong-un demanded complete security guarantees in return for denuclearization. Another request was economic aid to North Korea. The remaining demands were at the same time reduction of the joint South Korea–US military exercises and reducing US Armed Forces in South Korea. Pyongyang must find a survival way to feed itself. Nuclear weapons and ICBMs with enormous power have not directly solved a pledge to 25 million people on providing beef soup, silk clothing, and tile-roofed house, exactly the necessities of life. Through the third summit meeting between North Korea and China, Kim Jong-un was given no choice but to come up with a strategy to block China's participation in sanctions against the North, enjoying the economic benefits of denuclearization from the US. After meeting Kim Yong-chol at the White House in early June 2018, President Trump raised his voice on money issue like a casino businessman. "I think South Korea will do it," he told reporters, who asked about its stance on economic aid to North Korea, "To be honest, I think China and Japan will help North Korea too." At the same time, he reiterated, "I don't think the US will spend much money." In response, he cited physical distance for reasons of justification that the neighboring countries should support North Korea. "North Korea and the United States are thousands of miles away. But South Korea, China and Japan are neighboring countries of North Korea," Trump said like materialistic businessman and trader. Trump's unique statement on money means that the US government intends to divert much of its aid to North Korea into China, South Korea and Japan, which could lead to financial burdens. Trump bluntly expressed his position that the U.S. would not be the subject of North Korean version of "Nunn–Lugar Program". In fact, the US has been reluctant to inject money into the North Korean nuclear issue, rather than conventional thinking. In the 1994 Geneva agreement, the US imposed the financial ratio of 70%, 20% and 10% on Korea, Japan and the European Union (EU), respectively for the construction of a light-water reactor worth US$4.6 billion, which was the price for North Korean nuclear freeze. On the other hand, the US only sent 500,000 tons of heavy oil to North Korea each year. Trump's hidden intention as unconventional leader who prefers a pragmatic *condominium* alliance instead of a value-first alliance may be to save US funds in return for successfully achieving denuclearization. This is a logical consequence of a business leader who accumulated wealth in the real estate business. All the criteria for the US foreign policy are the mindset that begins with money and ends with money. He noted that even the North Atlantic Treaty Organization (NATO), which was in charge of European security after World War II, would collapse if its members do not bear the defense budget with 2% of gross domestic product (GDP). As far as money is concerned, it is a matter of vital interest to President Trump in North Korean denuclearization.

First financial backer for denuclearization is Inter-Korean Cooperation Fund

In this context, high-level officials in Trump administration are emphasizing private investment into North Korea rather than the aid from international organizations like the International Monetary Fund (IMF) and the Asian Development Bank (ADB). Secretary of State Pompeo recently said that in lieu of foreign aid, there will be investment, advancement and technical assistance to North Korea from the private sector. National Security Advisor John Bolton also noted that "if I were Kim, I would not seek economic assistance from the US." Instead of aid, Bolton proposed that North Korea to persuade US companies to do business or invest in the North. For example, Aurora Mineral Corp. in Colorado imported a magnetic site clinger from Dancheon City, North Hamgyong Province in 1990s. North Korea has a huge amount of the mineral. In particular,

Mike Pompeo made it clear that the US would not repeat the same mistake, noting that the previous administrations only helped develop nuclear weapons by providing huge amounts of money for food and energy aid to North Korea. After all, it reaffirmed its stance on continuing sanctions until denuclearization. But North Korea has consistently insisted that economic aid should precede or proceed at the denuclearization stage at the same time. It can be seen that the two sides will have a difficult time finding the financial solution in high- and working-level talks as well as summit meetings. In any case, the *decalcomania* that parallels North Korea's denuclearization, whether direct financial supports from South Korea, China, or Japan, or individual investment by US private companies, will be more significant than just easing sanctions against North Korea. Regardless, whether it is direct support from South Korea, China, Japan, or individual investment of US private companies, the *decalcomania* picture that can be combined with North Korea's denuclearization will be a kind of economic compensation or a brisk support that goes beyond simple lifting of sanctions. North Korea will use the noble phrase of peace on the Korean Peninsula as a step toward denuclearization, but in proportion, it will seek to profitably secure the source and route of the financial backer. Pyongyang will slow down denuclearization if the gain is not concretely seen in short time.

North Korean power elite's interest in money is as great as that of President Trump as enterpriser. It is easy to understand how many North Korean diplomats are bent on economic aid and compensation. When US$25 million was frozen in the Macau-based Banco Delta Asia Bank in 2005, North Korean diplomats including Kim Kye-gwan confessed that they were a nervous wreck. Sixty North Korean diplomatic missions around the world should report to Pyongyang's Foreign Ministry the results of earning foreign money from illegal deal and trade like smuggle and expediential business. The project to excavate US soldiers' remains included in the agreement in Singapore is one of the most attractive foreign currency earnings projects. The US Congressional Research Service (CRS) said in a report *Foreign Assistance to North* (released on May 26, 2005) that the US Department of Defense has provided North Korea with about US$28 million for compensation of corpse returning since 1993. The flow of total money for North Korea's economic aid and compensation for the denuclearization process can be distinguished after denuclearization. First of all, the first safe would be the South Korea's Inter-Korean Cooperation Fund. The Inter-Korean Cooperation Fund, which is a trustee of the Export-Import Bank of South Korea, was worth US$1.41 billion as of the first half of 2018. The fund was set up under the South–North Cooperation Fund Act, which was established in January 1990 with the aim of promoting inter-Korean exchanges and cooperation and recovering the national community. The government and the ruling party are considering a sharp increase in next year's budget, as North Korea's denuclearization is expected to sharply increase demand for funds. The implementation of the Panmunjom Declaration in April 2018, which is the key to inter-Korean exchanges and aid to North Korea, will require an increase in funds. The recent inter-Korean project to connect railways and roads also entails significant costs. Lee Sang-joon of the Korea Research Institute for Human Settlements predicted that the cost of linking railways would be at least US$3.6 billion from a maximum of US$39.8 billion. The maximum is the basis for building new facilities and the minimum is the cost of remodeling and repairing levels. In addition to social overhead capital such as ports and electricity, construction of agricultural-based fertilizer, agricultural chemicals, agricultural machinery, and other agricultural-related plants to solve food problems will increase costs exponentially. Including forestry cooperation and other environmental sectors requires astronomical budgets. The size of the Inter-Korean Cooperation Fund cannot handle the aforementioned initiatives, so the South Korean government and the ruling party stress the increase.

Lack of investment, not a shortage of money

At the request of the Unification Ministry of the South Korean government in 2003, this author conducted a study on the current status of the South–North Cooperation Fund and the efficient mid- to long-term operational direction. It proposed measures to raise inter-Korean cooperation funds that would increase demand in the future and investigated ways to operate them at the business level. However, it was not easy to come up with innovative measures. Due to the structure of the South Korean government's budget planning, which has a high proportion of the rigid budget like military and social welfare expenses, it was limited to raise the funds from the government. Therefore, the following measures were specifically considered: New Unification Purpose Tax through the enactment of the special act; the issue of long-term government bonds; tariffs on the profits of inter-Korean exchange and cooperation projects; investment in SOCs, such as roads, railroads, ports and power plants; 1% of the annual budget going to North Korea; overseas financing; International Consortium to Support North Korea and so on. Under the current law, North Korea is not subject to foreign economic cooperation funds. Therefore, it is necessary to revise the law in South Korea to support North Korea after denuclearization. None of the proposals is a magic trick for large-scale funding. It is difficult to come up with a landmark alternative to funding North Korea, which is uncertain about its future value. In particular, with the tax burden rate of the Korean economy rising, the increase of the quasi-taxable Inter-Korean Cooperation Fund will be inevitable for the public to resist taxes. In the end, the South Korean government should persuade the public that the Inter-Korean Cooperation Fund will reduce unification costs in the middle to long term.

If North Korea gets on the highway of denuclearization, the main source of funds for the North Korean economy will be the international community. A high-ranking official, who heads a financial group, claimed the following at the inter-Korean economic cooperation seminar. Many international financial institutions including South Korea lack investment destinations, not money. If an investment environment is created in North Korea, the capital transfer will be made quickly. The increase of ethnic Koreans appointed as high-ranking international organizations such as

World Bank President Kim Yong and Director of the Asian and Pacific Affairs Bureau of the International Monetary Fund Lee Chang-yong and the reduction of their role as investment banks of international financial institutions could be a driving force in creating a positive environment for international organizations to invest in North Korea. The first barrier to the current North Korean economy is the United Nations Security Council's sanctions. After North Korea's fourth nuclear test (January 2016), the UN adopted five sanctions resolutions. Financial sanctions were included in the 2270 (March 2016) and 2321 (November 2016) resolutions. The 2270 Resolution closed its overseas branches of foreign financial institutions and financial institutions in North Korea. The 2321 Resolution banned public and private financial aid to trade with North Korea. These constrained North Korean financial institutions. After North Korea's sixth nuclear test in September 2017, the UN adopted 2375 Resolution that prohibited the export of textile and clothes, and reduced 50% of the import of 4 million oil barrels in a year.

International financial organization's entry conditions: On-the-spot survey in Pyongyang

The next barrier is the designation of a state sponsor of terrorism. President Trump announced in November 2017 that he would re-designate North Korea as a state sponsor of terrorism. It had been nine years since the North had lifted its designation as a state sponsor of terrorism in 2008. He pointed out that North Korea had repeatedly supported international terrorism, including assassinations in overseas territories, in addition to its nuclear threats to the world. US law requires the US administration to unconditionally veto a terrorist sponsor's entry into an international financial institution. US and international financial institutions are banned from providing aid to North Korea as the country is designated as a sponsor of terrorism. IMF aid is also banned under the Bretton Woods Agreement Act. At the same time, international financial institutions are prohibited under the International Financial Organization

Act. In order for North Korea to receive funding from international financial institutions, the UN sanctions should be lifted, the country should be freed from the state sponsor of terrorism, and in principle be a member of international financial organization. The process of raising funds for North Korea from international organizations is divided into three stages. First is the post-engagement phase, second is the funding phase before joining the international institutions, and third is an establishment of a consortium for North Korea based on the assumption that it has no support from international organizations. The will of the North Korean authorities is crucial for the North to join the international financial organization. North Korea needs to join an international organization to receive economic aid, but the North has a political burden of disclosing its regime to the outside world including IMF's on-the-spot survey in Pyongyang. It suggests that North Korea has a lot of resources to overcome if it wants to join the international financial organization. Financial support is available even before joining the international financial organization, but this is an exception such as the Palestine case. Improving ties with the US and Japan is essential for North Korea to join the World Bank.

Even if North Korea step by step joins the World Bank after its denuclearization, it is possible to review loans worth US$1 billion to US$4.5 billion a year. North Korea officially applied for the membership of ADB for the first time in February 1997, but was rejected due to opposition from major shareholders the US (12.7%) and Japan (12.7%). After the first inter-Korean summit in June 2000, North Korea also applied for membership in September 2000, but was rejected because security problems such as missile issues were not resolved. The US has maintained that it is possible for North Korea to join international financial institutions only by resolving security threats and converting to a transparent economic system. US Assistant Secretary of State for Economic, Business and Agriculture Ellen Larson said in a luncheon address at the Korea–US 21st Century Committee held in Washington, D.C. on April 9, 2002, "In order for North Korea to join the Asian Development Bank, IMF membership must be made first." In March 2001, North Korean Vice Foreign

Minister Han Sung-yul visited the US with the North's economic mission and expressed intention to join the IMF and the International Bank for Reconstruction and Development (IBRD), but was rejected because conditions were not created. The US said that it would allow the World Bank or IMF to provide unofficial technical assistance to North Korea, such as economic education or training, but would not provide any more funding. Since funding of international financial institutions is limited in principle to member countries, it is practically impossible for North Korea, a non-member country, to receive such funds. However, there are exceptions to the application of trust funds to Palestine and Yugoslavia. These examples were based on the fact that it would be difficult to achieve the support of international financial institutions in a short period of time, and that it would be possible in a long period even if international financial institutions were agreed upon by major parties.

Assistance with emergency funds before joining the international financial organization

Vietnam joined the international financial organization in 1986 through the reform of Doi Moi, but the actual funding was not realized until 1993 due to various procedures. At that time, the US proposed a roadmap to normalize relations with Vietnam by setting up a temporary liaison mission in Hanoi (1992) and allowing international financial institutions such as the IMF and the World Bank through the lifting of partial embargo. In July 1993, the US allowed international financial institutions to resume their loans in Vietnam. Vietnam promoted the introduction of foreign capital under IMF support, pushed for the introduction of direct investment by Asian neighbors and improved the environment of foreign direct investment. These exceptions show that the IMF's conditions, such as foreign exchange reserves, are greatly mitigated in comparison with the provision of emergency funding prior to entry to the international financial institution. In this regard, North Korea has been very interested in international organization. Vietnam established diplomatic relations with the US, whom it fought against during the

Vietnam War, and in 1995 accommodated 120% of the requirements of repatriating the remains of US soldiers who died in the 16-year conflict. Partner relations with the World Bank have contributed greatly to the economic growth of Vietnam. As of March 2017, the World Bank provided US$22.5 billion in subsidies, credit and positive loans to Vietnam. After his visit to Pyongyang, Pompeo went to Vietnam on July 9 and said, "Vietnam's miracle could belong to Kim Jong-un."

One of the short-term measures before joining the international financial institution will be the North Korea Support Consortium, which is participated by the International Bank. While North Korea is seeking to join the international financial organization, the South Korean government can establish a "Trust Fund for Democratic People's Republic of Korea" in the World Bank, including the US, Japan and the EU. North Korea does not have to meet strict data submission requirements when joining the IMF. Transparency of support should be secured through a certain level of policy dialogue with representative organizations of consortiums. If North Korea's denuclearization progresses considerably, the "Special Trust Fund Consortium" can be reorganized as a World Bank-led consultative group. Multilateral support could reduce the political burden of both donor and recipient countries and also increase transparency and efficiency of support. In addition, the government can prevent the donor fatigue by simply supporting consumers' consumption, such as food aid, and start full-scale development aid. If North Korea carries out various international obligations along with its denuclearization and joins the international financial institution, it will be able to provide financial aid rapidly to the regime. If North Korea joins the international financial organization, it could consider providing the financial aid to the North such as the IMF's Poverty Reduction and Growth Facility, the special fund from the World Bank's International Development Association, and fund from the Asian Development Fund. Considering the level of North Korea's national income, the North is highly likely to be included in the recipient country. Depending on the progress of the denuclearization process, North Korea could be considered an important region for Northeast Asia's stability. As the Asian Infrastructure Investment Bank, which has been strongly promoted by Chinese President Xi, is concentrated mainly on Southeast Asian region, North Korea and China should have good relationship for investment in Pyongyang. In the short term, China and Japan can support the ODA (official development assistance), but the amount will not be large as North Korea expects.

The maximum price for denuclearization is US$200 billion for a decade?

If North Korea faithfully implements the reform program of the IMF and the World Bank after joining the international financial institution while pursuing denuclearization with sincerity, Pyongyang will be able to enjoy various economic benefits. It is possible to write off foreign debt using the Heavily Indebted Poor Countries (HIPC) Initiative and the Cologne Initiative, which are led by the IMF and the World Bank. As of 2017, North Korea's foreign debt was estimated to be around US$3.45 billion, more than half of which were lent by the Paris Club creditors including Russia. The US economic magazine *Fortune* and the UK's Capital Research Institute predicted that North Korea would submit a US$2 trillion bill for a decade in return for denuclearization. *Fortune* explained that the figure was calculated based on the economic level of the two Koreas based on the amount of money West Germany contributed to East Germany during the reunification process (US$1.2 trillion). *Fortune* noted that North Korea, unlike East Germany, was given no choice but to pay higher prices because it had nuclear weapons. And it was expected to accelerate with US inflation, interest rate hikes and weak global stocks. However, the outlook for *Fortune* was higher than the general estimation because it assumed unification of the Korean Peninsula. In May 2017, Hong Kong's weekly news magazine *Chengming* claimed that North Korea would stop developing nuclear weapons on the condition of receiving US$60 billion in unconditional aid from China, Japan, Russia and South Korea over the next 10 years. What these claims have in common is that it takes a lot of money along with North Korea's denuclearization process. In recent years, the Japanese government has been reacting swiftly to the changes of the political situation in Northeast Asia. Japan foreign ministry experts are drawing up a roadmap by proposing the "Strategic Map of the Korean Peninsula for the Construction of Greater Northeast Asia Co-Prosperity Sphere", which was established in the 1930s. 70% of the North Korea's basic infrastructure frame such as power plants, ports, railways, and roads was built during the Japanese occupation. Since the Singapore Summit, both North Korea and the US have been focusing on follow-up measures to implement denuclearization. Accurately quantifying and negotiating the economic compensation and denuclearization process may be in line with the nature of both money-obsessed leaders. Trump said on Twitter that he would expect Kim Jong-un to keep the contract signed by Singapore, but it seems empty thus far. Even two lovers who strongly love each other must above all buy a house and earn salary in order to get married and lead a life together. Despite the talks in Singapore, the future talks are likely to follow in the footsteps of the Congress of Vienna (1814) unless specific cash flow is secured.

Chapter 7

DPRK's Nuclear Weapon and Geopolitical Dynamics in East Asia

The 21st century is the era of Asia

The 21st century has been dubbed "the era of Asia". After centuries of domination by the West in the wake of the first Industrial Revolution, Asia will finally take center stage. The continent is the world's largest piece of land and home to 60% of the world's population. Gross domestic product in terms of purchasing power, which had been less than 20% in the 1980s, now hovers at 40%. Asia's contribution to the world economy is likely to grow bigger. In ancient Assyria, Asia meant "the eastern land of the rising sun". In the 21st century, the sun has set on the West and risen in Asia. But it is too early for Asians to call the 21st century theirs. The United States and Europe still command enormous economic, political and military power. Economic growth in Asia has slowed, and so-called Asian capitalism has failed to address income inequality, financial instability and worsening environmental problems. Cooperation among Asian economies is as essential as individual expansion in order to make Asia the center of the world. Asian governments are closely dependent, but they do not have a cooperative system. The region can hardly strengthen systematic cooperation because of its weak sense of unity and gap in economic and military power. Conflicts over historical and territorial issues are deep. There is no political mechanism that can iron out differences when sovereignty claims and common regional interests collide.

The Northeast Asian regional order has been undergoing a reconfiguration since the early-to-mid 1970s. From World War II to at least the middle of the 1970s, the regional order was broadly structured by Cold War bipolarity plus national economic systems heavily buffered from outside penetration. As bipolar tensions eased and global economic and financial pressures mounted, regional relations became far less certain as governments have maneuvered to reshape their regional relationships. Broadly speaking, the results have been (1) increased regional economic interdependence; (2) regionalized multilateralism; and (3) a reduced focus on regional military power projection. As a consequence of all three, the region has witnessed a blurring of prior dichotomies between "friends" and "foes". Of particular note, political relations among China, Japan and South Korea became broadly positive. With differing speeds and levels of enthusiasm, all three moved in the direction of global, regional and trilateral interdependence, a deepening of regional institutions, a tempering of nationalist bombast, and cooperation at the expense of contestation. Particularly emblematic of this cooperation was their trilateral compromise in forging the 2010 Chiang Mai Initiative Multilateralization (CMIM), the initiation in 2008 of an annual trilateral summit, the subsequent creation of a Trilateral Secretariat based in Seoul, and the signing in 2012 of a three-way agreement governing trilateral investments.[108] The region is moving to a post-hegemonic order that is increasingly defined by balance of power calculations and logics. Great power politics is returning. But there are constraints on how far the region will move to a more volatile setting in which security rivalry and Cold War geopolitics will rule.

The American-led order in East Asia provided the foundation for the cascade of political and economic transitions that have marked the region. But at the same time, these great transitions have served to transform — and undermine — America's old relationship with the region. If the old order in East Asia was "partially hegemonic", the emerging order in East Asia is more multi-polar and shaped by balance of power impulses. With the rise of China, the United States is no longer the only major great power in the region. The region is in transition to a new sort of order, although the specific features and organizing logic remain unclear. Indeed, the rise of China is perhaps the defining drama of East Asia and the global order. The extraordinary growth of the Chinese economy — and its active diplomacy and military buildup — is already transforming East Asia. Future decades will almost certainly see further increases in Chinese power and further expansion of its influence on the world stage. This is a power transition with far-reaching implications for America's strategic interests and global position.[109]

Major issues in East Asia: Cooperation and conflict

China's soaring current account surplus, the largest in the world, and its foreign assets, most of which are held as official foreign exchange reserves, have significantly boosted not only Beijing's domestic decision-making autonomy but also its power and influence in the realm of international politics. The latter is most visible in Beijing's fast-growing government-to-government lending (especially in Africa and Southeast and Central Asia) and its influence over China's growing investments abroad by state banks and official agencies, which are highly sensitive to political signals from the Communist Party of China (CPC).[110] China's financial power, like that of Japan in the 1980s, is tied to its emergence as a major creditor country — the most dramatic symbol of which has been China's foreign exchange reserves, which reached a record US$3.7 trillion in 2015 (approximately 43% of China's gross domestic product). China's influence in the international community has increased through its staggering growth. It has created a new regional lender, the Asian Infrastructure Investment Bank, and wants to connect China and the West through a new Silk Road under the One Belt, One Road initiative. The Chinese yuan has joined the International Monetary Fund basket of special drawing right to gain global reserve status along with the US dollar, euro, British pound and Japanese yen. Chinese scholars are busy pitching the merits of Chinese capitalism and its unique growth model. Not surprisingly, discussion of China's rise, especially among the American, South Korean and Japanese media, has been dominated in recent years by the theme of a newly assertive China — one that, as it grows economically and militarily more powerful, becomes more comfortable politically in revealing its "true colors". Explanations of China's new assertiveness have focused on both international structure and China's domestic politics. In terms of international structure, pundits claim that, in the wake of the 2008 financial crisis, Chinese leaders perceived a dramatic shift in the global balance of power.[111] The perceived decline of American power and onset of a more multi-polar world, so the argument goes, emboldened Chinese leaders to be "more confident in ignoring Deng Xiaoping's longtime axiom not to treat the United States as an adversary, and in challenging the United States on China's interests.[112] As its oil platforms drill in disputed waters of South China Sea, China no longer speaks the language of "quiet rise". Rather, Xi Jinping's self-assured foreign policy stimulates fear in Vietnam, South Korea, Japan, Taiwan, the Philippines, and the United States. Nationalism is on the rise in the Asia-Pacific region. It will engender discourses and practices within the rising Chinese challenger that works to undermine the legitimacy of the established order. This will be true whether China's rise continues or stalls. Japan's nationalist turn, like China's new assertiveness, will make peaceful compromise in Asia more difficult. Mounting nationalism will also promote internal balancing among Beijing's neighbors but will, along with other alliance handicaps, inhibit their ability and desire to align with each other against China.

After the 9/11 terrorist attacks, much US attention was focused on the Muslim world and wars in Iraq and Afghanistan. China is a rising power and the US is well served by re-investing in its relationships with Japan, South Korea and the Philippines and forging new partnerships with Vietnam, India and Myanmar. President Barack Obama announced that the US government gave military presence in the Asia-Pacific a top priority in his speech in the Australian

Parliament on November 17, 2011. This speech was perceived to be the announcement of "Pivot to Asia" policy. Early in 2012, the US Department of Defense published a report to name the new policy as "rebalance toward the Asia-Pacific region". In August of that year, Secretary of Defense Leon Panetta disclosed a plan to reinforce the military presence in the Pacific to turn "the current 50/50 split between the Atlantic and Pacific Oceans into a 60/40 split favoring the Pacific" by 2020. The US government reinforced forces in the western Pacific to support relationships with allies and partnership countries in the region. The US government justified the rebalance with a view that the US's "relationships with Asian allies and key partners are critical to the future stability and growth of the region." In this sense, the Asia pivot had produced some tangible results. Obama also got China to agree to begin cutting carbon emissions by 2030. In 2015, he ironed out a deal with China on cyber-attacks to establish some rules of the road in this new field of power competition. But despite the rebalance and "Pivot-to-Asia" policy, President Obama had yet to do much about the elephant in the room, even though Beijing had aggressively moved in the South China Sea to dredge up new islands and laid claim to the territorial waters of other US allies like the Philippines. Its neighbors feared that China was unilaterally staking claim to the waterways — an economic lifeline of the region. Obama's administration had encouraged the Philippines to work out the dispute over artificial islands with China on its own. The White House supported for the Philippines's legal suit at The Hague Tribunal in July 2015 against China's claims to the waterways it had claimed. The rebalance was a response to the complex situations that condition the US strategic position: financial restraints, end of the war in the Middle East, China's military build-up and the growing economic and financial influence of Asia.[113] Despite the rhetorical emphasis on the importance of the US interests in the Asia-Pacific and the reiterated commitment by US government leaders, skepticism is rising in the US due to financial insufficiency and domestic weariness of overseas war.[114] It is Japan who fills in the deficiency of US finance and national will to support American commitment with an expanded role as a US ally. The Japanese government has shown a stern position against Chinese expansion into the East China Sea during the conflict with China on the sovereignty over the Senkaku/ Diaoyu islets. The US government has supported the Japanese in the defense of the islets, while the Japanese are willing to invest their tax money in the defense of islands on which the US military bases are located.

The trends of new Cold War in Northeast Asia: China, Russia, North Korea versus US, Japan, South Korea

North Korea carried out its sixth nuclear test on September 3, 2017 and boasted of a weapon light and small enough to be mounted atop a ballistic missile, a nightmare scenario for Seoul and Washington, which has military bases in the Pacific and on its west coast within Pyongyang's striking range. The latest test produced a more powerful explosive yield than the North's previous detonations, indicating that the country was making progress in its efforts to build a functional nuclear warhead. It was North Korea's most powerful test ever. After the test, the North's nuclear weapons institute issued a statement saying that the test was successfully conducted for a final check on the explosive power and other characteristics of a "nuclear warhead that has been standardized to be able to be mounted on" its ballistic missiles. The North also argued that the standardization of the nuclear warhead would enable the DPRK to produce at will and a variety of smaller, lighter and diversified nuclear warheads of higher strike power. North Korea conducted its fourth nuclear test on January 6, 2016, which it claimed was the successful detonation of a hydrogen bomb. The North Koreans successfully put a satellite into space on February 7, 2016, even as diplomats were negotiating the Resolution 2270. The claim, if true, signified that the isolated regime in Pyongyang had made a major leap in its nuclear weapons capabilities. Pyongyang had conducted three nuclear tests in 2006, 2009 and 2013. The North drew international condemnation by conducting its fourth nuclear test in January 2016. That was followed by a rocket launch which was regarded by many experts as a disguise for a test of its long-range missile technology. After the United Nations Security Council resolution, in defiance of mounting pressure from the international community, North Korea's leader claimed his country had miniaturized nuclear warheads and warned of an "all-out offensive" and "pre-emptive" nuclear strikes against Seoul and Washington. North Korean leader Kim Jong-un vowed a nuclear test "in a short time" as well as tests of several kinds of ballistic rockets capable of carrying nuclear warheads. Kim Jong-un allegedly led a test of a new technology that would allow a ballistic missile armed with a warhead to re-enter the earth's atmosphere, according to North Korea's state-run Korean Central News Agency.[115]

The communist neighbor's back-to-back provocations roiled the security conditions in Northeast Asia, a major spot for rivalry and cooperation between the United States and China. The North's provocations have also complicated South Korean government's diplomacy. It has especially driven a wedge between Seoul and Beijing, upending much of what former South Korean President Park Geun-hye did during 2012 to 2015. President Park Geun-hye attended China's key war anniversary event on September 3, 2016, demonstrating her resolve to build a bilateral strategic partnership. The US action of rebalance revealed a concrete feature when the strategic weapons of the US forces showed up in front of the North Korean military machines that enhanced the threat level tremendously in September 2016. The US and South Korean military leaders perceived the North Korean threat was more powerful than the previous atomic bombs. The mobilization of US strategic weapons was an action of strategic deterrence against the nuclear threat from the North. Rebalance toward the Asia-Pacific region is the US military arm penetrating the Regional Security Complex in the East Asian region. The US power is being projected to the East Asian region from the western Pacific. It is basically a maritime power conceptualizing an air-sea battle. The confrontation between North Korean and the US–South Korean forces on nuclear weapons test led to the deepening of Chinese intervention into the security dilemma on the Korean Peninsula.

US and South Korea versus China: THAAD deployment in Korean Peninsula

China has kept its balance between the two Koreas for the peace and stability on the Korean Peninsula. China is becoming a constituent part of the Regional Security Community (RSC) on and around the Korean Peninsula. One cannot think of a solution to the security problems on and around the Korean Peninsula without considering the constructive role of the Chinese government. The United States is a superpower maintaining predominance over both the Atlantic and the Pacific. The US as a superpower is interested in the building and reinforcing of the global order. The global order of the US is a liberal one based on the rule of law and multilateral institutions that support the freedom of navigation, commerce, protection of human rights and nuclear non-proliferation. The North Koreans invited the enhanced penetration of US power into the East Asian region through their violent challenge to the principle of nuclear non-proliferation. They have developed atomic bombs with delivery systems and were actually applying those weapons of mass destruction (WMDs) to threaten South Korea. Realist theorists interpret the US rebalance as pained and inevitable act of the US balancing against the rise of China. According to the theory of Professor John Mearsheimer, the US had grown into a superpower by achieving predominance over the American continent. He explained that a superpower does not want to see another great power growing into a competitive superpower. Thus the US strategic interest lies in the prevention of China from gaining predominance over the East Asian continent. The US needs to help the related countries to join in the Asian continent balance against China rather than bandwagon with it. The US penetration into the East Asian RSC is more than welcome to South Koreans. South Korea depends on the US's extended deterrence against the North Korean nuclear threat. It is China's strategic interest that has been hurt by the enhanced intervention of the US forces into the East Asian region, induced by the North Korean nuclear threat.

But the South Korean government made it clear that making a decision on whether to deploy a Terminal High Altitude Area Defense (THAAD) battery to the peninsula is Seoul's sovereign right, referring to objections regarding the issue voiced by China.[116] Even though Seoul argued that the decision would be made in accordance with national security and interests, and not due to other conditions, the complicated stance has been subtle. The remark was construed as downplaying speculation that Seoul and Washington provoked the THAAD issue to pressure China to join hands with them on producing harsher sanctions against Pyongyang, if Beijing does not want a THAAD battery to be placed on Korean soil. South Korea's basic position has been that the THAAD issue is not directly linked with Beijing's participation in the UN Security Council sanctions. China has been opposed to the THAAD deployment on the peninsula out of concerns that its radar could snoop on the country's military activities. The Obama administration's decision to deploy an advanced missile defensive system in South Korea also gave President Xi of China less incentive to cooperate with Washington on a North Korea strategy that could aim, for example, to freeze the North's nuclear capacity. China has strongly opposed to North Korea's nuclear weapons but at the same time opposed the missile defense system in South Korea. Beijing interpreted the THAAD deployment as another American effort to contain China. Even though President Obama said after meeting with Xi in Hangzhou, China in 2016 that the deployment did not target for China, China's officials argued that the THAAD radar could detect Chinese missiles on the mainland under its nuclear undermining. Despite tensions over North Korea's nuclear and missile tests, American scholars considered the issue less important than Middle Eastern problems, a rising China, tensions with Russia and even climate change, a survey showed on February 23, 2016.[117] The survey reflected widespread perceptions that North Korea stood low on the US priority list and that the administration of President Obama had little appetite for tackling the problem as it had been preoccupied with Middle Eastern issues, such as Iran's nuclear program and the militant group Islamic State. The United States would not engage in talks with North Korea if the discussions were not focused on denuclearization. Despite US's efforts and personal ties with President Xi, China had been lukewarm toward imposing painful new sanctions on the North in the initial stage after the nuclear test. Beijing had emphasized the need for dialogue as well instead of a sanctions-only approach. In order to actively deter and respond to North Korea's nuclear, weapons of mass destruction and missile threats, the US and South Korea agreed to utilize efforts in every category including South Korea's conventional capabilities and the US's extended deterrence. Both countries agreed the deployment of the US-led THAAD system in South Korea. China and Russia were fiercely opposed to South Korea's move to bring the US THAAD advanced missile defense system to the peninsula. During a Reuters interview, Chinese Foreign Minister Wang Yi criticized South Korea and the US for threatening its national security interests. Wang maintained that the coverage of the THAAD missile defense system, especially the monitoring scope of its X-Band radar, would go far beyond the defense needs of the Korean Peninsula. He also argued that by reaching deep into the hinterland of Asia, the THAAD deployment would not only directly damage China's strategic security interests, but also harm the security interests of other countries across the region. Concerns were growing over the fallout from the strain in the Seoul–Beijing relationship. After the fourth test of nuclear weapons in January 2016, Chinese Ambassador Qiu Guohong said the resolution was "paving a stone for political settlement of the nuclear issue on the Korean Peninsula, signaling a desire for a return to dialogue." Even if a UN Security Council resolution was adopted to punish the North, chances were slim that it would move toward denuclearization.

US versus China and North Korea: Peace agreement

The US had reportedly agreed to hold peace treaty talks with Pyongyang on condition that the discussion would deal with denuclearization before the Singapore Summit 2018. However, Washington insisted that denuclearization shall remain the focus of any talks, and made clear that a denuclearized peninsula will be an overriding priority. It was not clear that the US would not engage in concerted discussions with North Korea that did not place an emphasis on denuclearization. *The Wall Street Journal* report said that the US had conditionally agreed to accept the North's offer to hold peace treaty talks, just days before the North's nuclear test, but Pyongyang rejected the counter-proposal and went ahead with the fourth test on the January 6, 2016. The strategy was also shared by other partners of the six-party talks, including South Korea and Japan — partners of an ironclad alliance. The US has been consistently telling Pyongyang that it remains open to authentic and credible negotiations based on the agreement reached with all members of the six-party talks in September 2005.[118] It is not new that North Korea wants a peace treaty with the US to formally end the Korean War. DPRK for the first time proposed the initiative in 1974. Pyongyang had continued to iterate the argument. The consistent proposal was officially included in the September Agreement of 2005. Pyongyang pressed the demand harder after Foreign Minister Ri Su-yong made the demand during a speech at the UN General Assembly in October 2015. The US had said the demand was a nonstarter with the North pursuing nuclear ambitions. US officials had stressed that the communist regime had gotten the order wrong and should first focus on negotiations to end its nuclear program.

Territorial disputes are categorized into dominion territorial disputes and boundary or border disputes as well as "continent territorial disputes" and "sea territorial disputes". Here, dominion dispute refers to a dispute regarding a political decision related to the jurisdiction over and allocation of a territory. The territorial disputes of Northeast Asia acutely arose in sea territories rather than in inland territories after 1994, when the UN Convention on the Law of the Sea took effect. In other words, the territorial disputes between countries within the regions of this zone generally display the characteristics of disputes regarding dominion over islands, which affect the "maritime boundaries" in the surrounding regions and the dispute related to "dominion" itself as well as the disputes of other countries in other regions of the world.[119] The representative marine dominion dispute cases include the Kuril

Islands (Japan's northern territory) dispute, the China–Japan Diaoyu/Senkaku Island dispute, the East China Sea dispute, and the South China Sea dispute between China and some Southeast Asian countries.[120]

Since 2010, the Chinese government has been increasingly willing to follow popular nationalist calls to confront Western powers and adopt tougher measures in maritime territorial disputes with its neighbors. Thus, in November 2013, China unilaterally declared an Air Defense Identification Zone (ADIZ) over an area of the East China Sea that covers the Senkakus, the uninhabited islands administered by Japan but claimed by China, where they are also called Diaoyu. This move drew sharp criticism from both Tokyo and Washington. China was "attempting to alter the status quo by coercive measures," including "dangerous acts that could cause unintended consequences," said the Japan's Ministry of Defense in its annual defense White Paper released on August 5, 2014. The report went on to express concern that China's rapidly expanding maritime and airspace activities around the Senkaku Islands were ratcheting up tensions in the East China Sea that could trigger an unwanted clash. Similarly, China's sovereignty spats in the South China Sea with several Southeast Asian states came to a head in a prolonged naval standoff with the Philippines over the Scarborough Shoal (Huangyan Island). Tensions with Vietnam — another disputant to China's claims over South China Sea islands — also remain high. In 2014, China and Vietnam engaged in a two-and-a-half-month standoff over the Chinese rig known as HD 981, managed by the China National Petroleum Corporation and owned by the state-run China Offshore Oil Corporation, which was drilling in waters Vietnam claimed as its exclusive economic zone. Emboldened by Vietnam's inability to block HD 981, Beijing announced in July 2014 that it would place four more rigs in the South China Sea. The standoff over the rig was especially significant because it showed a high degree of interagency coordination among China's civilian maritime agencies, the People's Liberation Army, and the oil companies. Most important, it suggested that Chinese President Xi was quickly consolidating his power and is now aggressively pushing China's maritime claims.

Current situation and prospects of multilateral security cooperation mechanism in Northeast Asia

In discussions concerning the establishment of a regional security regime in the Asia-Pacific region, the Organization for Security and Cooperation in Europe (OSCE) is often referred to for comparison. In this regard, reviewing the initial conditions of the so-called Helsinki Process gives us some insights into establishing a similar mechanism in this region. Major factors that developed a security cooperation organization in Europe include a stable power structure, hegemonic leadership, solidarity displayed by neighboring countries, sharing of common values, and congruence of interests of the member states.[121] In other words, it becomes easier to reach a compromise acceptable to the states concerned if the level of tension between them is lower, the regional hegemony exerts strong leadership, states share common values, and states pursue mutual interests. The existence of a stable power balance between the East and the West and Europe's anti-war movement after the World War II facilitated discussions on comprehensive security issues. European countries displayed path dependency associated with continuance in a series of OSCE negotiations, which began with an informal meeting in 1972. They reached a decisive moment of concluding the Helsinki Accords in 1975 and accomplished the process of institutionalization at the Paris Conference in 1990. Still, efforts to adopt a European-style concept of security cooperation in Asia have not gone very far, as evidenced in the unsuccessful attempts to call for a "Pacific Ocean Conference along the lines of the Helsinki Conference" in 1986 and a proposal for Security Cooperation in Asia in 1990. Clearly, the Asia-Pacific region has not experienced the spillover effect of cooperation in non-military sectors spreading to military sectors. In reality, the ASEAN Regional Forum (ARF) remains at the level of discussion when it comes to addressing issues of common interests, as the multinational forum has not displayed concrete results in the settlement of problems. The registration of conventional weapons possessed by each country and the submission of annual reports, which were taken as part of trust building measures, are merely rudimentary measures. It is difficult to develop such a low level of institutionalization to a security regime in Europe without overcoming the following limitations. First, countries in the Asia-Pacific tend to avoid discussing sensitive security issues, such as those related to Taiwan, the Korean Peninsula, and the territorial disputes over the South China Sea. Second, they shuffle off responsibilities for the establishment of a cooperative security mechanism to other bilateral meetings or higher-level regional meetings. Third, they are divided over what types of institution should be developed. It should be pointed out that, in a situation like this, regional dialogue for the establishment of a security regime is likely to end up as nothing more than a cocktail party. It remains to be seen whether making practices of continuing multilateral dialogues is indeed a useful means of deterring threats and coping positively with real threats.[122]

Trilateral deterioration in the face of competing nationalism

Almost certainly, the United States and China will struggle and compete for leadership within East Asia. The region will become more decentralized and complex. Therefore, a straightforward hegemonic order or a traditional balance of power system will not be easily established through simple negotiation between two countries in the near future. The area will retain and evolve aspects of both hegemony and balance.[123] A cold peace will likely simmer within the region but not reach a boiling point. Outside the remote possibility of land warfare on the Korean Peninsula, East Asia's maritime geography encourages naval competition but militates against land invasions and occupations. Because of what Chicago University Professor John Mearsheimer called the "stopping power of water" and the fact that East Asia is a seascape, where "the spaces between the principal nodes of population are overwhelmingly maritime," the region will avoid the kind of great military conflagrations that took place on dry land in the 20th century even as nationalism continues to fuel tensions and disorder. In this leaderless but contested region of the world, threats are much more likely to be hot; danger will come frequently in the form of shooting wars among the regional powers over disputed islands more than diffuse disagreements over geopolitical, monetary, trade, and environmental issues. Problems and crises will arise more frequently and, whenever the United States and China try to take initiative away with territorial issues, will be resolved less cooperatively. Let us summarize the recent and future characteristics of geodynamics in Northeast Asia. First, Northeast Asia is forging a new regional order, the major parameters of which are still being worked out. Nevertheless, the previous order shaping interactions until the end of the 1980s or the beginning of the 1990s had disappeared. China and the US, for example, have become "frenemies (friend plus enemy)" on a range of global and regional security matters while becoming deeply interdependent economically. Economic and institutional linkages among Japan, China and South Korea have deepened. Meanwhile, within both Japan and the ROK, their respective alliances with the United States are undergoing reexamination; even as they are re-embraced they show enhanced complexity and greater independence for the previously junior partners. Second, external shifts in geopolitics and geo-economics have opened up political space within the domestic political economies of Northeast Asia for a rethinking and reconfiguring of security and economic policies. Third, however, in the past several years, a wave of competing nationalisms has derailed what had previously been a herky-jerky but nonetheless clear-cut trend toward greater trilateral cooperation. As was noted earlier, nationalism has deep roots in all three countries and hostility toward Japan has ebbed between latent and inflammatory in South Korea and China for decades. And within Japan, a burgeoning and introspective nationalism has been evident since the bursting of the economic bubble in 1990–91. Finally, Northeast Asia is gradually gripped by the perspective of a new Cold War connected with the uncertainty of Trump's diplomacy.

The approaching path of Northeast Asia will become more complicated, comparing to the pattern and characteristics of the old Cold War during 1950–80. The inauguration of the new US government has contributed to the unpredictability in East Asia. Whether or not Trump has followed through on his campaign pledges to diminish or possibly abandon American commitments to security alliances such as the North Atlantic Treaty Organization (NATO), Japan, and South Korea, his election victory forces nations around the world to begin preparing for the day they can no longer count on the American-backed order. That uncertainty puts pressure on allies and adversaries alike to position them, before Trump even took office, for a world that could be on the verge of losing one of its longest-standing pillars of stability. Allies in Europe or Asia, suddenly considering the prospect of facing a hostile power alone, cannot wait to see whether Trump means what he says, Professor James Goldgeier said, adding that they "will have to start making alternate plans now."[124] Trump's election came at a moment when rising powers were already pushing against the American-led order: China in Asia, Iran in the Middle East, and particularly Vladimir Putin's Russia in Europe. Those powers will be tempted to test their new limits. Prime Minister Shinzo Abe, who had been planning to meet Hillary Clinton in Washington in February 2016, tried to calm his country, as the yen surged and stocks stumbled. "Hand in hand with Trump, we will try to work together," he said. On the campaign trail, Trump singled out Japan. He claimed that Tokyo was not paying its fair share to support United States military bases, calling into question the American commitment to defend Japan in case of attack. A rising China could put a check on Trump's stated ambitions in Asia. He will decrease the commitment to Pacific security issues. But if he carries out such a policy, China will be much more authoritative and aggressive in the Pacific. And then most of the alliance countries and security experts in Washington will be against Trump's policies. It is a little difficult for Trump to just change all the old policies. Then South Korean President Park Geun-hye instructed her government to coordinate closely with Trump's transition team to ensure that her country and the United States would maintain sanctions and pressure on North Korea to stop its nuclear weapons program. "North Korea should not misjudge the solidity of our alliance with the United States and our joint ability to respond to provocations," said a government spokesman.

Trump unsettled South Koreans when he said that he might withdraw American troops from their country unless Seoul paid more for their presence in 2018. He also indicated that he might let Japan and South Korea protect themselves with nuclear weapons and that he might negotiate directly with the North Korean leader, Kim Jong-un. Trump's surprisingly strong performance caught analysts off guard, but it was welcome news for those in South Korea with the belief that their country must build its own nuclear weapons to defend against North Korea. As America draws down its armed forces in East Asia, many strategists worry that the Pacific will not remain pacific for long. They fear that the resulting power vacuum could set off a scramble for security. But that does not have to happen, not if America's diplomatic engagement intensifies as its military presence is reduced. The countries of the region are a diverse, disputatious lot whose trade rivalries and territorial conflicts are now breaking out of their cold war confines. South and North Korea which fear each other and Japanese resurgence vie for China's favor. Japan had been thwarted by Russia's refusal to return four islands seized at the end of World War II, and Russia was also angered at Japan's demands for their return. Both countries may want to ally with China as well. Meanwhile, renewed Chinese assertiveness in the Spratly Islands raises fear from India to Australia. And the whole region is engaged in a frenzy of arms purchases. To allay the insecurities and cool the conflicts, many countries in the region want Washington to remain engaged. But that does not have to mean maintaining the US military presence at current levels. US troops on the Korean Peninsula can continue to be pulled back from the 38th parallel and further reduced as talks between the North and South progress. US carrier task forces are not needed to show the flag; Aegis cruisers will do. And Navy operating tempos can slow.

But high-level US diplomatic attention cannot afford to recede. A multilateral forum with regular meetings might assure America's active engagement. The US, Japan, China and Russia are already brokering a ceasefire in Cambodia and coaxing North Korea to give up its nuclear ambitions and they could be guarantors of a more permanent peace. But this nascent Concert of Asia may best be left to operate informally. It would also be premature to create an Asian analogue of the Conference on the Organization for Security and Cooperation in Europe. A more promising forum for now may be the Association of Southeast Asian Nations if all four powers and other Asian countries can be made full participants. Engagement has inevitably risks. Regional conflicts may require Washington to take sides. But American disengagement is far riskier. That could set off an arms competition and shifting alliances that, sooner or later, lead to war.

Chapter 8

Contingency and Determinants of Stabilization Strategy in North Korea

Concept of contingency in North Korea

Should the contingency of regime collapse occur in North Korea, power shifts on the Korean Peninsula and in Northeast Asia will be inevitable. Upheavals in the North Korean political system will have significant impact on a Korean society that has longed for reunification for the last 70 years or so. To ensure peace and stability on the Korean Peninsula in the event of a sudden change, it is essential to establish an executive stabilization strategy that effectively responds to a turbulent situation within North Korea in its early stages. Various aspects of this stabilization strategy, including the military, foreign affairs, and governmental administration, need to be addressed in order to increase the chances of success even in an extremely chaotic situation. To achieve the minimal level of stabilization necessary for the government to take effective control, it is essential to implement transitional military governance in the initial political vacuum. For the purpose of this study, the North Korean contingency is assumed to have no civilian alternative to fill the political vacuum after the collapse of Kim Jong-un regime because of the serious factors like economic disaster and uprisings of unsatisfied people.

Military rule may be necessary to provide urgent humanitarian assistance and facilitate a smooth transition to civilian government in circumstances in which state institutions cannot properly perform day-to-day functions.

First, there should be fundamental measures to shore up the governing authorities and maintain rule of law when it would be very difficult to expect social stability. The police forces may not be enough to effectively contain with a crisis situation like contingency. Securing social order is paramount, preceding other priorities. Second, military rule allows for more effective stabilization operations. Stabilization operations are efforts to restore order and stability when many essential political, economic, and human elements that are critical to general security are absent.[125] Stabilization operations should be executed in close coordination with public administration as it concerns the society at large. Third, there needs to be more comprehensive measures, such as state reconstruction. After a contingency in North Korea, many North Korean residents want to see the establishment of a new, democratic government rather than the continuation of an oppressive regime. As more fundamental changes are demanded, there will be limitations to the extent of fully utilizing existing state apparatuses. Moreover, there might emerge strong resistance from the stakeholders of the old regime, particularly when they can mobilize their own military force.

Accordingly, military rule should be considered as a viable option to ensure successful stabilization operations. The military rule will be transferred to civilian rule as soon as certain conditions such as reconstruction and establishing democratic principles are met. Therefore, it is critical to understand the factors that contribute to the success and failure of stabilization strategies undertaken by previous military governments. Granted, stabilization efforts have produced different outcomes depending on each country's political, social and economic contexts and circumstances. For a North Korean contingency, its political and societal particularities also should be considered when devising a strategy for its stabilization. It is important to identify the different determinants of stabilization according to various contexts and circumstances drawn from the analysis of previous stabilization strategies of military governance. This research aims to draw useful policy implications for the Republic of Korea's response to a North Korean contingency by conducting a comparative structural analysis of different military governments since World War II and identifying key factors that determined the successes and/or failures of their respective stabilization policies.

A review of existing literature reveals the following criteria for discussion: the characteristics of political change in Third World countries;[126] the causes and outcomes of failed states that are potentially applicable to North Korea;[127] reconstruction cases following American interventions;[128] the causes of failure in the stabilization of Iraq;[129] and circumstantial outlooks of North Korean contingency.[130] Accordingly, this study lists a variety of factors related to stabilization addressed in previous research, and describes particular features of these factors through causality analysis. This study further examines selected factors to investigate their significance. Also, the study conducts a comparative analysis of different cases to verify the major determinants of stabilization.[131] This analysis is limited to military governments, civil-military affairs, and stabilization strategies implemented in the reconstruction process of four cases: the military governments of Germany, Japan, and Korea after World War II and the Coalition Provisional Authority (CPA) in Iraq which was established after the fall of Saddam Hussein in 2003. Important factors in the stabilization of a country include the maintenance of public security, human security, economic and infrastructural development, rule and maintenance of order, and other societal relationships.[132] The collapse and preservation of the state system are determined by the political, economic and societal factors, international relationships, and political ideologies of a particular nation-state.[133] In the case of North Korea, contingency or "sudden change" is based on the theory of state system collapse whereby a socialist regime transforms into democratic one. In particular, the leadership of the head of state, underlying ideologies, and the centralized state organizations are keys to the preservation of the system.[134] If these mechanisms fail, the state's durability will suffer.[135]

The Iraq War is another example following the United States' shift toward reconstruction efforts over battlefield success. The military victory was not sufficient to secure war-torn Iraq as the political power vacuum quickly created chaos and instability across the nation. The aftermath of the Iraq War highlighted the importance of successful military rule and stabilization efforts.[136] This builds a strong case for the necessity of quick restoration of the North Korean government's day-to-day functions after the contingency. Accordingly, there should be reconstruction efforts in North Korea similar to what took place in post-war Germany and Japan. However, this article bases its findings on the assumption that the ROK government extends its governing authority in restored areas after North Korea contingency rather than the establishment of a new government in North Korea.

Various factors have affected military governments' stabilization strategies. Based on previous research on systemic collapse and stabilization, this study assumes that military governments produce better outcomes in stabilization efforts with a centralized power in place. Thus, it is also assumed that governments which historically have decreased in structural authority may encounter severe difficulties in stabilization efforts. Additionally, external intervention in national politics can be considered a control variable, not an outright causal factor, in the outcomes of stabilization. The following lists the four factors considered in this study, and how they are defined. First, the "political factor" specifically refers to the degree of concentration of political power. In particular, it indicates how much power and administration belong to a central government. Whether or not power belongs to this government is a major determining factor of stabilization. Second, the "economic factor" refers to the degree of economic stability that exists during the process of state system transformation. Third, the "race factor" indicates racial differences. The study compares US military occupiers and the occupied population by their racial differences, to see whether they coincide with each other. Finally, this study uses the "social factor", which specifically aims to verify the existence and degree of social divisions. The study divides military governments into two categories: one which emerged in the management of defeated countries and liberated colonial states after World War II, and the other which emerged in the 21st century. The cases of Germany, Japan, and Korea belong to the first group, while the case of Iraq, which occurred in 2003, corresponds to the second group. Although there exists a wide time gap between the two groups, the review of previous research on military governments in similar cases, which occurred in extremely fragmented and decentralized societies, revealed that there are some major factors that determine the impact of military governments on stabilization regardless of time periods.[137] Comparative political research seeks to determine universalities, but universal analyses can be limited by regional particularities. Moreover, the political behaviors of Iraq and North Korea are very different from those of democratic countries, though, granted, the political systems of those two countries also highly differ from each other. Nevertheless, the authors have determined that the conditions relevant to the aims of this study can be comparable.[138] In order to explain the unique characteristics of North Korea's state system and political changes in Middle East, this study aims to identify diverse factors that form the backgrounds of political phenomena.[139]

Comparison of stabilization strategies in action

Germany (1945–1949)

As Hitler took power under the banner of National Socialism, the features of a nationalism-based unitary state intensified in Germany.[140] By accusing the Jewish people of being the sources of social ills in fact created by the German defeat in World War I, Hitler maximized the level of social division.[141] One of the characteristics of a totalitarian political regime is a monopoly of power; all political power is concentrated in, and is distributed from, the center.[142] Occupation by the Allied Forces was designed to eliminate Nazism and militarism, and to prevent Germany from threatening world peace again. Thus, the American military occupation in Germany was not for the purpose of liberating Germany, but to rule a defeated enemy state. Furthermore, the Allied Forces intended to hold high-ranking Nazis accountable for war crimes committed during World War II.[143] The US forces defined the concept of military government as the highest authority that a military could exercise, and encompassed all activities of governing the population and properties in areas reclaimed from the occupation of enemy forces. They also stipulated that the process of occupation could be accomplished through either agreement or force, and that occupation did not mean that the sovereignty of the occupied government was entirely handed over to the occupying force, but rather that only the right to control was handed over temporarily.[144] Initially, the US military government in Germany was established in the context of a very hostile relationship. Because of the differing perspectives held within the Allied Forces and ongoing post-war conflicts, the military government in Germany experienced several difficulties. In particular, the confrontation between the West and the Soviet Union, and the extreme economic hardship in Germany created much friction between the occupying forces and the people of the occupied territories. For instance, in Soviet occupied areas, the functions of the military government were carried out under the guidance of the Soviet Union leadership.[145] Later, however, as the political situation of Germany changed (through the de-nazification movement) and conditions for democratization improved, the US military government gradually evolved into a system that supported the establishment of democratic government by the Germans. Germans had the capacity and will to operate a centralized state power. The country had traditions of democracy and elections while the political party system, well developed before 1933, could easily re-emerge after 1945. Their capacity and will for autonomy were critical factors in swiftly ending the US military government.

Japan (1945–1952)

The reformist forces that led the Meiji Restoration changed the state structure of Japan into a Western system. While demolishing social groups and establishing central government organizations, Japan switched to a modern system in which power concentrated in the state and its emperor.[146] The centrality of the Japanese government was accentuated during World War II as the characteristics of a wartime state system were incorporated.[147] Compared to pre-1933 Germany, the Japanese party system was less developed and the tradition of democracy was more limited. On August 14, 1945, through "The Imperial Rescript Ending the War", the Japanese emperor warned that it would be against his will for the people to stir up trouble or social division as a backlash of their defeat. He asked the Japanese people not to fall behind in the development of their state by focusing on reconstruction after the defeat.[148] Thanks to the emperor's uniquely revered status in Japanese society, his words were a tremendous boost to the US military officials as they began to organize a military government in Japan.[149] As the place of the Japanese emperor in the postwar political setting was secured, the normalization of the defeated country proceeded relatively smoothly.[150] The authority of the Supreme Commander of the Allied Powers (SCAP) was unparalleled in the Japanese land. The Japanese government functioned under the governing authority of SCAP, which exercised general administrative power.[151] The military government was able to use both indirect rule, through Japanese government organizations, and direct rule.[152] Hence, although a degree of post-war tumult was inevitable when the US military government began, Japan restored stability relatively quickly after occupation.[153] The occupation was based on the still-functioning administration of Japan except for the temporarily decentralized police. Also, the post-1945 Japanese political parties partly adopted the war-time party systems.

South Korea (1945–1948)

When an American military government was established in South Korea, there already existed a centralized political system, which had begun before Japanese colonial governance.[154] The military government made sure that no political power among Koreans would replace the military government.[155] At first, the US government prevented Korean political leaders from holding leadership positions and also from intervening in the policy-making of the military government. Furthermore, it did not allow Korean politicians and organizations to play a specific role in, nor have extensive input on issues related to, policies that the US military authorities carried out.[156] By the autumn of 1946, Koreans assumed greater responsibility in each administrative department, with US military government providing consultation.[157] In February 1947, Koreans were appointed as heads of civil administration departments, and in May, the military government was renamed as the Korean interim government.[158] The low wages of military government employees fueled widespread corruption, and failure in price controls for consumer goods led to hyper-inflation. These were failures traceable to American military government.[159] According to the US Central Intelligence Agency (CIA), the new government successfully implemented the initial process of transition to democracy despite various limitations, such as lack of experience with the parliamentary system and power centralization within the President.[160] A number of different standards can be used in evaluating the success or failure of the US military government.[161] From the perspective of stabilization, the role of the military government can be evaluated as positive, in that a government that claimed to support democratic values was established, and that it ruled the country peacefully, based on laws and institutions. Gradual transition came successfully in spite of the armed conflicts with the *Namnodang*, the communist party of South Korea in 1946.

Iraq (2003–2011)

Historically, Iraq had failed to construct a solid, centralized state power. The Ba'ath Party regime inaugurated in 1968 faced various challenges. Internally, it needed a national integration that embraced the Kurds, and externally, it needed to end interventions by foreign powers (e.g., Iran and the US).[162] During Hussein's reign, the Sunnis gradually prevailed to exclusively wield power, and sectarian conflicts deepened due to the repression of Shias. In turn, the Iraqi government established after the fall of Saddam Hussein was predominantly Shiite, while the Sunnis, the power-holders under Hussein, were marginalized. When the United States waged the Iraq War, it expected to encounter serious challenges in operating a military government even following victory on the battlefield. In October 2002, Peter Pace, the deputy chairman of the Joint Chiefs of Staff, noted the possibility of ethnic and sectarian violence, the division of Iraqi territory, and the inevitability of post-war US intervention for more than a decade in a "Parade of Horrible" — a list of 29 disasters US would encounter during and after the invasion of Iraq. Ryan Croker, appointed US Ambassador to Iraq, warned in a memo titled "The Perfect Storm" of violent conflicts among different ethnic, sectarian, and racial groups, and the social division of Iraq after the end of the Hussein regime.[163] Specialized military power in sufficient volume was needed to ensure public security within an unstable domestic political situation.[164] Manpower numbering at least several tens of thousands would be needed for border control, and another hundreds of thousands of troops would be needed to control the entire territory of Iraq. During the war, the US dispatched a small number of troops who were unfamiliar with the Middle East. They were neither specialized in urban warfare nor able to effectively prevent foreign elements from flowing in across Iraqi borders.[165] Although sovereignty was handed over to the Iraqi government in June 2004, it was not capable of establishing a functioning democracy.[166] Instability and turmoil in Iraq continued because of the absence of a democratic tradition, as well as increasing confrontations between different ethnic groups. Sunnis violently fought back because they were politically excluded. Young Shias also led anti-government activism due to an unemployment crisis. Their conflict with the Kurds further remained an issue that was politically unaddressed.[167]

Implications of comparative analysis

This analysis highlights four factors, namely centralized power, economic stability, racial identity between the military government and the subjects, and the level of social division, that are most important in stabilization strategies. Chief among these is the power structure of the target state under the military government. In countries that have reasonably concentrated political power, the central government was powerful enough to control local administration. As long as the administrative systems of these countries are integrated, it is possible to carry out efficient governance and control of the society. In the case of both Germany and Japan, a centralized government was in place for a significant period before the military government, while Korea had an integrated social structure and culture inherited from traditional dynastic rule. Within Iraq, in contrast, the control of centralized power had been weakened after the fall of Hussein and social conflicts among different sectors and classes intensified. The economies of each country were all very weak when military governments assumed power. Thus, it is very difficult to distinguish differences in the impact of economic factors on stabilization. There are several cases in which stabilization failed despite American intervention in the form of economic aid intervention. Germany and Japan were special cases in which the extent of industrialization before military government was relatively high when compared to other countries, but this industry had been destroyed by the war.[168] At the beginning of the military government in Germany, the capacity for food distribution was very low.[169] Other factors may be more appropriate in determining stabilization.[170]

The nation-building cases led by the United States indicate that economic conditions were not the primary factor to determine the success of stabilization effort. However, it does not mean that economic conditions should be taken lightly as economic poverty incites social unrest, undermining the political authority. American authorities deemed it necessary to react to economic hardships when they generated instability, as in the case of South Korea in 1946. As seen in Iraq, even active US involvement could not reverse negative outcomes. There, resources were not efficiently distributed, and corruption responsible for the monopoly of wealth was widespread. In a survey in 2012, the transparency of Iraq was ranked 169th among 176 countries surveyed. Compared with previous survey in 2003, in which Iraq ranked 113th out of 133 countries, the situation had worsened.[171] This study also reveals that the level of social division was extremely serious in the cases of Korea and Iraq.

Table 8.1 Comparative analysis of stabilization strategies

Division		Germany	Japan	South Korea	Iraq	Characteristics	
						+	–
Variable	Central power	+	+	+	–	Concentrated	Fragmented
	Economic stability	–	–	–	–	Stable	Unstable
	Race	+	–	–	–	Same	Different
	Social division	+	+	–	–	Integrated	Disintegrated
Effect	Stabilization	+	+	+	–	Success	Failure

In Korea, the Joint Soviet–American Commission and ideological confrontations aggravated political confusion immediately after its independence. In Iraq, there had been long-term disruptions among the Sunnis, Shias and Kurds, and conflicts intensified further after Hussein's death. In Germany and Japan however, internal conflicts did not increase during the period of military government even though there were concerns about latent conflicts with the socialists. There were racial differences in all cases except for Germany, but no significant impact was found in this matter.[172]

Table 8.1 summarizes the comparison of the cases. Comparing the cases through a mixed system analysis that focuses on the variables mentioned earlier indicates that there is a meaningful correlation between stabilization and the structure and characteristics of power. The intervention by a foreign power can be seen as a control variable. Iraq is quite different from the other three cases in each respect. It lacked a developed party system and democratic traditions. Thus, internal structure and the ripple effect of foreign interference, which were confirmed in the case of Iraq, can be regarded as determinants of the failure in stabilization. This research adds a number of important insights into the discussion on structural problems and effects of foreign interventions in Iraq. First, this article tries to examine the clash of ethnic cultures and social conflicts as parts of structural problems in Iraq. Before the case of Iraq emerged, Samuel Huntington noted that, based on the theory of clashes of civilization, China and Islamic civilization would rise to collide with the Western civilization. He presented a war of civilizations as a virtual scenario.[173] In this regard, multi-layered identities in the Middle East challenged the transplantation of a Western democratic system. There are diverse variables such as tribalism, state nationalism and Arab nationalism, and Islamism coexisting in the region.[174] Discord among tribes was not overcome, even by a strong religious ideology. Instability is inevitable when a country is fragmented by tribal allegiances.[175] However, it cannot be asserted that differences in civilization are necessarily the cause of this tragic outcome. It can also be explained by the concept of multiple individual civilizations co-existing in various layers.[176] Second, this research looks at types of foreign interventions and their consequences. The extremists that support anti-government activities in Iraq had flown into the country through its porous borders with Syria and Jordan. The US-led military authority in Iraq initially judged that the opposition powers organized by the local population could be physically controlled. The US handled Iraq in this traditional approach.[177] Despite American intervention, however, the situation in Iraq deteriorated quickly and unexpectedly.[178] The Iraq's transition to democracy was more than an internal development in Iraq. Considering geographic proximity and cultural similarities between Iraq and its Arab neighbors, it would have had significant impacts on neighboring Arab states if democracy successfully had taken roots in Iraq. Middle Eastern countries were particularly sensitive to Iraq's political transition to democracy as they were either authoritarian kingdoms or dictatorial republics. Therefore, they were happy to allow insurgent fighters and material support for insurgency flow into Iraq.

Table 8.2 provides a comparison of policies promoted during the period of military government, which in each case indicates that their objectives and contents were similar. However, strategies for stabilization failed only in Iraq. Germany and Japan had successful stabilization efforts with no violent opposition. South Korea had favorable results after violent conflict with the *Namnodang*. This research compares different variables and tests the hypothesis that stabilization depends on the level of concentration of power and that stabilization can be

Table 8.2 Case study on military government and assessment of stabilization strategies

Country	Centralization of Power and Intervention of Neighboring Countries	Main Policy	Result
Germany	Concentrated central power	System transition (Democratization)	Establishment of democratic government
Japan		Replacement of privileged class (limited)	Political and social stability
South Korea	Concentrated central power	System transition (establishment of government) Humanitarian support Replacement of privileged class (limited)	Establishment of democratic government Construction of public services Political and social stability
Iraq	Fragmentation of power Neighboring countries' intervention	System transition (democratization) Humanitarian support Replacement of privileged class (complete)	Establishment of democratic government Corruption and weak distribution structure Occupation of land by anti-government powers

influenced by interference from neighboring countries. Despite similarities among stabilization strategies, the results of stabilization were different depending on contexts for the policy; in other words, the properties of political power.

Korean unification and stabilization strategies

Types of unification and contingency

Among different types of unification, this paper is only concerned with the scenario of sudden change that could occur due to the collapse of North Korea's political system. It cannot be ascertained that the current, unstable elements of the North Korean system will catalyze a contingency, such as the fall of Kim Jong-un, mass escape from North Korea, or a coup d'état any time in the near future. Furthermore, a realistic analysis should be limited in estimating the potential of a collapse.[179] The international trend of conflicts in the 21st century suggests that military clashes are very frequent, while large-scale wars between countries are relatively rare. Similarly, the majority of the wars that occurred during the Cold War were civil wars that took place during the process of decolonization.[180] The origin of the concepts of political contingency is not clearly defined; nor is there a related definition agreed upon among scholars.[181] By taking into account the situation in North Korea and the relationship between North and South Korea, it is defined here as "a series of processes related to unexpected circumstances, except for war, in North Korea, such as accidents involving the person in highest power, coup d'état, power struggle, or people's uprising, including extreme situations where the current political power and system break down."[182] However, if South Korean military intervention occurs before a full regime collapse, it may escalate the conflict as in the case of Syria, Libya and partly Iraq. Both a delayed and a premature intervention might be problematic. Thus, should sudden change occur, there must be a timely execution of the correct stabilization strategy, to prepare for a massive outflow of refugees from North Korea, violent insurgency, and large-scale social upheaval.

Circumstances for stabilization

During the period of military rule under the Soviet Union in the northern part of the Korean Peninsula above the 38th parallel, the consolidation of political power intensified in North Korea. In particular, deification of Kim Il-sung strengthened the monopoly on power, and a sole dominant system was established in 1956.[183] The control structure of Kim Jong-un's reign further solidifies the totalitarian regime based on one-man leadership. When sudden changes occur, it is highly likely that the ideology and values of the North

Korean people will cause conflicts, as their background deeply rooted in the formation of socialism and the special social structure of North Korea will collide with trends of reform and social change. Therefore, it is necessary to maintain the existing power structure in North Korea. Furthermore, if a military government is established in the northern half of the peninsula, some elements of the central administrative structure of North Korea can be useful for governance in the initial stabilization effort. If the centralized political system plays a positive role in the ruling via a military government in this process, the goal of stabilization will be achieved early.

The chronic economic crisis of North Korea can hardly improve without a fundamental reform of the state system, because it is inherent to the economic structure. If economic crisis is exacerbated during a period of sudden changes, social divisions within North Korea and between North and South Korea can deepen and widen. This study hypothesizes that the South Korean forces would lead the military government in the northern area, while American forces intervene only in air and maritime support operations and other limited areas. US military involvement is likely to generate North Korean or Chinese opposition because of the memory of the Korean War and geopolitical rivalry between the US and China. Given the racial factor, if South Korean forces run the military government in North Korea after the collapse, race-related conflict would not occur as long as the US forces do not directly participate. To achieve complete unification, however, the severe disparity between the South and the North that has developed over the past 70 years or so has to be addressed, despite the fact that North and South Koreans share the same ethnicity should be addressed, and national homogeneity should be recovered through various policies that Germany adopted after their reunification in 1990. If the unification is limited simply to the territory itself, the division between the two countries could increase, because of class conflicts between North and South Koreans. Therefore, the military government should enact integration plans in a manner to boost cultural homogeneity. When political contingency occurs in North Korea, social disruption will be grave, regardless of the existence of central power.

However, as confirmed through the case study, deepening social division does not necessarily lead to failure in stabilization. Two aspects should be taken into account if social division becomes severe. First, severe social divisions can either weaken the control of the central government or prompt specific interest groups to provoke social fragmentation, thus causing instability throughout the society.

Second, foreign forces sometimes intervene to disrupt the convergence of power or to support insurgents, thus aggravating social confusion. Like the case of Iraq, intervention by foreign forces may intensify instability. This is valid for both Chinese and ROK intervention if it happens before a full regime collapse. Thus, it is also necessary to review the possibility of foreign forces intervening in the Korean Peninsula during a period of sudden change. Sudden changes in North Korea will have significant ripple effects on the international political situation surrounding the Korean Peninsula. Hence, a stabilization policy should accommodate the interests of its surrounding countries. Especially in Northeast Asia, a balance of power is critical with the strengthened confrontation of four major powers and their respective alliances, the US, Japan, China, and Russia. Uncertainty and complexity of international situations are increasing, as shown in worldwide financial crisis, China emerging as a "G2 (Group of Two)" power, international demand for democracy, the instability of North Korean politics, and acceleration of efforts to develop weapons of mass destruction (WMDs) in North Korea.[184] These anxiety drivers are likely to continue, because of the structural characteristics of international politics in Northeast Asia. This suggests that the intervention of international power can be a critical variable to determine the stabilization of North Korea.

The power that intervenes in North Korea's contingency, other than South Korea, can be referred to as the "third party", "neighboring country" or "foreign power". Multiple definitions of such powers are possible, depending on alliance or other special relationships. In this paper, however, it is defined as all countries other than South Korea. First, this discussion addresses China, which is the closest among the countries that may intervene in issues on the Korean Peninsula. For China, North Korea has continuously played a pivotal role as a security buffer zone. China, which considers the stability of the peninsula to be paramount, is concerned about the potential fall of North Korea and will intend to prevent instability in its northeastern border regions and the influx of North Korean refugees into China in advance, by active involvement in North Korea.[185] Thus, North Korea's collapse may have a large impact on the Chinese calculation of national interests. As China and North Korea share a border of more than 1,000km, China, as the most directly affected country, is expected to promptly engage in its own stabilization strategies.[186] Second, if China intervenes, Russia, which traditionally has a relationship with North Korea, may bring its military forces into Hamgyong Province. Moreover, Japan may bring its Self-Defense Forces onto the Korean Peninsula to support the US operation, based on the country's right to collective self-defense.[187] Third, as a part of ROK–US alliance, the United States will execute various operational plans in close coordination with its ROK partner. Accordingly, it is likely that there will be combined military efforts in North Korea as the ROK and United States jointly advance into the North. This article does not include other types of contingencies in North Korea or the potential case of joint intervention by ROK and US in the event of North Korean contingency. These issues demand more discussion through future studies to clarify the thinking surrounding them. Table 8.3 provides a comparison of stabilization factors. Two different outlooks can be predicted for the future of North Korea if sudden changes occur. In Scenario A, the unified political system of the country is maintained, as the central concentration of power continues even after drastic change. In this case, control by central power is still valid, and thus, its integrated structure and administrative function are also valid or recoverable, even when factors that threaten the security of the system emerge. In Scenario B, the control of the central power dissolves, leading to the fragmentation of the existing structure. In this case, a number of competitive powers emerge, and the system of public administration and social safety net is destroyed. Stabilization succeeds in

Table 8.3 Comparative analysis of central power concentration among the stabilization factors in North Korea and Iraq

Classification		Iraq (Fragmentation)	North Korea (Future Contingency)		Characteristics	
			Unification Scenario (A)	Fragmentation Scenario (B)	+	–
Variable	Central power	–	+	–	Concentrated	Fragmented
	Economic stability	–	–	–	Stable	Unstable
	Race	–	+	+	Same	Different
	Social division	–	–	–	Integrated	Disintegrated
Effect	Stabilization	–	+	–	Success	Failure

Scenario A, but not in B. The scenario to be realized will depend on the early success or failure of stabilization strategies.

Contingency in North Korea and stabilization strategies

The comparison of stabilization's success and failure cases shows two differences. First, in Germany, Japan, and Korea (where the Japanese military was originally present), defeated countries were completely disarmed after the war under US leadership. In Iraq however, the US military and the new Iraqi government were unable to suppress the Sunni-led insurgency, and arms and supporting powers entered the country through its borders. Second, the population in Germany, Japan and Korea actively collaborated with the systemic transitions that unfolded after the occupation by the US forces because the majority of them had suffered under totalitarian regimes and colonial occupation. In Iraq by contrast, the power relationship between the dominant group and subordinate group changed in the political system transition process, leading to serious resistance from the former power. Controlling the North Korean forces effectively will be a challenging task. For efficient management, the majority of active soldiers can be labeled as "grey" (potential threats) and high-ranking officers as "black" (threatening elements).[188] An analysis of the military integration between East and West Germany should inform the design of a strategic approach tailored specifically for North Korea (indeed, North and South Yemen, which had armed conflict starting in 1994, may offer a better analogy.[189] Additionally, humanitarian issues that rise during initial confusion should be promptly addressed by enhancing relief activities. When South Korean military forces intervene in the event of sudden changes in North Korea, legal and normative boundaries must be considered, such as the Korean Constitution, treaties, international laws and codes, and the statements, announcements, and agreements signed between North and South Korea.[190] These laws and norms sometimes conflict with each other, and there are gaps between justification and benefits, and between theory and practice. Moreover, national interests and the interests of international society or neighboring countries do not always coincide. Thus, in preparing for North Korea's sudden changes, such legal problems and issues of international relationships should be reviewed and defined in terms of national laws of South Korea. At the same time, this approach should be accompanied by active diplomatic endeavors. For instance, discussing those problems and issues with international society and neighboring countries in depth is necessary.[191] Stabilization strategies can be established with two goals in mind. First, intervention by neighboring countries should be deterred, and collaboration between the military government and the occupied country's political and administrative system should be maximized. Second, public security in North Korea should be assured early in the stabilization strategies, and humanitarian support should be enhanced. Initially, territorial unification should certainly be established; later, conditions for integration should be established.[192] To achieve these two goals, stabilization strategies in North Korea should be made concrete. Although counterstrategies by different types of sudden changes should be secured, this paper presents strategies at the level of conceptual planning. Table 8.4 summarizes the case study of military government and stabilization strategies.

Table 8.5 summarizes past tailored stabilization strategies. It identifies the determinants of success in stabilization through a

Table 8.4 Case study of military government and tailored stabilization strategies in North Korea

Target	Factors for Success/Failure	Environment of Transition (Contingency)	Tailored Stabilization Strategies
Germany	Democratization of totalitarianism system	Lack of experience with democracy and market economy	Democratization and marketization
Japan	Collaboration of dominating groups	Agitation and desertion of dominating groups	Harmony between old and new powers
Iraq	Intervention of neighboring countries Resistance to international intervention Shortage of knowledge in peacekeeping	Potential of the intervention of neighboring countries, including China Internalized anti-American sentiment Simultaneous need for forceful maintenance of peace	Establishment of international collaboration Minimization of American Forces' intervention Specialization of stabilization operation
South Korea	Humanitarian support Construction of public services	Shortage of food and resources Disintegration of public services	Emergency relief Restoration of public services

comparative study and draws lessons accordingly. It further presents a tailored stabilization strategy for North Korean contingency, taking into account the different circumstantial contexts of North Korea from other case studies. First, in this light, border control and early assurance of public security are the most important and urgent tasks in the event of sudden changes in North Korea. As confirmed in the case of Iraq, border control is vital in order to prevent the fragmentation of power and deter intervention by foreign elements. The Iraqi government, which continued to be unstable even after democratization, recovered its capacity to lead only recently.[193] As it directs military operations independently, it begins to emerge from its past subordination to US military forces.[194] Arriving at this took a significantly long time because of initial failures in stabilization. Additionally, preventing internal unrest efficiently is also needed to

Table 8.5 Latent environment of North Korea and tailored stabilization strategies

Target	Main Policy for Stabilization	Environment of North Korea (Contingency)	Tailored Stabilization Strategies
National	Enhancing power of central authority	Lack of experience with democracy and market economy Agitation and desertion of the privileged	Democratization and marketization Harmony between old and new powers
Common	Restraining neighboring countries' intervention	Disintegration of public services Shortage of food and resources Simultaneous need for forcing and maintaining peace Internalized anti-American sentiment	Restoration of public services Emergency relief Specialization of stability operations units Minimization of the US force's intervention
International		Potential for the intervention by other countries, including China	Formation of international collaboration

allow for the early provision of humanitarian support.[195] Second, both national and international elements need to be accounted for in setting up stabilization strategies, because of overlap between certain national elements with international ones. For example, neighboring countries may intervene in the name of humanitarian support and foment internal instability. Consequently, intervention by neighboring countries may interfere with stabilization by reducing the control of the central power of the country. Thus, complex stabilization strategies that consider both national and international characteristics are required.

Third, depending on the strategies of the ROK–US Combined Forces in preparation for sudden changes in North Korea, US Force may be able to enter into North Korea.[196] However, in the process of performing stabilization operations in North Korea, the role of the US forces and the areas of the operation should be minimized. Reducing intervention by American forces is needed to deter the expansion of third-party intervention and internal social divisions in North Korea. The intervention of US forces should be designed to be minimal, especially when anti-American sentiment, the history of the rejection of foreign intervention, and national sentiment in North Korea are taken into account.[197] Fourth is the existence of an organization with specialized capacity to perform civil-military operations (CMO).[198] Peacekeeping capabilities to maintain and manage peace effectively are a necessary condition for the next stage — state reconstruction.[199] Civil control can be made possible in a stabilized context. Until a full-scale government is set up, the role of military organizations in maintaining public security is critical. However, military peacekeeping operations are far from simple. Maintaining and enforcing peace require a different approach to military operations and engagement rules. Thus, both cannot be accomplished perfectly. Comparing the characteristics of the Canadian and US armies, Francis Fukuyama pointed out that using a military that is performing combat duty for the purpose of peacekeeping is inappropriate.[200] It is therefore important to organize armies in multi-layered and multi-role structures to meet strategic need through appropriate operations or tactics. This structure becomes more complex if international organs, such as the United Nations, intervene.[201] Fifth, if the existing dominating elite class is efficiently replaced with new power in North Korea, and such new power is well supported, North Korea's early stabilization can be achieved. The replacement of dominant elite targets both the ruling class and the public. Fear of the collapse of the system should be minimized through proper coordination between old and new powers.[202] If the North Korean forces are dismantled early or abolished in controlled areas, they are likely to grow to become a threatening power within the North or toward South Korea.

Countries in which the controlling power of the central government was, or is being, lost are classified as fragmented countries. If government-guaranteed social welfare becomes wholly insufficient or chronic civil war continues in these countries, they are likely to become failed states even if state power still exerts control within their borders, and the concentration of central power will gradually diminish.[203] The concept of fragmentation is useful in explaining situations in which the central governing authority's power weakens. However, different variables, such as the concentration of power, capacity for government control, and decentralization, need detailed consideration. This study focuses on four variables to diagnose the possibility of success and failure of stabilization strategies undertaken through military governance. In addition to these variables, minute additional elements can influence outcomes in complex ways. First, because of the anti-American sentiments that emerged during the Korean War, it is very likely that North Korean forces and other fragmented power groups will continuously threaten the authority of military government, perhaps working in collaboration with China and other countries. During the Korean War, the United States all but razed North Korea to the ground through carpet-bombing operations by its overwhelmingly superior air force. It sowed terror through the inhumane threat of fiery death through the use of napalm bombs, killing many non-combatants in this manner.[204] North Korea described it as "brutal bombing".[205] North Korea's anti-American sentiment was created through the experience of the Korean War, and it deepened due to the post-war siege mentality. A situation where the US is actively involved in military governance in North Korea is very likely to prompt significant resistance.

The hostility toward foreign intervention is not confined to the United States alone. China and Russia, which supported North Korea during the early years of North Korea and the Korean War, are not immune from the backlash against foreign intervention. The US, China, and Russia inflicted heavy losses on North Korean residents as they sent troops to North Korea during the course of the Korean War. Any intervention from China will be met with a great level of skepticism and scorn due to China's numerous invasions of the Korean Peninsula historically. Japanese involvement in military operations around the Korean peninsula might also generate strong resentment and anger in both Koreas as the Japanese occupation of Korea is still bitterly remembered. It should be noted that the Iraqi memory of Western colonialism was also a key factor in generating widespread insurgency in wake of US invasion. Therefore, South Korean forces should lead the military government at the front, whereas the US should participate in the system by providing collaborative support in the backend during the initial stages. Second, to operate successful military governance in a society where a sole totalitarian system has been active as the fundamental power for more than 70 years, democracy and the merits of a market economy should be effectively established. In particular, addressing economic poverty through providing basic necessities in the beginning of military governance is essential to win North Korean support for the process of stabilization. Furthermore, it is possible that China, which is very likely to intervene in the Korean Peninsula because of their geographical proximity and previous military alliance, could incapacitate any effort toward military governance. From this, one can draw the conclusion that international diplomacy should precede the implementation of military governance in order to manage the China factor efficiently.[206] Thus in North Korea, the four variables will unfold very differently when compared to the military governments in Germany, Japan and Iraq in the past. Therefore, if drastic changes occur in North Korea, the results of the comparative analysis in this paper may be used to predict the determinants of stabilization. The analysis herein confirms that stabilization can succeed when the control of central power is assured and the intervention of "unwanted" foreign elements is deterred through effective military governance. The case of North Korea includes both relative advantages and disadvantages compared to the case of Iraq. Potential interventions by neighboring countries (e.g., China) and stubborn North Korean forces are negative factors for stabilization. On the other hand, centralized power and cultural conditions are advantageous factors. The potential for the success of stabilization in North Korean contingency increases when disadvantageous factors are minimized and advantageous factors are maximized. To maximize the potential for success, it is necessary to plan for these various possible contingent scenarios and design respective countermeasures.

Chapter 9

Unification of Korean Peninsula: Is It Possible?

Feasible scenarios for unification

One of the songs that South Koreans commonly sing today is "Our wish is unification." North and South Korea on the Korean Peninsula, a racially homogeneous nation with a history of 2,000 years, was a unified nation for 1,300 years after the unification during the seventh century. It has been around 70 years since it was divided as a result of the Cold War of the 1940s. All Koreans in South and North Korea are looking for unification since the division of 1945. Reunification will be determined not only by the ideology and will of the two Koreas, but also by the international politics of Northeast Asia. Despite the aspirations of both Koreans, the latter factor may act more strongly. The reunification of the Korean Peninsula will be possible only in conjunction with their national power and the desire of the two Koreas, based on the positive circumstances of international situation of Northeast Asia, which are favorable to the nation. This author proposes three feasible scenarios for unification of the Korean Peninsula and introduce related strategies. The types of unification expected on the Korean Peninsula will be divided into the different types according to the subject, speed, and method of unification.

As a subject of unification, it is divided into bottom-up and top-down type. Depending on the speed of unification, it can be divided into radical and progressive style. Radical reunification takes place through the process of absorption and incorporation into the other through the transformation of either side, which means the ultimate annihilation of any one state or regime and requires a period of about three years or more after unexpected changes like sudden death of leader and coup d'état in North Korea. Progressive unification is a step-by-step type by agreement between the two Koreas, which takes about 30 years. In the past, the Korean government's unification plan entered the second stage of inter-Korean coalition stage (capable of developing by federal stage) through the first stage of reconciliation cooperation (1 nation, 2 states, 2 governments and 2 systems). The integration stage (such as the unification treaty) is finally reached. Transitional anomalies take about 15 years in a form that can be achieved at an intermediate point between rapid and gradual unification. Also, unification can be divided into peaceful and armed unification. There are German peaceful reunification and Vietnamese-style unification by armed force. The process of unification can be divided into "de-facto reunification" and "juridical reunification" by analyzing the process of unification in terms of time and procedural concept under the real situation where the surrounding great powers are involved in the problem of the Korean Peninsula. It requires at least about 30 years for a unified Korea through legal and institutional unification to join the United Nations as a single country, in case of international recognition as a complete reunification based on one government and one system. However, the legal unification of the Korean Peninsula should be preceded by consensus of neighboring countries such as the G2, the US and China. A significant level of international consensus is definitely needed, such as the East–West German Unification Treaty. With West Germany's continuous eastern policy toward East Germany during many years and economic strength, West Germany suddenly demonstrated its diplomatic ability to capture the "window of opportunity" when the Berlin Wall collapsed. South Korean government should raise its national strength so that it can exercise appropriate diplomatic power in time. It should be preceded by continuing to whisper the logic that the unification of the Korean Peninsula becomes a plus for the four major powers, and reaching the point of exercising national power to pursue it in real diplomacy.

The three kinds of unification scenarios based on changes in the internal situation of North Korea are as follows. First, A type happens in emergency case due to sudden change of North Korean leader. A prepared contingency plan is necessary for the swift solution of chaos in North Korea. Peaceful unification will take a year after leadership change (Y + 1). Second, B type will be established by reform and opening up of North Korea. This unification will take 15 years (Y + 15). Third, C type will be "one country, two systems" formula like the unification of China and Hong Kong, the latter being a special administrative region of the country. The unification will need at least 30 years (Y + 30). This author shall explain the scenarios of "emergency type due to sudden change". The North Korean nuclear issue was not solved in a short period of time. North Korea announced the completion of its uranium facilities on specific point of time. International pressure intensified on North Korea, including the United States, as a result of Pyongyang's unreasonable military provocations against South Korea and the US military bases on the Korean Peninsula. As North Korean dictator Kim Jong-un has not improved its economic hardship after the third succession, the North Korean economy is rapidly depressed by the increasing cynicism, criticism and desperation of the people and the North Korean leadership is gradually losing control. As the overall durability of the Kim Jong-un regime is seriously degraded, the internal crisis of the power is accelerated. The Chinese leadership is actively involved in the problem of the Korean Peninsula. China offers alternatives to the emergence of abnormalities in the operation system of the North Korean power. There will be coup d'état and popular uprising that are instigated by the continued trial and error of the leadership due to insufficient authority of Kim Jong-un's leadership. China and Russia have a compromising policy that does not strongly object to the unification of the Korean Peninsula, if the necessary and enough condition that there is no US's military intervention in the north of the 38th parallel on the Korean Peninsula is fulfilled, even though North Korean regime collapses. It is necessary and sufficient condition that a unified Korea establishes balanced diplomatic ties with the neighboring countries, in light of complex international politics in East Asia. China does not actively oppose unification under the premise of establishing a new leadership system by elections throughout the northern part of the Korean Peninsula.

There is a high possibility that the sudden changes of unprecedented situations such as the outflow of weapons of mass destruction to the Middle East and other countries, and massive refugees and mass starvation caused by food shortage may arise in North Korea. It is urgent for South Korea and international society to manage North Korea during the early probationary period. They should try to coordinate the concerns of the interested parties so that the confusion of North Korea will not spread to international disputes. It took around a total of 36 months for Germany to achieve peaceful reunification through the Two-Plus-Treaty of 1990, considering the transition period of 11 months after the collapse of the Berlin Wall. It will cost a huge amount of reunification money in order to quickly manage the crisis and confusion in North Korea and to swiftly have various systems similar to South Korea's political and economic realms in a short period of time. With the excessive cost of unification, it will be a major task for South Korean government to prevent the spread of negative perceptions of unification among South Koreans in case of first scenario. The enormous cost of initial crisis management due to social disorder management is needed. Various costs related to mitigate social disruption such as massacres, plundering and arson are increasing because of high probability that there will be an illegal leakage of weapons of mass destruction. The costs of emergency relief resources such as food, medical supplies, etc., as well as social welfare and personnel management due to the large-scale migration of North Koreans also increase. In addition, there is a considerable expense to normalize the social system and economic order while fixing the mess of the North Korean society in a short period after a sudden change. It will also take much money to establish a rational administrative system for restoring various economic and demographic facilities such as census and social statistics. If the North collapses in a state of sudden change without opening and reform, the average annual reunification cost will be US$72 billion. This scenario is expected to cost about seven times more than the gradual unification case because the cost of initial investment is enormous. In reality, the budget is concentrated in the short term, but benefits are also calculated early and the total cost is estimated too much, so it is expected to increase about three times, which is less than seven times estimated from the existing point spread type. As various unification benefits such as reduction of armaments and various country risks are also provided in the short term, an accrual calculation method which deducts benefit from unification cost should be introduced.

The following is B type. It is a scenario for step-by-step integration of "reformed and open-ended type" unification (Y + 15). Kim Jong-un will pursue proactive foreign policy like improvement of the US–North Korean relationships in order to resolve the severe economic difficulties. With the weakening of the young leader's power, a new collective leadership system is established in which the military and labor parties are combined. A collective leadership system was formed during the post-Stalin era of Soviet state and the post-Mao period of China. A new North Korean leadership replacing Kim will announce a prospect for denuclearization, underlining reforms and opening up policies like the promotion of North Korea–US diplomatic ties and revitalization of inter-Korean relations. There will be the establishment of an inter-liaison office where mutual representatives play a role in Seoul and Pyongyang, respectively. A preliminary infrastructure for unification over a minimum period of time (15 years) will be planned. Five ports, including Nampo, Hamheung, Wonsan, Sinuiju, and Haeju of North Korea, have been designated as special economic zones, attracting capital from South Korea and the international community. The atmosphere of unification will be spread. The methods and timing of unification will be discussed through the agreement between the two Koreas, and preparatory mechanisms will be prepared for concrete integration. There will be the establishment of various organizations and institutions for the inter-Korean coalition. Chinese President Xi Jinping supports the reform and openness of North Korea, while the United States, Russia and Japan agree on the peaceful and gradual unification of the two Koreas on the premise of denuclearization of the Korean Peninsula and obtain international recognition of reunification through the conclusion of a unification treaty between North and South Korea. The two Koreas build various organizations for unification. North Koreans can gain a level of improved living and political freedom in the integration process. However, they can soon recognize the relative deprivation and cannot exclude the possibility of social unrest. Considering the serious unemployment problem in North Korea and the vulnerability of the social security system, the positive aspect of gradual reunification should be gradually highlighted by removing some anxiety factors through the minimum expenditure of social security.

Reformed and open-ended reunification will minimize the adverse effects that were experienced during the reunification process of East–West German unification by covering the burden of the unification cost under a mid- and long-term plan. This type of reunification will give North Korea the time and space to nurture the difficult economy through creating a structure to finance itself for development. By designating the northern part of Korean Peninsula as a special economic development zone that benchmarks South Korea's economic growth during the 1960s and 1970s, Pyongyang will reduce unification costs by investing in North Korean infrastructures such as railways, roads, and ports through domestic and foreign capital attraction methods before unification. It also seeks ways to reduce the burden on the government by expanding the participation of South and North Korean private and international communities in inter-Korean economic exchange cooperation. The cost of unification excluding the initial crisis management and rebuilding the emergent North Korea is required in the mid-to-long term and stepwise manner. Therefore, the cost of gradual unification declines rather than the radical unification. It is urgent to concentrate on the human development for job conversion according to the reduction of large-scale troop. There are also the growing social costs including education, health and welfare for North Koreans, and the establishment of legal and institutional order. Progressive economic integration should precede legal and institutional reunification according to the market economy logic.

Once political unification is achieved, North Koreans will have the same rights and obligations as South Koreans. Therefore, there will be considerable hassles on the efficiency of realizing equal economic rights for residents of North and South Korea through radical economic integration. Despite the gap in the proportion of one to four of economic power in the reunification process of East and West Germany, an actual exchange of money and wages at a ratio of one to one resulted in huge economic distortions. As North Korea abandons its nuclear program and gradually increases its self-reliance with the support of the international community, the cost of unification can be reduced if North Korea continues its high economic growth rate. In the peaceful unification method, the period of expenditure for unification is divided into early (one year), middle (two to three years), and long term (after four years). In the first year of unification, discussions on the unification method and procedures, it is expected that total administrative expenses will be US$22 billion including administrative support, system integration, and economic reconstruction. Institutional integration costs at the initial stage include the budgets of new currency issuance and support for privatization of enterprises, household subsidies for price reforms, foreign debt acquisition, and administrative system integration. During the medium term (two to three years) of the reunification, one needs to discuss the sectorial integration of the two Koreas. During the long-term unification period (after four years), it is expected to be worth US$1 trillion to promote development and investment in North Korea.

Finally, it is C type. It is a unification scenario of the "Chinese–Hong Kong-style" one country, two systems. There is a special situation in which the North Korean regime is forced to promote reunification with South Korea due to the deteriorating economic situation, increasing pressure to abandon nuclear weapons and improve human rights record, the unfavorable international environment, the weakening of the North Korean supreme leader's authority, and the opposition of the people. On the other hand, Chinese President Xi has a stance that the balance of power shall not be broken by the US increasing power in the Korean Peninsula, and therefore advocates the unacceptable position of early reunification by expanding and strengthening of the Korea–US alliance on the Korean Peninsula. The position of the unified Korea in the new great power relations becomes the most important agenda of China in Northeast Asian international politics. China will be reluctant to overcome the division unless there is firm confidence that the unified country adheres to balanced stance with US and China. While maintaining the status quo of "Two Korea" on the Korean Peninsula, it is inevitable for South Korea to favor a compromise model that achieves the positive integration effect of the two Koreas. Therefore, North Korea will not be incorporated into the capitalist economy of South Korea for the time being, but the US and China will agree to operate the socialist political system, while maintaining reform and openness in the northern part of Korean Peninsula. Even if North Korea does not release weapons of mass destruction including the asymmetric nuclear weapons to the outside world, it is difficult for Washington to justify rejection of China's demands. It is a realistic scenario that without nuclear weapons, North Korean regime governs the country through socialist political system and market economy. Intermediate measures are needed to ensure the vested interests of the North Korean power elite in order to prevent social upheaval. It adopts the unification method as a national referendum after running the mixed Chinese–Hong Kong style system which is a combination of socialism in politics and market economy, for 30 years as a transitional period. In accordance with the principles of the national sovereignty system, China recognizes the autonomy of Hong Kong, so that the two Koreas maintain different systems as Hong Kong keeps its existing capitalist system and lifestyle.

The Korean Peninsula is a key geographical region in Northeast Asia where continental and maritime forces are in sharp conflict.

West Germany Prime Minister Helmut Kohl had a summit with Soviet President Mikhail Gorbachev, the last romantic socialist of the Soviet Union when the Berlin Wall collapsed. The then Prime Minister Helmut Kohl proposed an economic cooperation worth DM3 billion (US$1.5 billion) and called for no military intervention in case of the fall of Berlin Wall that symbolized the end of the Cold War between the East and West. West Germany's then Foreign Secretary Hans-Dietrich Genscher requested for the signing of the East–West German Unification Treaty, during a meeting with the then French President François Mitterrand in Paris and the then British Prime Minister Margaret Thatcher in London. The opposition of both countries was serious, but West Germany presented dozens of memorandums and overcame them with economic and diplomatic strength. Germany effectively used the beginning of the European Union (EU) during the early 1990s. Unless Germany was included in the European integration, the situation at the time when the meaning of integration had to be cut down was very positive for Germany to achieve unification. It is necessary for South Korea to have diplomatic capacity to build confidence that unification on the Korean Peninsula is not unfavorable to China and Russia through diplomacy based on the South Korea–US alliance.[207]

It is very important for Seoul to secure international support for unification. Specific policies are needed to make unification a national issue across the country. In addition, it is necessary to use a "strategic complex engagement policy" that mixes the Eastward policy of West Germany and US operation of intelligence agencies during the Cold War era for the Soviet Union's opening policy. Instead of the simple "embracement policy" toward North Korea, let the North Korean human rights and economic reality contact a hot breath of South Korean capitalism and liberal democracy. It is also necessary to benchmark various closed projects that the US Central Intelligence Agency (CIA) used to knock on the doors of the former Soviet Union. Systematic but quiet engagement inside North Korea can allow the winds of freedom to enter Pyongyang. Various activities and operations for information injection are inevitable for North Koreans who do not exactly recognize the outside world. It is necessary to develop a business that establishes the material basis of the unified economy through inter-Korean exchange and cooperation. Through human and material exchanges, the North Korean people should pursue large-scale projects to experience capitalism. It is also necessary to implement policies to increase food production, such as North Korean forest greening and cooperative farm support. There is also a need to change the people's consciousness by injecting market-oriented economy and capitalism into the closed territories and ensuring the survival of the people. South Korean goods and information should be distributed from markets such as Pyongyang, Wonsan, and Shinuiju. Residents should be aware that this material and information originates from Seoul. This project needs much time. It also takes a huge budget. Especially, it should be pursued secretly. If one mentions it in the media in Seoul, it will be forced to stop due to massive crackdowns by North Korean regime. Until the level of information flowing into Pyongyang reaches the threshold, it should not be publicized.

Notes

Chapter 1: The Beginning and Progress of North Korea's Nuclear Development

1. Kim Il-sung pledged in his writing that his father Kim Hyung-jik emphasized the following statement: "When burglars come into the house and threaten you with a sword, no matter how much you ask the burglary to save your life, the burglary can't save your life. If the guy outside the house is also a robber, hearing the clamor, other peoples can't help you. In order to defend my life, I must fight the robbers with my own strength. When you fight a robber who is holding a sword, you have to fight with a knife to win." "Contents of the Pledge," in Kim Il-sung, *Kim Il-sung Memoir I* (Pyongyang: Chosun Labor Party Publishing Company, 1992), p. 47.
2. Tae Young-ho, *Password of the Third Floor Secretariat* (Seoul: Giparang, 2018), pp. 41–42
3. The link to the press conference is: https://www.trumanlibrary.org/publicpapers/index.php?pid=985&st=&st1=. Harry S. Truman, The President News Conference (November 30, 1950), *Public Paper of the Presidents of the United States.*
4. Douglas MacArthur, *Reminiscences: General of Army* (New York: McGraw-Hill, 1964), p. 384.
5. Lee Jae-hak, "Determination of non-use of nuclear weapons by the Truman administration during the Korean War in terms of situational deterrence theory", *The Journal of International Politics* 54 (3), International Politics Association (2014), pp. 79–112.

6. Roger Dingman, "Atomic diplomacy during the Korean War", *International Security* 13 (3) (Winter, 1988–1989), pp. 72–76.
7. Kim Il-sung, "Current Situation and Current Task", *Kim Il-sung Collection 6* (Pyongyang: Labor Party Publishing House, 1980), p. 45.
8. The outcome of the review of the Nixon administration's defense policy is important in two respects. One is that the Nixon administration revised the US military doctrine from a "two and a half war strategy" to a "one and a half war strategy". What is important in these revisions is that China is separated from the Soviet Union. It acknowledged the perpetuity of the confrontation between China and the Soviet Union and reflected the dramatic fact that the US ended its assumption in the US strategic plan to fight the small and medium communist countries. Um Ho-gun, *North Korea's Nuclear Development: Background and Contents* (Seoul: Baksanjarwon, 2009), pp. 220–224; and Henry Kissinger, *White House Years* (Boston, MA: Little Brown and Company, 2009). Another is that the United States was seeking to liquidate past relationships and practices, even if it had promised to keep its existing commitments. Combined with the Nixon Doctrine's policy, the United States cut its East Asian forces from 744,000 in 1969 to less than 420,000 in June 1971. Of those, 265,000 were cuts from Vietnam, but 50,000 were cuts from other Asian countries, including Korea. US Department of State, *1969–70: A Report of the Secretary of State* (Washington, D.C.: Government Printing Office, 1971).
9. Sun Woo-jung, The heaven and earth gangster scam, *Chosun Daily Newspaper*, March 21, 2018.
10. Han Yong-seop, *The Fate of Nuclear Weapon in North Korea* (Gyeonggi-do Paju: Park Youngsa, 2018).
11. Joseph S. Bermudez, Jr., "North Korea's nuclear programme", *Jane's Intelligence Review* 3 (9) (September 1991), p. 405.
12. Kim Il-sung, *Kim Il-sung Collection 19* (Pyongyang: Chosun Labor Party Publishing Company, 1982), pp. 214–215.
13. North Korea, *Labor Newspaper*, October 26, 1965.
14. Kim Il-sung, *Kim Il-sung Collection 12* (Pyongyang: Chosun Labor Party Publishing Company, 1958), p. 112; Social Science Publishing Company, *Economic Dictionary 1* (Pyongyang: Social Science Publishing Company, 1977), p. 569; and Kim Il-sung, *1977 New Year's Address* (Paperback), p. 9.
15. Joseph S. Bermudez Jr., *The Armed Forces of North Korea* (London: I.B. Tauris Publisher, 2001), pp. 217–219.

16. *The Economist*, June 24, 2004.
17. Oli Heinonen, North Korea has started nuclear development since the signing of Geneva Agreement in 1994, *Joongang Daily News Paper*, May 18, 2018, p. 10.

Chapter 2: North Korea's Nuclear Quest and Complexity

18. David Albright, Frans Berkhout, and William Walker, *Plutonium and Highly Enriched Uranium 1996: World Inventories, Capabilities and Policies* (Oxford: Oxford University Press, 1997).
19. Richard R. Paternoster, *Nuclear Weapon Proliferation Indicators and Observables* (Tech rept. LA-12430-MS. Los Alamos, N.M.: Los Alamos National Laboratory, December 27, 2011).
20. Charles Glaser, "Realists as optimists: Cooperation as self-help", *International Security* 19 (1994/1995), pp. 50–90.
21. Kathleen C. Bailey, *Strengthening Nuclear Nonproliferation* (Boulder: Westview Press, 1993).
22. Michael J. Mazarr, *North Korea and the Bomb: A Case Study in Nonproliferation* (New York: Macmillan Press, 1997).
23. Selig H. Harrison, *Korea Endgame: A Strategy for Reunification and U.S. Disengagement* (Princeton: Princeton University Press, 2002).
24. Victor D. Cha, "Korea's place in the Axis", *Foreign Affairs* 81 (3) (2002), pp. 79–92; and Victor D. Cha and David C. Kang, *Nuclear North Korea: A Debate on Engagement Strategies* (New York: Columbia University Press, 2003).
25. Michael O'Hanlon and Mike Mochizuki, *Crisis on the Korean Peninsula: How to Deal with a Nuclear North Korea* (New York: McGraw-Hill, 2003).
26. James C. Moltz and C. Kenneth Quinones, "Getting serious about a multilateral approach to North Korea", *The Nonproliferation Review* 11 (1) (Spring 2004), pp. 136–144.
27. Snyder, Scott, "North Korea's Nuclear Program: The Role of Incentives in Preventing Deadly Conflict", in David Cortright, ed., *The Price of Peace: Incentives and International Conflict Prevention* (Lanham, MD: Rowman & Little, 1997), pp. 55–81; and Snyder, Scott, "North Korea's challenge of regime survival: Internal problems and implications for the future", *Pacific Affairs* 73(4), Special Issue: Korea in Flux (Winter, 2000–2001), pp. 517–533.

28. Nicholas Eberstadt, "North Korea's interlocked economic crisis: Some indications from "mirror statistics", *Asian Survey* 38 (3) (March, 1998), pp. 203–220.

Chapter 3: After the Fifth and Sixth Nuclear Tests of DPRK, the Situation in Northeast Asia and the US Response

29. North Korean leader Kim Jong-un signed an order to carry out a hydrogen bomb test on December 15, 2015. The North's Korean Central Television (KCTV) disclosed photos of his signing right after the official announcement of the test's success. The North then fired six short-range projectiles on March 3, 2016 and two Scud-type short-range missiles on March 10, 2016. On both occasions, the missiles were fired into the sea off its east coast. On March 18, 2016, firing of the mid-range missiles was the first since March 2014. A Rodong missile has a maximum range of 1,200km, covering all of South Korea and much of Japan.
30. Global credit appraiser Moody's Investors Service, meanwhile, earlier said the shutdown would have only a limited impact on South Korea, as the zone contributed around 0.04% of the country's annual gross domestic product.
31. The way in which Wang expressed opposition to THAAD during the Reuters interview is preposterous. Wang used an ancient Chinese saying from the Chu–Han Contention (206–202 B.C.); "Xiang Zhuang performed the sword dance as a cover for his attempt on Liu Bang's life." The saying comes from the Feast of Hong Gate in 206 B.C., during a power struggle for supremacy over China between Xiang Yu and Liu Bang (Emperor Gao), the founder of Han dynasty. Xiang Zhuang, a younger cousin of the warlord Xiang Yu, attempted to thrust his sword at Liu Bang on numerous instances. The saying is used to describe a situation where one does something to disguise an attack on another person. Wang was metaphorically describing Korea as a subordinate of the US acting on its instructions to hurt China. This kind of derogatory remark is an affront to Korea and its people. It shows that the top Chinese diplomat regards Korea as a client state of the US and expressed his outdated perception through an irrelevant metaphor. For a foreign minister to voice such a view about a close neighbor, with

which his country enjoys significant economic and cultural relations, is an unthinkable breach of diplomatic protocol. The Ministry of Foreign Affairs of South Korea should lodge a complaint about Wang's inappropriate description of Korea in the interview and make sure that such instances are not repeated.

32. The South Korean government faces a totally new circumstances in which it cannot delay discussions on the deployment any more after Pyongyang conducted its fourth nuclear test and third flight test of submarine-launched ballistic missiles (SLBMs). Given the North's alarming speed in developing nuclear weapons and the SLBMs, the government cannot simply wait for the development of the Korean Air and Missile Defense (KAMD) system, which was an earlier plan that China would have been far more comfortable with. But the THAAD deployment could require a massive investment by the US. Not to mention the cost of ₩3 trillion (US$2.49 billion) per artillery battery, the system calls for significant additional expenditures for maintenance and repairs. In addition, opponents contend that the system would not be effective in intercepting high-altitude missiles on the Korean Peninsula due to the relatively short distance they would fly.
33. The *Foreign Policy* magazine's survey of about 700 scholars currently teaching or researching at colleges and universities throughout the US listed the conflict in the Middle East as the most important foreign policy issue followed by climate change and renewed Russian assertiveness. It appears that concerns about WMD (weapons of mass destruction) proliferation had gone down among these experts, despite the recent North Korean missile tests. "Only 10 percent of scholars listed WMD proliferation in their top three issues compared to 14 percent in our previous survey," the magazine said. WMD proliferation ranked only as the 11th most important issue. Other issues listed as more important foreign policy matters than WMD proliferation included transnational terrorism, China's rising military power, failed states, global wealth disparities, global poverty and China's rising economic influence. *Korea Times*, February 23, 2016. https://www.koreatimes.co.kr/www/nation/2019/03/120_198712.html
34. In September 2005, the George W. Bush administration, working through the China-led six-party talks (Russia, South Korea and Japan being the other involved parties) reached an agreement to denuclearize North Korea. After a promising start with five working groups addressing every issue of interest to Pyongyang, from energy and economic aid to a

peace treaty, the North decided to walk away. Then it was Obama's turn. Despite the fact Pyongyang answered his call for a dialogue by conducting a nuclear test in 2009, three years later the US reached what would be known as the leap day deal, in which Pyongyang agreed to freeze its nuclear missile programs in exchange for aid. The accord fell apart only days later when Pyongyang disagreed with the US on its interpretation.

35. About US$44 million would be needed for the next five years to implement a North Korea sanctions bill that Congress had overwhelmingly approved in response to Pyongyang's nuclear and missile tests, the Congressional Budget Office estimated. Of the total, US$33 million was necessary to carry out provisions for radio broadcasting and other programs to improve access to information to North Koreans and humanitarian assistance to North Korean refugees, the office said in a cost estimate report.
36. On February 7, 2016, the North sent what it called a satellite into orbit, a move which Seoul and Washington viewed as a covert test of ICBM technology. Kim Jong-un said that the rocket liftoff came even as hostile forces were getting "ever more frantic to suffocate" the North, stressing that the North's push for scientific research should be continued.
37. The statement of the spokesman for the National Defense Commission, carried by the North's KCNA, came out one month after the United Nations imposed its harshest-ever sanctions against North Korea on March 3, 2016 in reaction to the North's fourth nuclear test, conducted on January 6, and long-range missile test, conducted on February 7. "The synonymous Leningrad blockade, the most severe sanctions in world military history, and the Caribbean Cold War crisis, cannot even be compared to today's situation on the Korean Peninsula," the statement said, adding that the sanctions are "anachronistic and rashly suicidal, although they do not know it yet."

Chapter 4: The US Denuclearization Policy toward North Korea: Trump's Choices — Diplomacy and Military Options

38. Malcolm Chalmers, "Preparing for war in Korea", *Whitehall Reports* (Royal United Services Institute for Defense and Security Institute, September 27, 2017).

39. The Council on Foreign Relations, What the US can do about North Korea, *Foreign Affairs* August 10, 2017, https://www.foreignaffairs.com/audios/2017-08-10/what-us-can-do-about-north-korea?cid=inted&pgtype=hpg%AEion=br3&sp_mid=55084168&sp_rid=bmFtc3VuZ0Brb3JlYS5hYy5rcgS2&spMailingID=55084168&spUserID=NTY0NTU0NTU1NTQS1&spJobID=1260979917&spReportId=MTI2MDk3OTkxNwS2 (date of searching: 2017.10.6).
40. Lee Sang-hyun and Woo Jung-yeop, "U.S. policy toward North Korea after North Korea's sixth nuclear test", *Policy Briefing* 2017-26 (Sejong Institute, 2017).
41. In his speech in the Australian Parliament on November 17, 2011, President Barack Obama announced a policy of giving "top priority" to military presence in the Asia-Pacific. Former Secretary of Defense Leon Panetta: Atlantic/Pacific military presence from 50/50 to 40/60 by 2020. But increasing domestic weariness of overseas troops and financial insufficiency. https://en.wikipedia.org/wiki/East_Asian_foreign_policy_of_the_Barack_Obama_administration (date of searching: 2017.10.9).
42. *Yonhap News*, October 21, 2017, http://www.yonhapnews.co.kr/bulletin/2017/10/21/0200000000AKR20171021033700083.HTML?input=1179m (date of searching: 2017.10.21).
43. Vladimir Putin urged the international community to provide a sense of security for North Korea, saying that the North will not give up its nuclear weapons and missiles and must be resolved through diplomacy. *News 1*, October 5, 2017, http://news1.kr/articles/?3095309 (date of searching: 2017.10.5).
44. *Yonhap News*, October 6, 2017, http://www.yonhapnews.co.kr/bulletin/2017/10/06/0200000000AKR20171006024151014.HTML?input=1179m (date of searching: 2017.10.9).
45. *Yonhap News*, October 22, 2017, http://www.yonhapnews.co.kr/bulletin/2017/10/22/0200000000AKR20171022003051080.HTML?input=1179m (date of searching: 2017.10.23).
46. "First-strike invasion of North Korea is the prelude to a suicide, the focus of training about our top leaders and key strategic targets focused on 'precision strike'. The fact that warlords are openly talking about the execution of the massive retaliation operation plan is another indication." North Korea, *Rodong Sinmun*, October 12, 2016.

47. *Yonhap News*, September 29, 2017, http://www.yonhapnews.co.kr/bulletin/2017/09/29/0200000000AKR20170929201151080.HTML?input=1179m (date of searching: 2017.09.30)
48. When something happens on the Korean Peninsula, there is a principle that China always talks about. This is the so-called "three principles of the Korean Peninsula". "Maintaining peace and stability on the Korean Peninsula", "realization of denuclearization on the Korean Peninsula", and "resolution through dialogue and negotiations". In this context, "peace and stability on the Korean Peninsula" and "denuclearization of the Korean Peninsula" are China's two main goals on the Korean Peninsula, and dialogue and negotiations are the means to realize these goals. China has a fourth principle that it does not talk about on the surface. It is to maintain and expand its influence on the Korean Peninsula. Shin Jong-ho, China Insight, *Joongang Daily Newspaper*, October 12, 2016.
49. "The North Korean government has made North Korea nuclear weapons because of the US threat, and now it is well equipped to transport them. Therefore, the talks to discuss denuclearization of North Korea are not what the North Korean government wants right now. North Korea was not disappointed in China at all. China is doing what it has to do and North Korea is doing what it has to do. North Korea, which has nuclear weapons in its constitution and party conventions, will no longer return to the six-party framework under the premise of giving up its nuclear weapons."
50. Nam Sung-wook, "Research on contingency and determinants of stabilization strategy in North Korea", *International Journal of Korean Unification Studies* 25 (1) (2016), pp. 129–161.
51. "Trump is a wise politician and visionary. The US should choose Trump over Hillary's stupid." *DPRK Today*, June 2, 2016.
52. "The US government's move to crush the control North Korea cannot avoid bankruptcy. The Obama administration's 'strategic patience' policy has put more pressure on the new administration. In addition, the former US government's North Korea policy has become a burden to its successor. The snowballing burden is now directly linked to America's fate." *Rodong Sinmun*, November 10, 2016.
53. According to an opinion poll on diplomatic and security perceptions of American people released by the conservative think tank Charles Cork, when asked how much US military power should be used abroad compared to the past 15 years, 51.1% said it should be used less and 25% more. Shin,

Bo-young, *Munhwa Daily News Paper,* October 27, 2016, http://www.munhwa.com/news/view.html?no=20161028010701301160001 (date of searching: 2017.5.2).

54. *Yonhap News,* October 23, 2017, http://v.media.daum.net/v/20171023104421253?f=o (date of searching: 2017.10.23).
55. Kim Hyun-wook, IFANS Analysis on Major Global Issue, 2017-11 (Institute of Foreign Affairs and National Security, April 4, 2017).
56. *DongA Daily Newspaper,* October 8, 2017, http://news.donga.com/3/all/20171008/86651680/1
57. Former Director of National Intelligence James Clapper says he doesn't see any path to a denuclearized North Korea. *Huffpost,* August 14, 2017, http://www.huffingtonpost.kr/2017/08/14/story_n_17747448.html (date of searching: 2017.8.14); and KCNA, November 8, 2016.
58. H.R. 1644: Korean Interdiction and Modernization of Sanctions Act, H.R. 479: North Korea State Sponsor of Terrorism Designation Act of 2017, H.Res. 92: Condemning North Korea's development of multiple intercontinental ballistic missiles, and for other purposes.
59. The Bank of Korea, North Korean economic statistics, June 21, 2016, http://www.bok.or.kr/broadcast.action?menuNaviId=2236 (date of searching: 2017.10.1).
60. US Ambassador to the United Nations Nikki Haley argued that the measure would be the most severe.
61. KOTRA, August 25, 2017, http://news.kotra.or.kr/user/globalBbs/kotranews/10/globalBbsDataView.do?setIdx=247&dataIdx=160554 (date of searching: 2017.10.2).
62. Jeong Han-beom, "A theoretical discussion on the effectiveness of US-led economic sanctions against North Korea", *The Journal of Peace Studies* 18 (3), The Korean Association of Peace Studies (2017), pp. 193–216.
63. The sanctions were based on the "Korean Interdiction and Modernization of Sanctions Act" proposed by Ed Royce, chairman of the House Foreign Affairs Committee. In particular, the bill included comprehensive sanctions such as blocking North Korea's import of crude oil and oil products, banning North Korean workers from being hired, stopping North Korean ships from operating, prohibiting the trading of North Korean online goods and blocking gambling sites. *Yonhap News,* October 26, 2017.
64. *Yonhap News,* September 21, 2017, http://www.yonhapnews.co.kr/bulletin/2017/09/12/0200000000AKR20170912122300009.HTML?input=1179m (date of searching: 2017.10).

65. International sanctions on North Korea have led to higher energy prices, and in some cases, the value of the North Korean won against the US dollar could plunge, according to a report. *Yonhap News*, October 8, 2017, http://www.yonhapnews.co.kr/bulletin/2017/10 / 08/0200000000AKR20171008020400009.HTML?input=1179m (date of searching: 2017.10.9).
66. Nam Sung-wook, *Seoul Economic Daily*, September 12, 2012.
67. *Joongang Daily Newspaper*, October 2, 2017, http://news.joins.com/article/21988888?cloc=joongang|home|newslist2 (date of searching: 2017.10.3).
68. Former German Chancellor Gerhard Schröeder criticized Trump, saying, "No one knows what the US wants." Foreign policy should be predictable, but President Trump is saying this on social networking sites today and tomorrow. This unpredictability shakes the country. Seoul Traffic Broadcasting, September 15, 2017, http://www.tbs.seoul.kr/news/bunya.do?method=daumhtml2&typ_800=6&seq_800=10239750 (date of searching: 2017.10.4).
69. Nixon tried to prevent other countries from making provocations against the United States by instilling the international community with the perception that the US did not know what to do. In 1969, North Vietnam and its former Soviet Union launched nuclear bombers for three consecutive days to end the Vietnam War. *Chosun Daily Newspaper*, September 21, 2017, http://news.chosun.com/site/data/htmldir/2017/09/20/2017092003586.html (date of searching: 2017.10.7).
70. H.R. Haldman, *The Ends of Power* (New York: Times Books, 1978).
71. Schlesinger said the spread of Castro's idea of self-reliant problem-solving could stimulate poor and underprivileged people who demand decent human life opportunities in many parts of the world. This theory has since formed the basis of US foreign policy. The roots of the Madman Theory can be traced back to Machiavelli (1469–1527). The core of Machiavelli's leadership skills is that people around an individual cannot prepare for his next actions and have unpredictable behaviors to fear you. Nathan Miller, *Star-Spangled Men: America's Ten Worst Presidents* (New York: Scribner, 1998).
72. Henry Kissinger also attributed the 1970s invasion of Cambodia to Nixon's symptoms of instability. The 1995 confidential research report released by the United States Strategic Command (USSTRATCOM), which oversees strategic nuclear weapons under

the Freedom of Information Act, suggested that the theory had not been discarded.

73. John J. Mearsheimer, *The Tragedy of Great Power Politics* (New York: W.W., 2004).
74. Woo Jung-yeop, "U.S. policy towards North Korea following the sixth nuclear test", *Sejong Commentary* 2017-36 (Sejong Institute, September 6, 2017).
75. *Yonhap News*, October 20, 2017, http://v.media.daum.net/v/2017 1020101602623?f=o (date of searching: 2017.10.20).
76. US National Security Adviser H.R. McMaster explained that some of the four to five scenarios are relatively more intense. He said North Korea cannot tolerate completing the development of a ballistic missile with a nuclear warhead. Regarding the possibility of dialogue with North Korea, he said, "The negotiations can only take place if North Korea allows inspection of its nuclear facilities and announces its intention to stop its nuclear weapons development." *Joongang Daily Newspaper*, September 26, 2017, http://news.joins.com/article/21971630 (date of searching: 2017.10.2).
77. *Yonhap News*, September 12, 2017, http://www.yonhapnews.co.kr/bulletin/ 2017/09/120200000000AKR20170912061400009.HTML?input=1179m (date of searching: 2017.10.4).
78. At the final talks held in Vienna, Austria on July 14, 2015, Iran and the US, Britain, France, Germany, China and Russia reached an agreement to lift various sanctions imposed on Iran instead of restricting Iran's nuclear program. The agreement was reached to allow IAEA inspectors access to all facilities suspected of developing nuclear weapons, including the military facilities of Iran, which was the biggest issue of negotiations until the Iran nuclear talk's agreement. However, Iran had decided to coordinate the IAEA's request for special inspections through mediation, with the involvement of six major countries. Iran's research and development of nuclear technology centered on the new centrifuge was limited to Natanz facilities, while its concentration of enriched uranium was 3.67% or less (low-concentration uranium), and its size was 300kg. It also prohibited Iran from storing enrichment, research, and nuclear materials in a facility that it did not disclose. *Yonhap News*, September 23, 2017, http://terms.naver.com/entry.nhn ?docId=2851891&cid=43667&categoryId=43667 (date of searching: 2017.10.2).

79. The US independent proposal on North Korea, which came after the UN Security Council Resolution 2321 after the fifth nuclear test, contained the blocking of North Korea's transactions at the Society for Worldwide Interbank Financial Telecommunication (SWIFT), a financial network where financial institutions settle trade payments and transfer money.
80. North Korea's nominal gross domestic product (GDP) in 2016 was around ₩36,103 trillion, while its export volume was only about ₩3.2 trillion.
81. The US administration's North Korea policy on October 26, 2017 is the third sanctions under the strengthened sanctions against the North, which went into effect in February 2016. The State Department released a report on human rights violations and censorship in North Korea, and the Treasury Department imposed additional sanctions on seven individuals and three organizations. The sanctions sought to reduce slavery by some 120,000 North Korean workers in 42 countries around the world. There would be a setback in foreign currency earnings of US$1 billion a year. Nam Sung-wook, *Munhwa Daily Newspaper*, October 30, 2017.
82. *Voice of America*, July 1, 2017, https://www.voakorea.com/a/3923416.html (date of searching: 2017.10.3).
83. *Munhwa Daily Newspaper*, October 1, 2017, http://www.munhwa.com/news/view.html?no=20171001MW11483680813 (date of searching: 2017.10.3).
84. *Hankook Daily Newspaper*, October 1, 2017, http://www.hankookilbo.com/v/d9b1774e631a4bb4830f37c3d5a830d3 (date of searching: 2017.10.4).
85. "I told Rex Tillerson, the great Secretary of State, that he was wasting time trying to negotiate with the 'Little Rocket Man'," Trump said in a Twitter post. "Little Rocket Man" is a nickname that President Trump gave to North Korean leader Kim Jong-un, who continues nuclear and missile provocations. "Rex, save your energy. We will do what we have to do. The New Yorker, a US news magazine, reported on the day that what we should do is a military option against North Korea." "I don't think I'm going to fail," Trump tweeted, asking, "Why is it going to work now after 25 years of being nice to the Rockets?" he asked. "Clinton has failed, Bush has failed, Obama has failed," he said.
86. A senior US government official said in an anonymous interview with Reuters, citing a series of provocations from North Korea. President

Trump did not believe it was time to negotiate with the North. The focus of the diplomatic channels between Washington and Pyongyang was on ensuring the return of Americans detained in North Korea.

87. *The New York Times* analyzed that President Trump did not completely exclude diplomatic solutions, even though he made remarks drawing a line with North Korea in anger. Trump was believed to be trying to increase the negotiating power of his aides, including Tillerson, by using former President Richard Nixon's "Madman Theory" to describe his preference for force. However, some argue that it was a dangerous choice, as North Korean leader Kim Jong-un used the same "Madman Theory" as he could conduct a nuclear test in the atmosphere or launch an attack on Seoul under the circumstances of misjudgment.
88. Susan Rice, former national security adviser to the Obama administration, wrote in *The New York Times* on September 10, 2017 that there seemed little chance that North Korea would give up its nuclear weapons and that she proposed North Korea's permission to possess nuclear weapons compared to the former Soviet Union during the Cold War. Susan Rice, It's not too late on North Korea, *The New York Times*, September 10, 2017, https://www.nytimes.com/2017/08/10/opinion/susan-rice-trump-north-korea.html (date of searching: 2017.10.7).
89. *Joongang Daily Newspaper*, October 6, 2017, http://news.joins.com/article/21991940 (date of searching: 2017.10.6).
90. *Chosun Daily Newspaper*, October 29, 2017, http://news.chosun.com/site/data/html_dir/2017/10/29/2017102900869.html (date of searching: 2017.10.29).
91. Park Hwee-rak, "An analysis of a pre-emptive strike on North Korean nuclear weapons: Theories, international law and necessity", *New Asia* 21 (4), New Asia Research Institute (2014), pp. 31–56.
92. Park Yongsoo. "The competitive foreign policy management style of the former South Korean President Kim Young-sam in the process of First North Korean Nuclear Crisis", *The Korean Journal of International Relationship* 55 (4), The Korean Association of International Studies (2015), pp. 139–168.
93. *MK News*, September 20, 2017, http://news.mk.co.kr/newsRead.php (date of searching: 2017.10.30).
94. *Yonhap News*, October 5, 2017, http://www.yonhapnews.co.kr/bulletin/2017/10/05/0200000000AKR20171005014200071.HTML?input=1179m (date of searching: 2017.10.7).

95. Unlike the kinetic weapons system, CIA Director Mike Pompeo mentioned in September 2017.
96. President Trump said he just heard North Korea's foreign minister address to the UN and said that if he recited the idea of a "little rocket man (Kim Jong-un)", they would not last long.
97. After completing the UN General Assembly schedule on September 23, 2017, Foreign Minister Ri said in a statement released in front of the Hilton Hotel in New York, "As long as the US declares war, we will have all the right to defend ourselves."
98. *The Washington Post* pointed out that the North had taken the most direct and threatening response since President Trump's speech at the UN General Assembly, which mentioned "completely destroy" North Korea. *The New York Times* reported, "We should pay attention to North Korea's claim that it has the right to pursue US strategic bombers, even if they are not airspace." *Bloomberg* also said, "Li Yong-ho's claim for self-defense is based on the UN Charter," adding, "When the US strategic bomber, B-1B Lander, flew to the northernmost international airspace, we have to wait and see why he made such remarks."
99. *ABC News* of the US introduced David Gillespie's secret recipe for "Kim Jong-un taming". In his article "North Korea: Why dealing with Kim Jong-un is like managing a psychopathic boss", Gillespie suggested a strategy to respond to North Korea, such as possessing strong deterrence and strengthening of the South Korea–US alliance. *Segye Daily Newspaper*, October 2, 2017, http://www.segye.com/newsView/20171002000984 (date of searching: 2017.10).
100. Park Hwee-rak, "An evaluation and tasks of South Korean nuclear preparedness as a prerequisite for the unification: Focused on consistency among ends, ways and means", *Korea Association of Unification Strategy* 17 (2), Korea Association of Unification Strategy (2017), pp. 18–23.
101. President Trump made a series of mysterious comments on North Korea's nuclear and missile issues. Immediately after discussing the issue of North Korea and Iran with the top military leaders, he said, "(now) calm before the storm," and repeatedly mentioned the theory of dialogue and negotiation with the North via Twitter on October 7, 2017. However, there are many interpretations of his remarks because he did not disclose details. *Yonhap News*, October 7, 2017, https://news.nate.com/view/20171008n02484?mid=n0208 (date of searching: 2017.10.8).

102. After meeting with top military leaders, President Trump kept quiet for a second day about the meaning of his comment before the storm. When reporters asked what "quiet before the storm" meant, President Trump said, "You'll know." When reporters asked him "What does it mean other than military action?" he said, "Let's see," and left. *Yonhap News*, October 7, 2017, http://news.nate.com/view/20171007n01008?mid=n0208 (date of searching: 2017.10.7).
103. According to a poll released by Cable News Network (CNN) on September 8, 2017, 50% of respondents said they support military action against the North (43%). In particular, 74% of Republican supporters said they support it. With North Korea's sixth nuclear test, American public opinion is expected to get stronger.
104. Lee Hun-kyun, "The empirical approach on sanctions and effectiveness of the UN and international society against North Korea", *Unification Strategy* 17 (3), Korean Association of Unification Strategy (2017), pp. 264–267.

Chapter 5: Diplomatic Negotiation between US and DPRK: Summit

105. Tae Young-ho, *Password on the Third-Floor Secretarial Room* (Seoul: Giparang, 2018).

Chapter 6: Denuclearization and Financial Issues

106. Ashton B. Carter and William J. Perry, *Preventive Defense: A New Security Strategy for America* (Washington, D.C.: Brookings Institution Press, 1999).
107. William J. Perry, *My Journey at the Nuclear Brink* (Stanford University Press, 2015).

Chapter 7: DPRK's Nuclear Weapon and Geopolitical Dynamics in East Asia

108. T.J. Pempel, "Domestic drivers of Northeast Asian relations", *International Journal of Korean Unification Studies* 23 (2) (2014), pp. 65–95.

109. G. John Ikenberry, "From hegemony to the balance of power: The rise of China and American grand strategy in East Asia", *International Journal of Korean Unification Studies* 23 (2) (2014), pp. 41–63.
110. Victor Shih, *Factions and Finance in China: Elite Conflict and Inflation* (New York: Cambridge University Press, 2007).
111. For examples of this type of commentary, see Michael Swaine, "Perceptions of an assertive China", *China Leadership Monitor* 32 (May 2010), p. 10.
112. Alastair Iain Johnston, "How new and assertive is China's new assertiveness?" *China Leadership Monitor* 32 (May 2010), p. 35.
113. Alessandro Ricardo Ungaro, "Developments in and obstacles to the US Pivot to Asia: What alternatives for Europe?" *IAI Working Papers* (December 24, 2012), p. 3.
114. Bruce Klinger. "The U.S. Pivot to Asia and maritime security in Northeast Asia", paper presented in the International Sea Power Symposium held by the ROK Navy on 6 September 2013, pp. 119–130.
115. North Korean leader Kim Jong-un signed an order to carry out a hydrogen bomb test on December 15, 2015. The North's KCTV disclosed photos of him signing right after the official announcement of the test's success.
116. The South Korean government faces a totally new circumstance in which it cannot delay discussions on the deployment any more after Pyongyang conducted its fourth nuclear test and third flight test of submarine-launched ballistic missiles (SLBM). Given the North's alarming speed in developing nuclear weapons and the SLBMs, the government cannot simply wait for the development of the Korean Air and Missile Defense (KAMD) System, which was an earlier plan that China would have been far more comfortable with. But the THAAD deployment could require a massive investment by the US. Not to mention the cost of ₩3 trillion (US$2.49 billion) per artillery battery, the system calls for significant additional expenditures for maintenance and repairs. In addition, opponents contend that the system would not be effective in intercepting high-altitudes missiles on the Korean Peninsula due to the relatively short distance they would fly.
117. The *Foreign Policy* magazine's survey of about 700 scholars teaching or researching at colleges and universities throughout the US listed the conflict in the Middle East as the most important foreign policy issue followed by climate change and renewed Russian assertiveness.

"It appears that concerns about WMD (weapons of mass destruction) proliferation have gone down among these experts, despite the recent North Korean missile tests. Only 10 percent of scholars listed WMD proliferation in their top three issues compared to 14 percent in our previous survey," the magazine said. WMD proliferation ranked only as the 11th most important issue. Other issues listed as more important foreign policy matters than WMD proliferation included transnational terrorism, China's rising military power, failed states, global wealth disparities, global poverty and China's rising economic influence. *Korea Times*, February 23, 2016, https://www.koreatimes.co.kr/www/nation/2019/03/120_198712.html (date of searching: 2017.10.23).

118. In September 2005, the George W. Bush administration, working through the China-led six-party talks (Russia, South Korea and Japan were also involved) reached an agreement to denuclearize North Korea. After a promising start with five working groups addressing every issue of interest to Pyongyang, from energy and economic aid to a peace treaty, the North decided to walk away. Then it was Obama's turn. Despite the fact Pyongyang answered his call for a dialogue by conducting a nuclear test in 2009, three years later the US reached what would be known as the leap day deal, in which Pyongyang agreed to freeze its nuclear missile programs in exchange for aid. The accord fell apart only days later when Pyongyang disagreed with the US interpretation of it.
119. Yun Yeongmi and Park Kicheol, "Structural restrictions of territorial disputes in Northeast Asia", *The Journal of East Affairs* 27 (2) (Fall/Winter, 2013), pp. 89–111.
120. Yun Yeongmi, *Contemporary Russian Politics and International Relations* (Seoul: Doonam, 2012), pp. 280–281.
121. Andreas Hasenclever, Peter Mayer, and Volker Rittberger, "Interests, power, knowledge: The study of international regimes", *Myerson International Studies Review* 40 (1996), pp. 177–228.
122. Jina Kim, "Prospects and limitations of establishing a security regime in the Asia-Pacific", *Korea Defense Issue & Analysis*, Korea Institute for National Defense (2012), pp. 2–5.
123. G. John Ikenberry, p. 60.
124. Max Fisher, Uncertainty over Donald Trump's foreign policy risks global instability, *The New York Times*, November 9, 2016.

Chapter 8: Contingency and Determinants of Stabilization Strategy in North Korea

125. Joint Chiefs of Staff, *Stability Operations JP 3-07* (Washington, D.C.: Joint Chiefs of Staff, 2011), pp. I-1–I-2.
126. Charles F. Audrain, *Political Change in the Third World* (Boston: Unwin Hyman, 1988).
127. Francis Fukuyama, *State Building: Governance and World Order in the 21st Century* (Croydon: Profile Books, 2005); and Francis Fukuyama, ed., *Nation Building* (Baltimore: Johns Hopkins University Press, 2006).
128. James Dobbins, ed., *America's Role in Nation-Building from Germany to Iraq* (Santa Monica: RAND, 2003).
129. SIGIR, *Hard Lessons: The Iraq Reconstruction Experience* (Washington, D.C.: US Independent Agencies and Commissions, 2013).
130. Bruce W. Bennett, *Preparing for the Possibility of a North Korean Collapse* (Santa Monica: RAND, 2013).
131. For greater details about the method, see John P. Frendreis, "Explanation of variation and detection of co-variation: The purpose and logic of comparative analysis", *Comparative Political Studies* 16 (2) (1983), pp. 255–272.; and Ingo Rohlfing, *Case Studies and Causal Inference* (Hampshire: Palgrave Macmillan, 2012), pp. 97–124.
132. Joint Chief of Staff, *Stability Operations: JP 3-07* (Washington, D.C.: Joint Chiefs of Staff, 2011), pp. I-2–I-3.
133. Lee Dongkyu, Seo Inseok, and Yang Gigeun, "Long-term foresight study of North Korea system collapse from system collapse viewpoint — Take advantage of dynamic modelling analysis technique", *Journal of Safety and Crisis Management* 7 (1) (2011), pp. 85–88.
134. Jaroslaw Piekalkiewicz and Alfred Wayne Penn, *Politics of Ideocracy* (Albany: State University of New York Press, 1995), pp. 118–123.
135. The model of analysis is applicable if North Korea fully collapses. But a partial collapse or internal civil war might evolve into situations that had happened in Libya and Syria.
136. Mark T. Berger, "Nation-Building to State-Building: The Geopolitics of Development, the Nation-State System and the Changing Global Order", in Mark T. Berger, ed., *From Nation-Building to State-Building* (New York: Routledge, 2008), p. 2.
137. James Dobbins, ed., *America's Role in Nation-Building from Germany to Iraq* (Santa Monica: RAND, 2003), pp. 157–160.

138. *Fragile States Index*, http://fsi.fundforpeace.org/(accessed: 2015.8.20).
139. In Namsik, "The characteristics and implications of the political upheaval in Arab states in 2011", *The Korean Journal of International Studies* 51 (4) (2011), pp. 247–250.
140. Otto Dann, trans. Oh Insuk, *Nation und Nationalismus in Deutschland 1770–1990* (Seoul: Hanul, 1996), pp. 140–258.
141. Robert C. Tucker, *Politics as Leadership* (Columbia: University of Missouri Press, 1981), pp. 89–91.
142. Juan José Linz, *Totalitarian and Authoritarian Regimes* (Colorado: Lynne Rienner Publishers, 2000), p. 70.
143. Earl F. Ziemke, *The US Army in the Occupation of Germany 1944–1946* (Washington, D.C.: US Government Printing Office, 1975), pp. 325–327.
144. *Military Government and Civil Affairs: FM 27-5* (Washington, D.C.: Department of the Army and Navy, 1943), p. 1.
145. US Central Intelligence Agency, *Soviet Control Mechanism in Germany* (May 1949).
146. Jia Yoo, "National seclusion and openness: The contradiction and revolution the Japanese modernization process shows", *Journal of Joong-Ang Historical Studies* 27 (June 2008), pp. 155–157.
147. Kweon Sugin, "Ethnicity in contemporary Japan: New dimensions", *The Korean Journal for Japanese Studies* 19 (2004), pp. 184–187.
148. National Archives of Japan, *The Imperial Rescript Ending the War*, https://www.digital.archives.go.jp (accessed: 2015.6.10).
149. Carl J. Friedrich and Douglas G. Haring, "Military government for Japan", *Far Eastern Survey* 14 (3) (1945), p. 38.
150. US Central Intelligence Agency, *Japan Peace Treaty Problems, Issues and Reactions* (November 1947).
151. Ralph J.D. Braibanti, "Administration of military government in Japan at the prefectural level", *The American Political Science Review* 43 (2) (1949), pp. 258–259.
152. Eiji Takemame, trans. Song Byungkwon, *GHQ–Supreme Commander of the Allied Powers* (Seoul: Commonlife Books, 2011), pp. 188–191.
153. Ralph J.D. Braibanti, "Occupation controls in Japan", *Far Eastern Survey* 17 (18) (1948), pp. 215–216.
154. Choi Jangjip, *Democracy after Democratization* (Seoul: Humanitas Books, 2005), p. 60.
155. Meade E. Grant, *American Military Government in Korea* (New York: King's Crown Press, 1951), pp. 29–30; and Ibid., pp. 58–60.

156. US Army and Navy, *Manual of Military Government and Civil Affairs: FM 27-5* (Washington, D.C.: US Government Printing Office, 1943), p. 10.
157. Ibid., pp. 9–10.
158. Lee Wanbom, "Relationship between local political groups South Korea and the US, after liberation, 1945–1948", in Park Jihyang *et al.*, *New Light on the History of Pre- and Post-Liberation* (Seoul: Chaeksesang, 2006), p. 79.
159. Liem Channing, "United States rule in Korea", *Far Eastern Survey* 18 (7) (April 1949), pp. 77–79.
160. US Central Intelligence Agency, *Prospects for Survival of the Republic of Korea* (October 28, 1948), pp. 1–8.
161. Richard D. Robinson, trans. Jung Miok, *Betrayal of a Nation* (Seoul: Science and Idea, 1988); and Jung Yongok, *Research on US Military Occupational Documents* (Seoul: Seon-In, 2003), pp. 117–179.
162. Liam Anderson and Gareth Stansfield, *The Future of Iraq: Dictatorship, Democracy, or Division?* (New York: Palgrave Macmillan, 2003), p. 50.
163. SIGIR, *Hard Lessons*, pp. 12–13.
164. R. Royce Kneece Jr., *Force Sizing for Stability Operations* (IDA, 2010); Bruce W. Bennett, *Preparing for the Possibility of a North Korean Collapse* (Santa Monica: RAND, 2013); and Lee Geunuk, "Preparing for contingency in North Korea: A critique to Bruce W. Bennett's estimates for military manpower requirements", *Journal of National Defense Studies* 57 (3) (September 2014).
165. Larry Diamond, "What Went Wrong and Right in Iraq", in *Nation Building*, pp. 174–175.
166. Lee Geunuk, *The Iraq War* (Paju: Hanul, 2011), p. 185.
167. Larry Diamond, "What Went Wrong and Right in Iraq", in *Nation Building*, p. 181.
168. James Dobbins, ed., *America's Role in Nation-Building from Germany to Iraq* (Santa Monica: RAND, 2003), pp. 160–161.
169. Dennis L. Bark and David R. Gress, *From Shadow to Substance 1945–1963* (Oxford: Blackwell, 1993), pp. 128–135.
170. James Dobbins, ed., *America's Role in Nation-Building from Germany to Iraq* (Santa Monica: RAND, 2003), pp. 157–159.
171. "Transparency International Annual CPI report" quoted from Michael E. O'Hanlon and Ian Livingston, *Iraq Index Tracking Variables of Reconstruction & Security in Post-Saddam Iraq*, www.brookings.edu/iraqindex (accessed: 2015.6.15)

172. This study considers the concept of race like many other social cleavages such as culture and religion.
173. Samuel P. Huntington, *The Clash of Civilizations and the Remaking of World Order* (NewYork: Simon & Schuster, 1996).
174. In Namsik, *Study on the Application of Constructivism on the Middle East Identity Layers* (Seoul: IFANS, 2011).
175. Francis Fukuyama, *The Origins of Political Order* (New York: Farrar, Straus and Giroux, 2011), pp. 192–196.
176. Kang Jungin, "Theory of Clash of Civilizations", in Woo Chulku and Park Kunyoung, eds., *Contemporary Theories of International Relations and Korea* (Seoul: Sapyoung, 2004), pp. 568–569.
177. Paul Staniland, "Defeating transnational insurgencies: The best offense is a good fence", *The Washington Quarterly* 29 (1) (2005), pp. 21–40.
178. Thomas Heghammer, "The rise of Muslim foreign fighters", *International Security* 35 (3) (Winter, 2010/11), pp. 53–94.
179. Park Youngho, "Theoretical study on North Korean collapse", in *Tasks and Measures for Korean Contingencies* (National Security and Defense Academic Conferences Sourcebook, November 14, 1997).
180. Monty G. Marshall and Benjamin R. Core, *Global Report 2014: Conflict, Governance, and State Fragility* (Vienna: Center for Systemic Peace, 2014), pp. 11–14.
181. Jung Sangdon, Kim Jinmoo, and Lee Kangkyu, *Reunification Policy of West Germany and the Sudden Change of East Germany* (Seoul: KIDA Press, 2012), p. 20.
182. Nam Sung-wook, "Crisis of Korean Peninsula and Efficient Contingency Plan: Economic Aspects", in National Development Institute, Center for North Korean Studies of Korea University, ed., *Contingency Plan for North Korea's Crisis* (Seoul: Hanul, 2007), p. 93.
183. Choi Wankyu, ed., *Study on the Changing State Character of North Korea: Solidification of Exceptional State* (Seoul: Hanul, 2001).
184. Ministry of Unification, *2013 White Paper* (Seoul: Ministry of Unification), pp. 17–18.
185. Adam P. Liff, "U.S. policy toward North Korea: The China fallacy", *Pacific Forum CSIS* (October 8, 2009), p. 1, available at http://www.pacforum.org (accessed: 2015.6.12).
186. Bruce W. Bennett, *Preparing for the Possibility of a North Korean Collapse* (Santa Monica: RAND, 2013), pp. 87–101.
187. Jeong Cheolho, *ROK's Security Strategy for Chinese Military Intervention in North Korean Contingency* (Seongnam: Sejong Institute, 2014).

188. *Civil-Military Operations: TC 07-3-10* (Daejeon: Training & Doctrine Command of Army, 2007), pp. 5–48.
189. Park Yunghwan, *Study on the Possibility of Applying German Model for Inter-Korean Military Integration* (Seoul: Korea Research Institute for Strategy, 2004), p. 62.
190. Kim Myunggi, "Legal issues of ROK intervention in North Korean Contingency", *Korean Contingency and International Law* (Korea Institute of National Unification, Korean International Law Symposium, November 8, 1997); and Shin Bumchul, "Legal issues of the sudden collapse of North Korea", *Seoul International Law Journal* 15 (1) (2008).
191. Michael Walzer, *Just and Unjust Wars* (New York: Basic Books, 2006), pp. 91–108.
192. *Joint Stability Operations: JM 3-12* (Seoul: Joint Chiefs of Staff, 2010), pp. 96–98.
193. Dafna H. Rand and Nicholas A. Heras, "Iraq's Sunni reawakening", *Foreign Affairs* 16 (March 2015).
194. Jeremy Binnie, US sidelined from tacit offensive, *Jane's Defense Weekly*, March 5, 2015.
195. Lee Shinwha, "State failure and Responsibility to Protect (R2P) practical implication for North Korea", *Korean Political Science Review* 46 (1) (2012).
196. Paul B. Stares and Joel S. Wit, *Preparing for Sudden Change in North Korea* (Washington: Council on Foreign Relations, 2009), pp. 7–8.
197. Kim Jong-il, *Kim Jong-il Works 9* (Pyongyang: Workers Party Press, 1997), p. 32.
198. *Joint Civil-Military Operations: JM 3-6* (Seoul: Joint Chiefs of Staff, 2005), pp. 6–7.
199. Joint Chiefs of Staff, *Peace Operations: JP 3-07.3* (Washington, D.C.: Joint Chiefs of Staff, 2012), p. I-8.
200. Francis Fukuyama, "Guidelines for Future Nation-Building", in *Nation Building*, pp. 232–234.
201. Department of Peacekeeping Operations, Department of Field Support, *United Nations Peacekeeping Operations* (New York: United Nations, 2008), pp. 66–74.
202. For further information on the properties of the North Korean elite, refer to Lim Jaecheon, *Kim Jong-il's Leadership of North Korea* (London: Routledge, 2009); and Jina Kim, "An analysis of political instability in

the DPRK: Identity, interest, and leader-elite relations", *The Korean Journal of Defense Analysis* 25 (1) (March 2013), pp. 87–107.

203. Erin K. Jenne, "Sri Lanka: A Fragmented State", in Robert I. Rotberg, ed., *State Failure and State Weakness in a Time of Terror* (Washington, D.C.: Brookings Institution Press and the World Peace Foundation, 2003), pp. 219–223.
204. Bruce Cumings, *North Korea: Another Country* (New York: The New Press, 2004), pp. 15–31.
205. Kim Il-sung, *Kim Il-sung Works 8* (Pyongyang: Workers Party Press, 1980), p. 12.
206. For further information on the strategy cooperation for contingency, refer to Nam Sung-wook, Park Yong-han, and Cho Pyungse, "Effective stabilization and integration strategy after North Korea contingency", *Journal of National Defense Studies* 59 (1) (April 2016).

Chapter 9: Unification of Korean Peninsula: Is It Possible?

207. Nam Sung-wook *et al.*, *South Korea's 70-Year Endeavor for Foreign Policy, National Defense and Unification* (Singapore: Palgrave Macmillan, 2018), pp. 249–260.

References

Adam P. Liff, "U.S. policy toward North Korea: The China fallacy", *Pacific Forum CSIS* (October 8, 2009), p. 1, available at http://www.pacforum.org (accessed: 2015.6.12).

Alessandro Ricardo Ungaro, "Developments in and obstacles to the US Pivot to Asia: What alternatives for Europe?" *IAI Working Papers* (December 24, 2012).

Andreas Hasenclever, Peter Mayer, and Volker Rittberger, "Interests, power, knowledge: The study of international regimes", *Myerson International Studies Review* 40 (1996).

Ashton B. Carter and William J. Perry, *Preventive Defense: A New Security Strategy for America* (Washington, D.C.: Brookings Institution Press, 1999).

Bruce Cumings, *North Korea: Another Country* (New York: The New Press, 2004).

Bruce Klinger. "The U.S. Pivot to Asia and maritime security in Northeast Asia", paper presented in the International Sea Power Symposium held by the ROK Navy on 6 September 2013.

Bruce W. Bennett, *Preparing for the Possibility of a North Korean Collapse* (Santa Monica: RAND, 2013).

Carl J. Friedrich and Douglas G. Haring, "Military government for Japan", *Far Eastern Survey* 14 (3) (1945).

Charles F. Audrain, *Political Change in the Third World* (Boston: Unwin Hyman, 1988).

Charles Glaser, "Realists as optimists: Cooperation as self-help", *International Security* 19 (1994/1995).

Choi Jangjip, *Democracy after Democratization* (Seoul: Humanitas Books, 2005).

Choi Wankyu, ed., *Study on the Changing State Character of North Korea: Solidification of Exceptional State* (Seoul: Hanul, 2001).

Dafna H. Rand and Nicholas A. Heras, "Iraq's Sunni reawakening", *Foreign Affairs* 16 (March 2015).

David Albright, Frans Berkhout, and William Walker, *Plutonium and Highly Enriched Uranium 1996: World Inventories, Capabilities and Policies* (Oxford: Oxford University Press, 1997).

Dennis L. Bark and David R. Gress, *From Shadow to Substance 1945–1963* (Oxford: Blackwell, 1993).

Department of Peacekeeping Operations, Department of Field Support, *United Nations Peacekeeping Operations* (New York: United Nations, 2008).

Douglas MacArthur, *Reminiscences: General of Army* (New York: McGraw-Hill, 1964).

Earl F. Ziemke, *The US Army in the Occupation of Germany 1944–1946* (Washington, D.C.: US Government Printing Office, 1975).

Eiji Takemame, trans. Song Byungkwon, *GHQ–Supreme Commander of the Allied Powers* (Seoul: Commonlife Books, 2011).

Erin K. Jenne, "Sri Lanka: A Fragmented State", in Robert I. Rotberg, ed., *State Failure and State Weakness in a Time of Terror* (Washington, D.C.: Brookings Institution Press and the World Peace Foundation, 2003).

Fragile States Index, http://fsi.fundforpeace.org/ (accessed: 2015.8.20).

Francis Fukuyama, ed., *Nation Building* (Baltimore: Johns Hopkins University Press, 2006).

Francis Fukuyama, *State Building: Governance and World Order in the 21st Century* (Croydon: Profile Books, 2005).

G. John Ikenberry, "From hegemony to the balance of power: The rise of China and American grand strategy in East Asia", *International Journal of Korean Unification Studies* 23 (2) (2014).

Han Yong-seop, *The Fate of Nuclear Weapon in North Korea* (Gyeonggi-do Paju: Park Youngsa, 2018).

Harry S. Truman, The President News Conference (November 30, 1950), *Public Paper of the Presidents of the United States.*

Henry Kissinger, *White House Years* (Boston, MA: Little Brown and Company, 2009).

H.R. Haldman, *The Ends of Power* (New York: Times Books, 1978).

In Namsik, "The characteristics and implications of the political upheaval in Arab states in 2011", *The Korean Journal of International Studies* 51 (4) (2011).

In Namsik, *Study on the Application of Constructivism on the Middle East Identity Layers* (Seoul: IFANS, 2011).

Ingo Rohlfing, *Case Studies and Causal Inference* (Hampshire: Palgrave Macmillan, 2012).

James C. Moltz and C. Kenneth Quinones, "Getting serious about a multilateral approach to North Korea", *The Nonproliferation Review* 11 (1) (Spring 2004).

James Dobbins, ed., *America's Role in Nation-Building from Germany to Iraq* (Santa Monica: RAND, 2003).

Jaroslaw Piekalkiewicz and Alfred Wayne Penn, *Politics of Ideocracy* (Albany: State University of New York Press, 1995).

Jeong Cheolho, *ROK's Security Strategy for Chinese Military Intervention in North Korean Contingency* (Seongnam: Sejong Institute, 2014).

Jeong Han-beom, "A theoretical discussion on the effectiveness of US-led economic sanctions against North Korea", *The Journal of Peace Studies* 18 (3), The Korean Association of Peace Studies (2017).

Jeremy Binnie, US sidelined from tacit offensive, *Jane's Defense Weekly*, March 5, 2015.

Jia Yoo, "National seclusion and openness: The contradiction and revolution the Japanese modernization process shows", *Journal of Joong-Ang Historical Studies* 27 (June 2008).

Jina Kim, "An analysis of political instability in the DPRK: Identity, interest, and leader-elite relations", *The Korean Journal of Defense Analysis* 25 (1) (March 2013).

Jina Kim, "Prospects and limitations of establishing a security regime in the Asia-Pacific", *Korea Defense Issue & Analysis*, Korea Institute for National Defense (2012).

John J. Mearsheimer, *The Tragedy of Great Power Politics* (New York: W.W., 2004).

John P. Frendreis, "Explanation of variation and detection of co-variation: The purpose and logic of comparative analysis", *Comparative Political Studies* 16 (2) (1983).

Joseph S. Bermudez, Jr., "North Korea's nuclear programme", *Jane's Intelligence Review* 3 (9) (September 1991).

Joseph S. Bermudez Jr., *The Armed Forces of North Korea* (London: I.B. Tauris Publisher, 2001).

Juan José Linz, *Totalitarian and Authoritarian Regimes* (Colorado: Lynne Rienner Publishers, 2000).

Jung Sangdon, Kim Jinmoo, and Lee Kangkyu, *Reunification Policy of West Germany and the Sudden Change of East Germany* (Seoul: KIDA Press, 2012).

Jung Yongok, *Research on US Military Occupational Documents* (Seoul: Seon-In, 2003).

Kang Jungin, "Theory of Clash of Civilizations", in Woo Chulku and Park Kunyoung, eds., *Contemporary Theories of International Relations and Korea* (Seoul: Sapyoung, 2004).

Kathleen C. Bailey, *Strengthening Nuclear Nonproliferation* (Boulder: Westview Press, 1993).

Kim Hyun-wook, IFANS Analysis on Major Global Issue, 2017-11 (Institute of Foreign Affairs and National Security, April 4, 2017).

Kim Il-sung, *Kim Il-sung Collection 12* (Pyongyang: Chosun Labor Party Publishing Company, 1958).

Kim Il-sung, *Kim Il-sung Collection 19* (Pyongyang: Chosun Labor Party Publishing Company, 1982).

Kim Il-sung, "Current Situation and Current Task", *Kim Il-sung Collection 6* (Pyongyang: Labor Party Publishing House, 1980).

Kim Il-sung, *Kim Il-sung Memoir I* (Pyongyang: Chosun Labor Party Publishing Company, 1992).

Kim Il-sung, *Kim Il-sung Works 8* (Pyongyang: Workers Party of Korea Press, 1980).

Kim Il-sung, *New Year's Address* (Paperback) (Pyongyang: Social Science Publishing Company, 1977).

Kim Jong-il, *Kim Jong Il Works 9* (Pyongyang: Workers Party of Korea Press, 1997).

Kim Myunggi, "Legal issues of ROK intervention in North Korean Contingency", *Korean Contingency and International Law* (Korea Institute of National Unification, Korean International Law Symposium, November 8, 1997).

Kweon Sugin, "Ethnicity in contemporary Japan: New dimensions", *The Korean Journal for Japanese Studies* 19 (2004).

Lee Dongkyu, Seo Inseok, and Yang Gigeun, "Long-term foresight study of North Korea system collapse from system collapse viewpoint — Take advantage of dynamic modelling analysis technique", *Journal of Safety and Crisis Management* 7 (1) (2011).

Lee Geunuk, "Preparing for contingency in North Korea: A critique to Bruce W. Bennett's estimates for military manpower requirements", *Journal of National Defense Studies* 57 (3) (September 2014).

Lee Geunuk, *The Iraq War* (Paju: Hanul, 2011).

Lee Hun-kyun, "The empirical approach on sanctions and effectiveness of the UN and international society against North Korea", *Unification Strategy* 17 (3), Korean Association of Unification Strategy (2017).

Lee Jae-hak, "Determination of non-use of nuclear weapons by the Truman administration during the Korean War in terms of situational deterrence theory", *The Journal of International Politics* 54 (3), International Politics Association (2014), pp. 79–112.

Lee Sang-hyun and Woo Jung-yeop, "U.S. policy toward North Korea after North Korea's sixth nuclear test", *Policy Briefing* 2017-26 (Sejong Institute, 2017).

Lee Shinwha, "State failure and Responsibility to Protect (R2P) practical implication for North Korea", *Korean Political Science Review* 46 (1) (2012).

Lee Wanbom, "Relationship between local political groups South Korea and the US, after liberation, 1945–1948", in Park Jihyang *et al.*, *New Light on the History of Pre- and Post-Liberation* (Seoul: Chaeksesang, 2006).

Liam Anderson and Gareth Stansfield, *The Future of Iraq: Dictatorship, Democracy, or Division?* (New York: Palgrave Macmillan, 2003).

Liem Channing, "United States rule in Korea", *Far Eastern Survey* 18 (7) (April 1949).

Lim Jaecheon, *Kim Jong-il's Leadership of North Korea* (London: Routledge, 2009).

Malcolm Chalmers, "Preparing for war in Korea", *Whitehall Reports* (Royal United Services Institute for Defense and Security Institute, September 27, 2017).

Mark T. Berger, ed., *From Nation-Building to State-Building* (New York: Routledge, 2008).

Max Fisher, Uncertainty over Donald Trump's foreign policy risks global instability, *The New York Times*, November 9, 2016.

Meade E. Grant, *American Military Government in Korea* (New York: King's Crown Press, 1951).

Michael O'Hanlon and Mike Mochizuki, *Crisis on the Korean Peninsula: How to Deal with a Nuclear North Korea* (New York: McGraw-Hill, 2003).

Michael Swaine, "Perceptions of an assertive China", *China Leadership Monitor* 32 (May 2010).

Michael Walzer, *Just and Unjust Wars* (New York: Basic Books, 2006).

Ministry of Unification, *2013 White Paper* (Seoul: Ministry of Unification).

Nam Sung-wook, "Crisis of Korean Peninsula and Efficient Contingency Plan: Economic Aspects", in National Development Institute, Center for North Korean Studies of Korea University, ed., *Contingency Plan for North Korea's Crisis* (Seoul: Hanul, 2007).

Nam Sung-wook, "Research on contingency and determinants of stabilization strategy in North Korea", *International Journal of Korean Unification Studies* 25 (1) (2016).

Nam Sung-wook *et al.*, *South Korea's 70-Year Endeavor for Foreign Policy, National Defense and Unification* (Singapore: Palgrave Macmillan, 2018).

National Archives of Japan, *The Imperial Rescript Ending the War,* https://www.digital.archives.go.jp (accessed: 2015.6.10).

Nathan Miller, *Star-Spangled Men: America's Ten Worst Presidents* (New York: Scribner, 1998).

Nicholas Eberstadt, "North Korea's interlocked economic crisis: Some indications from "mirror statistics", *Asian Survey* 38 (3) (March, 1998).

Oli Heinonen, North Korea has started nuclear development since the signing of Geneva Agreement in 1994, *Joongang Daily News Paper,* May 18, 2018.

Otto Dann, trans. Insuk Oh, *Nation und Nationalismus in Deutschland 1770–1990* (Seoul: Hanul, 1996).

Park Hwee-rak, "An evaluation and tasks of South Korean nuclear preparedness as a prerequisite for the unification: Focused on consistency among ends, ways and means", *Korea Association of Unification Strategy* 17 (2), Korea Association of Unification Strategy (2017).

Park Yongsoo. "The competitive foreign policy management style of the former South Korean President Kim Young-sam in the process of First North Korean Nuclear Crisis", *The Korean Journal of International Relationship* 55 (4), The Korean Association of International Studies (2015).

Park Youngho, "Theoretical study on North Korean collapse", in *Tasks and Measures for Korean Contingencies* (National Security and Defense Academic Conferences Sourcebook, November 14, 1997).

Park Yunghwan, *Study on the Possibility of Applying German Model for Inter-Korean Military Integration* (Seoul: Korea Research Institute for Strategy, 2004).

Paul B. Stares and Joel S. Wit, *Preparing for Sudden Change in North Korea* (Washington: Council on Foreign Relations, 2009).

Paul Staniland, "Defeating transnational insurgencies: The best offense is a good fence", *The Washington Quarterly* 29 (1) (2005).

Ralph J.D. Braibanti, "Administration of military government in Japan at the prefectural level", *The American Political Science Review* 43 (2) (1949).

Ralph J.D. Braibanti, "Occupation controls in Japan", *Far Eastern Survey* 17 (18) (1948).

Richard D. Robinson, trans. Jung Miok, *Betrayal of a Nation* (Seoul: Science and Idea, 1988).

Richard R. Paternoster, *Nuclear Weapon Proliferation Indicators and Observables* (Tech rept. LA-12430-MS. Los Alamos, N.M.: Los Alamos National Laboratory, December 27, 2011).

Robert C. Tucker, *Politics as Leadership* (Columbia: University of Missouri Press, 1981).

Samuel P. Huntington, *The Clash of Civilizations and the Remaking of World Order* (New York: Simon & Schuster, 1996).

Selig H. Harrison, *Korea Endgame: A Strategy for Reunification and U.S. Disengagement* (Princeton: Princeton University Press, 2002).

Shin Bumchul, "Legal issues of the sudden collapse of North Korea", *Seoul International Law Journal* 15 (1) (2008).

SIGIR, *Hard Lessons: The Iraq Reconstruction Experience* (Washington, D.C.: US Independent Agencies and Commissions, 2013).

Snyder, Scott, "North Korea's Nuclear Program: The Role of Incentives in Preventing Deadly Conflict", ed. David Cortright, *The Price of Peace: Incentives and International Conflict Prevention* (Lanham, MD: Rowman & Little, 1997).

Snyder, Scott, "North Korea's challenge of regime survival: Internal problems and implications for the future", *Pacific Affairs* 73 (4), Special Issue: Korea in Flux (Winter, 2000–2001).

Social Science Publishing Company. *Economic Dictionary 1* (Pyongyang: Social Science Publishing Company, 1977).

South Korea Joint Chiefs of Staff, *Joint Civil-Military Operations: JM 3-6* (Seoul: South Korea Joint Chiefs of Staff, 2005).

South Korea Training & Doctrine Command of Army, *Civil-Military Operations: TC 07-3-10* (Daejeon: South Korea Training & Doctrine Command of Army, 2007).

Sun Woo-jung, The heaven and earth gangster scam, *Chosun Daily Newspaper*, March 21, 2018.

Tae Young-ho, *Password of the Third Floor Secretariat* (Seoul: Giparang, 2018).

The Economist, June 24, 2004.

Thomas Heghammer, "The rise of Muslim foreign fighters", *International Security* 35 (3) (Winter, 2010/11).

T.J. Pempel, "Domestic drivers of Northeast Asian relations", *International Journal of Korean Unification Studies* 23 (2) (2014).

Um Ho-gun, *North Korea's Nuclear Development: Background and Contents* (Seoul: Baksanjarwon, 2009).

US Central Intelligence Agency, *Soviet Control Mechanism in Germany* (May 26, 1949).

US Central Intelligence Agency, *Japan Peace Treaty Problems, Issues and Reactions* (November 17, 1947).

US Central Intelligence Agency, *Prospects for Survival of the Republic of Korea* (October 28, 1948).

US Department of State, *1969–70: A Report of the Secretary of State* (Washington, D.C.: Government Printing Office, 1971).

US Department of the Army and Navy, *Military Government and Civil Affairs: FM 27-5* (Washington, D.C.: Department of the Army and Navy, 1943).

US Joint Chiefs of Staff, *JP 3-07: Stability Operations* (Washington, D.C.: US Joint Chiefs of Staff, 2011).

US Joint Chiefs of Staff, *JP 3-07.3: Peace Operations* (Washington, D.C.: US Joint Chiefs of Staff, 2012).

Victor D. Cha, "Korea's place in the Axis", *Foreign Affairs* 81 (3) (2002).

Victor D. Cha and David C. Kang, *Nuclear North Korea: A Debate on Engagement Strategies* (New York: Columbia University Press, 2003).

Victor Shih, *Factions and Finance in China: Elite Conflict and Inflation* (New York: Cambridge University Press, 2007).

Voice of America, July 1, 2017, https://www.voakorea.com/a/3923416.html (date of searching: 2017.10.3).

William J. Perry, *My Journey at the Nuclear Brink* (Stanford University Press, 2015).

Woo Jung-yeop, "U.S. policy towards North Korea following the sixth nuclear test", *Sejong Commentary* 2017-36 (Sejong Institute, September 6, 2017).

Yonhap News, October 21, 2017, http://www.yonhapnews.co.kr/bulletin/2017/10/21/0200000000AKR20171021033700083.HTML?input=1179m (date of searching: 2017.10.21).

Yun Yeongmi, *Contemporary Russian Politics and International Relations* (Seoul: Doonam, 2012).

Yun Yeongmi and Park Kicheol, "Structural restrictions of territorial disputes in Northeast Asia", *The Journal of East Affairs* 27 (2) (Fall/Winter, 2013).

Index

CPSIA information can be obtained
at www.ICGtesting.com
Printed in the USA
JSHW022330291019
2157JS00001B/3